THE CULINARY

The New

ALSO BY THE CULINARY INSTITUTE OF AMERICA

Bistros and Brasseries • The Culinary Institute of America Cookbook • Vegetables
A Tavola! • Gourmet Meals in Minutes • Cake Art • Breakfasts & Brunches • Grilling

INSTITUTE OF AMERICA
Book of Soups

Over 160 New and Improved Recipes for Soups and Stews of Every Variety,
with Illustrated, Step-by-Step Techniques from the World's Premier Culinary College

PHOTOGRAPHY BY BEN FINK

LEBHAR-FRIEDMAN BOOKS
NEW YORK • CHICAGO • LOS ANGELES • TOKYO

THE CULINARY INSTITUTE OF AMERICA

President: Dr. Tim Ryan

Vice-President, Dean of Culinary Education:
Mark Erickson

Senior Director, Educational Enterprises:
Susan Cussen

Director of Publishing: Nathalie Fischer

Editorial Project Manager:
Mary Donovan

Editorial Assistant:
Shelly Malgee

Food Stylist:
Jessica Bard

Recipe Tester:
Kathleen M. Citera

LIBRARY OF CONGRESS CATALOGING-IN-PUBLICATION DATA
Cataloging-in-publication data for this title is on file with the Library of Congress.
ISBN 978-0-86730-860-0

LEBHAR-FRIEDMAN BOOKS
A company of Lebhar-Friedman, Inc., 425 Park Avenue, New York, New York 10022

Publisher: Maria Tufts

Art Director: Kevin Hanek

Manufactured in Singapore on acid-free paper

CONTENTS

Soup Basics

From the most delicate broth to light, cool fruit soups, and on to hearty purées, it is possible to find a soup to suit nearly any menu. Soups may serve as a single course of a meal or they may be its centerpiece.

Soups can be among the best teachers of important culinary lessons. They fill your mouth completely and instantly, giving you a simultaneous experience of aroma, texture, taste, and temperature. You can taste and evaluate soups at virtually any stage of preparation: if something goes awry, you can usually fix it as you go.

Soups are a good practice ground, for they rely on the most basic skills to prepare something truly delicious. Most soup recipes are extremely adaptable, and can be easily adjusted to meet the needs of the moment, especially when you want to add or substitute ingredients or flavorings. And, when you need a head start on a satisfying meal for busy days, soup is a convenient answer. Most soup recipes are easy to double for a big batch, so you can make them when time permits, then refrigerate or freeze whatever you aren't serving right away to keep for another meal.

Ingredients

Choose flavorful ingredients for your soup. This is the place to use richly flavored and well-exercised cuts of meat, such as the shank or shin, or mature stewing hens. Gentle simmering will tenderize these tougher cuts. A turkey neck gives a soup extra body and a subtle flavor.

The aromatics and other ingredients that you choose—onions, carrots, celery, leeks, herbs, spices, mushrooms, or tomatoes—can change a basic broth suitable for a chicken noodle soup into one perfect for a spicy Thai-inspired soup.

PREPARING THE MAIN INGREDIENTS

The main ingredients for all soups fall into three basic categories:

- the main flavoring ingredient(s)
- the liquid base
- supporting flavors and seasonings

Most soups include vegetables, whether they are included for supporting flavors or they are the main ingredients. The actual steps involved in preparing vegetables varies depending upon the vegetable itself. Some may need to be trimmed to remove stems and roots; some require only peeling. The way you cut them once they are prepared has an effect on the cooking time and the flavor of the soup. The smaller you cut them, the more quickly they will cook.

If you are going to purée the soup before serving it, neatness isn't extremely important, but a relatively consistent size is, which permits the vegetables to cook evenly. If you are making a soup that is not strained or puréed, pay a bit more attention to the appearance of the cuts for a more attractive finished dish.

If your soup is built from beef, lamb, pork, or game meats, opt for cuts that are the most flavorful. Cuts from the neck, hocks (or shank), or short ribs are usually more exercised, and thus have more intense flavors. More mature animals have more developed flavors as well. Young chickens simply don't have the depth of flavor that older birds have. Stewing hens are the best foundation for chicken-based broths and soups.

Trim meats to remove as much of the visible fat as you can. Some recipes call for large cuts to be tied before using them to prepare a soup. This helps the meat cook evenly for a better flavor in the finished soup. Others may call for the meat to be cut into pieces. Try to cut the meat into pieces that are about the same size.

Fish or shellfish should be perfectly fresh. If you are preparing a broth, you may include bones and the head, but you should remove the gills. Fish to be prepared in soups can be of any sort from salmon to tuna to monkfish. Whole fish should be filleted and skinned, and then cut into uniform pieces so that it cooks evenly and quickly once you've added it to the soup.

Shellfish like mussels and clams can be cooked in soups directly in their shells; be sure that you have cleaned them thoroughly as described on page 47. Shrimp, crab, lobster, and crayfish may be cooked separately, and then disjointed and/or shelled to add to the soup, or you may simply add them directly to the soup still in the shell.

The liquid base for your soup should be fresh and flavorful. We've included recipes for basic broths in this book on pages 15–18. There are other options as well, including purchased broths and stocks, milk, fruit and vegetable juices, and water.

THICKENERS

If your soup is to be thickened, as you would a cream soup or bisque, be sure to add any additional thickeners, like flour or potatoes, at the point suggested in the recipe. If these ingredients don't have enough time to cook thoroughly, the soup might end up tasting and feeling starchy or pasty.

Options for Finishing Soups

Soups can be finished with something as simple as a pinch of fresh chives, a squeeze of lemon juice, or a few grinds of black pepper. Heavy cream, sour cream, crème fraîche, or yogurt can be stirred into the soup right before it is served or simply added as a dollop to each bowl. Grated parmesan, shredded gruyere, or grated cheddar are options for some soups. A few drops of a fruity extra-virgin olive oil, a fragrant vinegar, or swirl of pesto are also good ways to make your soups special.

Garnish options range from something chefs call an "integral garnish," meaning simply that the garnish is cooked right in the soup; minestrone is a good example. Cream soups are traditionally garnished with small, neat pieces of the main ingredient; use a few perfect asparagus tips for your cream of asparagus soup, for instance.

Crackers and breads are important accompaniments to virtually any soup, but some soups include them as part of the recipe. Onion soup is served with a piece of toasted bread; New England clam chowder would be "lonely" without oyster crackers.

Soup Pots and Stock Pots

Soup and stock pots come in a variety of materials, shapes, sizes, and capacities. If you love soups, invest in a good pot. Look for the following quality indicators:

- **ENOUGH ROOM FOR THE SOUP TO EXPAND:** Pots come in a variety of sizes; pots that hold about 8 quarts are fine for the soups in this book. A larger pot, up to 12 quarts, is perfect for making broths and stocks. (You can use a stock pot to make soups, of course.) The reason that the pot should be much larger than the final yield is to leave plenty of room between the top of the soup and the top of the pot. The soup needs space—it will expand as it cooks and bubble while boiling. You need to have enough room to easily skim the surface while the soup cooks.

- **TALLER THAN WIDE:** Soup and stock pots have relatively narrow openings. This controls the amount of evaporation. Some evaporation is important to develop a rich flavor, but not so much that you end up with far less soup than you had expected. Most soups simmer for 30 minutes up to one or two hours. With a wide surface area, you might lose a noticeable amount of volume. A narrow surface area slows down evaporation.

- **HEAVY BOTTOM:** A solid, heavy, flat bottom is best for any pot, but is especially important for long simmering soups. If the pot has a thin bottom, it could easily develop hot spots as it sits on the burner that might burn or scorch the soup or cause the pot's bottom to buckle.

- **A LID:** You will want a lid for your soup pot to control the soup's cooking speed. Covering the pot tightly will slow or stop the evaporation of the soup, but also traps the heat inside the pot as well as making it easy to forget to look at the soup from time to time. Partially covering the pot by setting the lid slightly ajar, means that you can still easily keep an eye on the soup without letting it cook away.

- **EASY TO HANDLE:** Stock and soup pots are produced in a range of materials from stainless steel to aluminum (plain or anodized) to enameled cast iron. Most have two loop-style handles to make it easy to lift the pot. Test drive the handles to be sure your hands fit comfortably. Choose a pot that feels heavy, but that you can lift comfortably.

TOOLS FOR STRAINING

Sieves and strainers are made from fine mesh, and can be shaped like cones, drums, or bowls. Use a sieve or colander lined with a double layer of dampened cheesecloth for straining solids from soups. Colanders are strainers with plenty of large holes well suited for separating meats and vegetables from broths.

Skimmers, made of perforated metal or mesh, are useful for removing foods from hot fat or liquids or skimming foam from a simmering stock. Cheesecloth, a light, fine-mesh gauze made from white cotton, can be used alone or to line a colander or sieve for straining broth. Small squares are used to make spice sachets for infusing stocks and soups with flavor as explained on page 13.

☼ TIME-SAVING TIPS

Preparing soups within a time constraint can sometimes be a challenge; however, there are many ways you can adapt a soup recipe to meet your schedule by choosing and preparing ingredients wisely:

➡ *USE PREPARED BROTH OR STOCK:* A variety of broths, stocks, and other liquids, including water, vegetable essences, milk, or juices can be used as the base for soup. Select a good quality prepared stock or broth. Look for brands that are low in sodium with a pleasing flavor, so that the broth supports you soup rather than overpowering it. You can personalize and adjust the taste of prepared broths by adding a few more aromatic vegetables or seasoning ingredients while the soup simmers.

➡ *CHOOSE WATER INSTEAD OF BROTH OR STOCK:* If you don't have canned or prepared broth at the ready, don't be afraid to use water and an array of flavorings. A few sprigs of parsley or other herbs, a splash of lemon juice, dried or fresh mushrooms, a dash of salt and pepper, chiles, fortified wines, vinegar, or a bit of hot sauce are all excellent choices for a flavor adjustment; they can intensify the taste, complement the recipe, and add a whole new flavor dimension to your soup.

➡ *USE FROZEN VEGETABLES:* Fresh seasonal vegetables are great for full-bodied soups, but at certain times of the year, you may prefer to substitute good quality frozen vegetables: spinach, lima beans, collard greens, peas, corn, okra, winter squashes like acorn or butternut, green beans, and broccoli are just some examples. Some are ready to use as is, even without thawing, and cut down significantly on the amount of trimming, peeling, and chopping you need to do.

➡ *USE CANNED VEGETABLES:* Tomatoes, peeled or diced, are good to have on hand for soup making. Another canned food that you might want to keep in your pantry is beans—chickpeas, kidney beans, black beans, or cannellini. You can add them to many soups even if the recipe doesn't specify them.

Preparing Soups

Cook soups at a gentle simmer until they are flavorful. The only important caution is this: Don't let your soup overcook. Soups left to simmer for hours and hours lose nutrients, texture, and colors. Taste the soup carefully once all of the ingredients are properly cooked. You may find that you need a bit more salt and pepper, or you may want to add ingredients like lemon or lime juice, citrus zest, chopped fresh herbs, or a dash of wine.

Vegetables may be added in a staggered manner. Some vegetables are very dense, starchy, or fibrous. Those vegetables are added near the start of cooking time. Tender or quick-cooking vegetables like peas or corn are added in the final minutes of cooking time. Stir the soup from time to time to keep starchy ingredients like pasta, potatoes, carrots, or flour from sticking to the bottom of the pot.

Use a skimmer or ladle to remove any scum or foam that rises to the top of the soup as it simmers for the best flavor, texture, and appearance.

Taste the soup frequently as it cooks. When the flavor is fully developed and all of the ingredients are tender, it is ready to finish or garnish and serve right away, or you may prefer to cool and store the soup to serve later.

ADJUSTING CONSISTENCY

Thick soups, especially those made with starchy vegetables or dried beans, may continue to thicken during cooking and storage. As a general rule, purées, creams, and bisques should be about as thick as heavy cream and liquid enough to pour from a ladle into a bowl. The following steps may be taken to adjust consistency. For a soup that has become too thick, water or an appropriately flavored stock or broth may be added in small amounts until the proper consistency is reached. The seasoning should be rechecked before serving.

For a soup that is too thin, a small amount of diluted cornstarch or arrowroot may be added. The soup should be at a simmer or slow boil when the starch is added. It should be stirred continuously and should continue simmering for 2 or 3 minutes.

ADJUSTING FLAVOR AND SEASONING

Soups should be seasoned throughout the cooking process. Meat or poultry glaze may be added to bolster the flavor of a weak broth or consommé; however, this will affect the clarity of the finished soup.

Chopped fresh herbs, a few drops of lemon juice, Tabasco sauce, Worcestershire sauce, or grated citrus rind may be added to brighten a soup's flavor. These items should be added a little at a time and the seasoning carefully checked after each addition. Salt and pepper to taste may be added just prior to serving when the soup is at the correct temperature.

COOLING AND STORING

One of the best things about soups is that they are perfect to make ahead. You can double most soup recipes with no worries, as long as your pot is big enough. The soups in this book indicate the exact point at which you can stop the cooking process to cool the soup and serve it later. Some are cooked part-way; others are cooked completely but left ungarnished. The procedure is as follows:

Pour or ladle the soup into a wide, shallow pan or bowl. While you don't want to have too much surface area while you are cooking the soup, having a lot now means that the soup will cool faster.

➡ *MAKE AN ICE BATH:* To cool the soup rapidly, you will need to create an ice bath in a large bowl or in your sink. If you use a bowl, choose one that is large enough to hold plenty of cold water and ice as well as the bowl or dish filled with the soup you need to cool. Add ice and then enough cold water to fill the bowl or the sink halfway. Pour the soup into a metal bowl. Set the bowl in the ice bath and make sure it can't tip over. Stir the soup occasionally as it cools. This step cools the soup more rapidly by mixing the hot soup from the inside of the bowl with the cool soup closer to the edge.

Once the soup is cooled to room temperature (about 70°F), transfer it to storage containers. Cover the containers securely, make a label that gives the name of the soup as well as the date it was prepared, and then put it into the refrigerator or freezer. Most soups will last in the refrigerator for up to 1 week and in the freezer for a minimum of 2 months.

REHEATING

Try to reheat only the amount of soup you need. Repeated reheating will eventually have a poor effect on the soup.

Bring clear soups just up to a boil over high heat, and then check their seasoning and consistency. A little salt and pepper, a few drops of lemon juice, sherry, or other additions can make all the difference.

Reheat thick soups, such as creams, purées, or bisques, gently. Before you add the soup to a pot, put a thin layer of water or stock in the pot to act as a buffer between the soup and the heat. Put the pot over low heat and stir frequently as the soup softens slightly. Then you can increase the heat slightly and bring the soup up to a simmer. As always, be sure to check the seasoning carefully once the soup is at a simmer and make any adjustments you like. If the soup has become too thick or too thin, you can also adjust its consistency (see page 5 for more information about adjusting consistency).

Serving Soups

Serve hot soups very hot and cold soups very cold. Try heating the bowls for hot soups, using one of the following techniques: put the soup plates or bowls into a 200°F oven for 10 minutes or so or put the bowls in your sink and pour a pot of boiling water over them. To chill the bowls for cold soups, put them into the refrigerator or freezer for 10 or 15 minutes.

☀ SHOPPING FOR SOUP INGREDIENTS

FRUITS	AMOUNT	EQUAL TO
Apples	1 lb	3–4 medium 3 cups sliced
	1 medium	1 cup diced or sliced ¾ cup chopped
Apricots, dried	6-oz package	1 cup dried
Apricots, fresh	2 medium 1 lb	½ cup sliced 2 cups halves or slices 8–12 medium
Berries (strawberry, blueberry, raspberry)	1 dry pint	2–3 cups
	1 lb	3½ cups
Honeydew Melon	1 (4 lbs)	4 cups diced
Lemons	1 medium	2–3 tbsp juice 2–3 tsp grated peel

Limes	1 medium	1½–2 tbsp juice 1–2 tsp grated peel
Oranges	1 medium	⅓–½ cup juice 1½–2 tbsp grated peel
Papaya	1 lb	1 medium 2 cups sliced/cubed
Pineapple, fresh	1 medium	2 lbs 3 cups chunks/cubes
Plums, fresh	1 lb	8–10 small 6 medium 5 large 2–2½ cups pitted
Strawberries, fresh	1 dry pint	2½ cups whole 1¾ cup sliced 24 medium
Strawberries, frozen, whole	20-oz package	4 cups, whole

SEAFOOD AND TOFU	AMOUNT	EQUAL TO
Clams, in shell	8 quarts	1 quart, shucked
Clams, shucked	1 quart	2–3 cups, chopped
Crab, in shell	1 lb whole	6–7 oz meat; ⅔ cup flaked
Crabmeat, canned	6½ oz	1 cup flaked
Lobster	1 medium, 2½ lbs	2 cups cooked meat
Mussels, unshucked	1 qt	25 mussels; 1 cup meat
Oysters, shucked	1 lb	12 medium 1 pint
Shrimp, in shell	1 lb	extra colossal: less than 10; colossal: 10–15; jumbo: 21–25; extra large: 26–30; large: 31–35; medium: 43–50; small: 51–60
Tofu, firm	1 lb	2½ cups cubed

HERBS	AMOUNT	EQUAL TO
Basil	½ oz fresh	1 cup chopped leaves
Parsley, fresh	2 oz (about 1 bunch)	1½ cups chopped leaves
Rosemary, fresh	4-inch stem	¼ tsp dried leaves
Sage, fresh	12 leaves	1 tbsp chopped
	1 tbsp chopped	1 tsp dried
Thyme, fresh	1 sprig	½ tsp dried
Saffron	4–6 threads	¼ tsp crushed powder

DRY GOODS	AMOUNT	EQUAL TO
Beans, dried (black, red, white, navy pinto, kidney, red, split-pea, black-eyed pea, etc.)	1-lb bag 1 cup	2–2½ cups uncooked; 5½–6 cups cooked 7 oz dry; 2½ cups cooked
Fava Beans, dried	1 lb	2 cups dried; 4½ cups cooked
Great Northern Beans, dried	1 lb	6–7 cups cooked
Hominy, canned	15 oz can	1¾ cups
Hominy, uncooked	1 lb 1 cup	2½ cups uncooked 4½ cups cooked
Pine Nuts	5 oz	1 cup
Bread	1 lb loaf 1 slice dry 1 slice soft	16–18 slices; 12 cups croutons ⅓ cup fine crumbs ¾ cup coarse crumbs; ¾ cup cubes
Rice, aromatic, uncooked	1 cup	3 cups cooked
Rice, brown, uncooked	1 cup	4 cups cooked
Rice, wild	1 lb	3 cups uncooked; 9–10 cups cooked

CHEESES	AMOUNT	EQUAL TO
Cheese, firm (Cheddar, etc.)	1 lb 1 cup shredded	4–5 cups, shredded 4 oz (approximately)
Cheese, hard (Parmesan, etc.)	8 oz 1 cup, grated	1½ cups, grated 5 oz (approximately)

VEGETABLES	AMOUNT	EQUAL TO
Asparagus, fresh	1 lb	16–20 spears 3 cups trimmed
Avocados	1 lb	2 medium 1½ cups cubed
Beans, green, fresh	1 lb	3 cups trimmed 2½ cups cut, cooked
Beet Greens	1 lb	1½ cups cooked 8 oz leaves
Beets without tops	1 lb	2 cups cooked sliced/diced 10 medium beets
Broccoli, fresh	1 lb 1 bunch	2 cups florets 3 cups cooked, chopped
Broccoli, frozen	10 oz	1½ cups chopped
Cabbage	1 med. head 1 lb raw	1¼–1½ lbs 3½–4½ cups shredded
Carrots, fresh	1 lb	5–7 medium 2½ cups shredded/sliced
Cauliflower, fresh	1 med. head 1 lb	1¾–2¼ lbs 1½ cups, cut up
Celery	1 bunch 2–3 med. ribs	1 lb untrimmed 2 cups, sliced/diced 1 cup chopped or sliced
Collard Greens, fresh	1 lb	6–7 cups raw 1½ cups cooked
Corn, fresh	3–4 ears	1 cup kernels

Corn, frozen	10 oz	1¼ cups kernels
Cucumber	1 lb	2 medium 2½–3 cups peeled, sliced/chopped
Fennel, bulb	1 lb	3 cups sliced
Garlic	1 clove, small 1 clove, large	½ tsp minced 1½ tsp minced
Ginger, fresh	1-inch piece	1 tbsp grated or chopped
Green Beans, fresh	1 lb	3 cups trimmed
Green Beans, frozen	10 oz	1½ cups
Green Peas, in pod	1 lb	1 cup shelled
Green Peas, frozen	10 oz	1½–2 cups
Jerusalem Artichokes	1 lb	12 medium; 2½ cups peeled, sliced
Jicama	1 lb	4 cups shredded
Kale, fresh	1 lb	6 cups raw leaves; 1¼ cups cooked leaves
Leeks	1 lb	1 bunch; 2 large or 3 medium 2 cups chopped or sliced (white part) 1 cup chopped, cooked (white part)
Lemongrass	2 stalks	1 tbsp finely chopped
Lima Beans, fresh, shelled	1 lb	3 cups
Lima Beans, frozen	10 oz	1¾ cups cooked
Lima Beans, in pod	1 lb	¾–1 cup shelled
Mushrooms, dried	2½–3 oz	equal to 1 lb fresh when reconstituted

Mushrooms, fresh	1 lb	2 cups, sliced, sautéed
		18–20 medium
Mustard Greens, fresh	1 lb	6–7 cups leaves
Okra, fresh	1 lb	35 pods
		1½–2 cups sliced
Okra, frozen	10 oz	1¼ cups chopped/ sliced
Onions, white or yellow	1 small	3 oz
		⅓–½ cup chopped
	1 medium	4–5 oz
		½–⅓ cup chopped
	1 lb	2 large/3 medium
		2–2½ cups chopped
Parsnips	1 lb	4 medium parsnips
Peppers, sweet fresh	1 small	¼ cup chopped
	1 medium	½ cup chopped
	1 large	1 cup chopped
	1 lb	3 large or 5 medium; 3–4 cups chopped
Peppers, sweet frozen	10-oz package	2¼ cups diced
Potatoes, new	1 lb	9–12 small
Potatoes, red	1 lb	7–9 small
	1 lb	5–6 medium
	3 medium	2¼ cups peeled, diced
Pumpkin, fresh	1 medium (1 lb)	4 cups peeled, cubed
	5 lbs	4½ cups cooked, puréed
Radishes	1 bunch	12 radishes; 1 cup sliced
Rutabaga	1 medium	2–3 lbs; 5 cups cubed

Scallions, with tops	1 bunch	6–8 scallions; 1 cup sliced
Shallots, fresh	1 medium	½–1 oz; 1 tbsp minced
Snow peas, fresh	4 oz	1½ cups trimmed
Snow peas, frozen	6 oz	1½ cups
Spinach, fresh, bunch	1 lb	4 cup torn leaves
Spinach leaves, fresh, packaged	10-oz bag	6 cups leaves
Spinach, frozen	10-oz package	1½ cups
Squash, winter (acorn, hubbard, pumpkin, etc.)	1 lb	1 cup cooked, mashed
Squash, winter, frozen	12-oz package	1½ cups sliced
Sweet potatoes, fresh	1 lb	2 large or 3 medium; 2 cups cubed or sliced
Swiss Chard, fresh	1 lb	4 cups stems plus 5–6 cups leaves
Tomatillos	1 lb	12–16 medium
Tomatoes, canned	28 oz	2 cups drained
Tomatoes, canned, diced	16 oz	2 cups pulp & juice
Tomatoes, fresh	1 medium	1 cup chopped
	1 lb	2 large, 3 medium, 4 small
		1–1½ cups peeled, seeded, chopped
Tomatoes, sun-dried	1 oz	10 tomatoes
Turnips	1 lb	3–4 medium
Watercress	1 bunch	2 cups chopped
Zucchini	1 lb	3 medium; 1 cup sliced

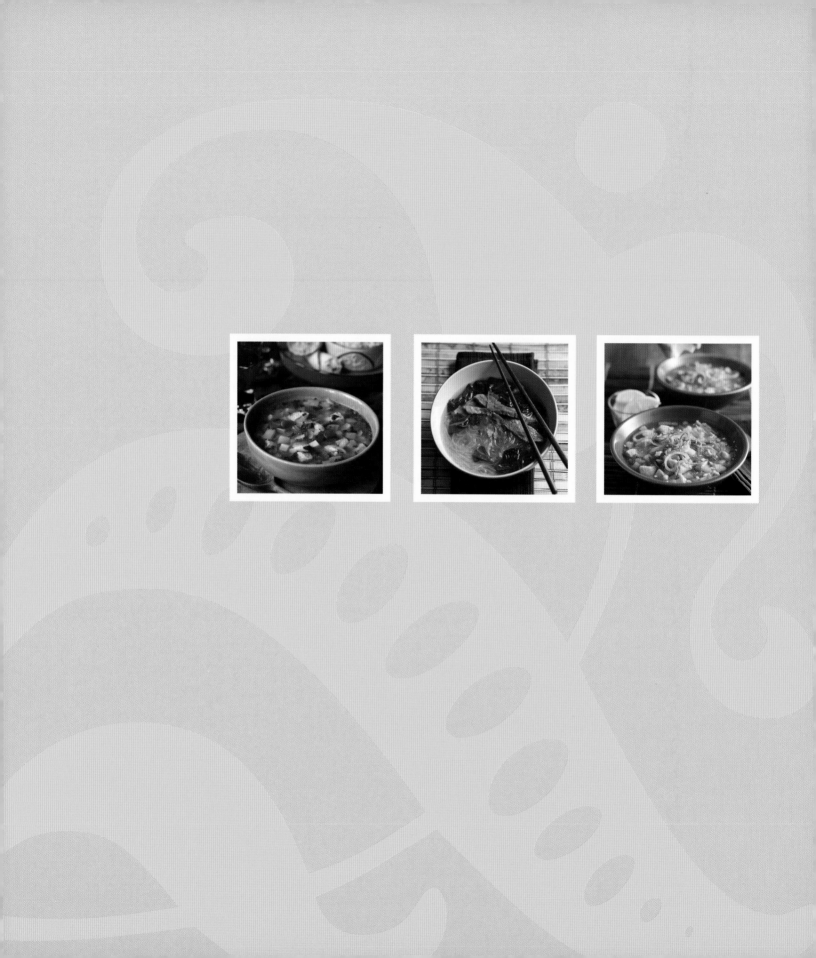

Broths

BROTHS ARE THE basic material of any dedicated soup-maker. A perfect broth is clear, with a light but noticeable body, and a rich, distinctive flavor. Its quality depends upon a combination of elements: the best ingredients, the right proportion of flavoring ingredients to liquid, careful temperature regulation, thorough skimming, adequate cooking time, and adjustments to the broth's seasoning throughout cooking time. The flavor depends upon the way you combine main flavoring ingredients, aromatics, and seasonings.

A simple broth can most certainly be served on its own. Presented piping hot in a soup cup, it is a warming and nourishing dish. Adding garnishes greatly expands the possibilities, turning a broth into a main dish. The way you add the garnish can change the soup's texture. If you simmer a combination of vegetables and some noodles in a broth (Chicken, Corn, and Noodle Soup, page 23), the broth is lightly thickened, giving it a more robust texture. If you prepare the garnish separately and add it to the broth just long enough to reheat it, the broth remains clear and light.

Although there is time involved in preparing a good broth, they are easy to make in large batches to freeze for later use. Use the chart on pages 6–9, *Shopping for Soup Ingredients*, to help make the best selections with the least waste. Broths can become a staple "convenience" food that eliminates the need for canned broth or bouillon cubes. Rich homemade broths may be served with whatever you have on hand in the refrigerator for a quick lunch or a Sunday evening supper: a little chopped meat and some leftover cooked grains, vegetables, or beans; some noodles or pasta; a big crouton topped with grated cheese; even an egg that you let "poach" directly in the broth.

Main Ingredients for Broths

Broths are a liquid essence of flavor, so the best broths are made from the most flavorful meats, fish, vegetables, and aromatics. Frequently, the meat or poultry used to prepare broths can work for other preparations, as long as it is cooked just until fully tender and *no longer*. The meat can then be julienned or diced to use as a garnish.

Observe the following guidelines for a broth that has a deep, complex flavor and a full body. To make 2 quarts of broth combine:

- 4 or 5 pounds of meat or poultry with 3 quarts cold water

- 5 or 6 pounds of fish or shellfish with 3 quarts cold water

- 3 to 4 pounds vegetables with 3 quarts cold water

Whatever your main flavoring ingredient, prepare it properly before you add it to the pot. Trim heavy stem or root ends from vegetables and scrub them thoroughly. Check your recipe to see if they should be peeled, and then cut them into the size suggested in your recipe; the size of the cut is usually related to how long the broth is supposed to simmer.

Many broths begin with the simplest of all liquids: cool, fresh water. Using a stock or broth as the base liquid will produce what is sometimes referred to as a "double broth."

Supporting Flavors

The point of making a broth is to produce a rich, flavorful liquid. For a well-balanced, interesting broth, you can introduce the appropriate seasoning and flavorings in the role of supporting flavors as the broth simmers.

Vegetable combinations, herb or spice mixtures, wines, and even some specific vegetables can be considered for the role of supporting flavor in a broth. You can vary the time you add these ingredients as well as the way in which they are prepared before they are added. This permits you to modify a basic broth formula to make a variety of broths, ranging from a traditional double broth to a Japanese-style miso broth.

As you taste your simmering broth, be conscious of these supporting flavors. If you are new to broth-making, remember to leave aromatic vegetables in large pieces so you can fish them out of the pot if necessary. A broth that seems too sweet might have too many carrots. If the herbs and spices are coming on too strong, you can remove them before they become overwhelming, especially if you've added them in the form of a sachet (see below) or bouquet garni (page 126). Use our recipes as a basic set of instructions to get comfortable with the process. After that, you can easily improvise until you've got the recipe that you like the best.

HANDLING AROMATICS FOR BROTHS

Aromatic herb and vegetable combinations such as mirepoix (usually two parts onion, one part carrot, and one part celery), a spice sachet (generally consisting of parsley stems, thyme, cracked black pepper, and bay leaves), or bouquet garni (similar to a spice sachet but wrapped in leek leaves) are traditional. Other traditional bases of flavor include the Cajun Trinity (onions, peppers, and celery), and sofrito (tomatoes, onions, and garlic cooked down to a flavorful paste). Contemporary broths may call for such ingredients as dried tomatoes, lemongrass, wild mushrooms, or ginger to give the broth a unique character.

➡ *MAKING A SPICE SACHET:* A basic sachet that will flavor 2½ to 3 quarts of liquid contains 5 or 6 cracked peppercorns, 3 or 4 parsley stems, 1 sprig fresh thyme or ½ teaspoon dried thyme, and 1 bay leaf. Add or substitute other spices to complement the flavors in a specific dish. For example, use cardamom, chiles, or star anise to flavor an Asian-style soup.

1. Place the herbs and spices on a square of cheesecloth large enough to contain them. If you prefer, enclose the herbs and spices in a large tea ball in place of the cheesecloth and hook it to the side of the pot.

2. Twist the corners of the cheesecloth together and tie securely with one end of a long piece of string.

3. When adding to the pot, tie the other end of the string to the pot handle for easy removal later.

4. At the end of cooking, gently pull out the bundle, untie the string from the pot handle, and discard.

ADDING AROMATIC VEGETABLES TO BROTHS: SWEATING, SMOTHERING, AND PINÇÉ

The degree to which the aromatic vegetables (onions, leeks, peppers, chiles, mushrooms, celery, carrots, garlic, shallots, and ginger, for instance) are cooked *before* they are combined with the rest of the broth has a strong influence on a soup's final flavor and color. Some recipes ask you to cook them until they are just limp and translucent; professionals refer to this as "sweating" the vegetables because the vegetables actually start to release some of their own moisture. If you cover the pot, it helps to cook the aromatics a little more quickly; this technique is known as "smothering." Other recipes may instruct you to cook the aromatics until they develop a golden or even rich golden brown color. Cooking the aromatics to this darker, caramelized stage is referred to as *pinçé*, or creating a *pinçage*. A *pinçage* often includes a tomato product, such as tomato paste, that is cooked to a deep, brick-red color before the liquid is added.

GARNISHING BROTHS

Garnishing broths adds visual and textural interest. Simple garnishes, such as a very fine dice of vegetables (brunoise) or a small bit broken from a sprig of a fresh herb (pluches), are traditional. Other choices include diced or julienned meats, pieces of fish or shellfish, croutons, dumplings, quenelles, wontons, noodles, and rice. The recipes found in this book and in many other books illustrate the breadth of possibilities.

☼ BASIC METHOD FOR BROTHS

When assembling the equipment, select a pot large enough to accommodate the broth as it cooks. There should be sufficient room at the top of the pot to allow for some expansion during cooking, as well as to make it easy to skim away any impurities from the surface. The pot should be tall and narrow rather than short and wide. If available, select a pot with a spigot to make it easier to strain the broth. You will also need skimmers and ladles, storage or holding containers, strainers, tasting spoons and cups, and a kitchen fork to remove any large pieces of meat.

The same basic method applies to making a broth from either poultry, meat, or fish:

➡ *CHOOSE THE INGREDIENTS:* Choose meat cuts from more exercised parts of the animal because the more fully developed the muscle, the more pronounced the flavor. The same is true of poultry broths, where stewing hens or more mature game birds are the best choice for deep flavor.

Select fish and shellfish for broths carefully. Freshness is of primary concern, as is the relative leanness or oiliness of the fish. It is best to use lean, white-fleshed fish such as sole, flounder, halibut, or cod. Richer, oilier types of fish, such as bluefish or mackerel, tend to lose their flavor when their delicate oils are subjected to high temperatures for even short periods. Shellfish and crustaceans cooked in their shells in a small amount of liquid produce excellent broth. It must be strained very carefully to remove all traces of grit or sand.

➡ *PREPARE THE BROTH INGREDIENTS FOR COOKING:* Trim away excess fat on the surface of meats or poultry. Remove the gills from fish and scrub any shellfish. Depending upon the results you want, you may choose to sear some meats to develop a deeper color and more pronounced flavor.

➡ *ADD THE AROMATICS:* Add any aromatics that your recipe calls for in the correct sequence. You may simply combine everything all at once, or you may add them in a staggered manner. Herbs and spices are usually added only during the final half hour of cooking time.

➡ *COMBINE THE INGREDIENTS WITH A COOL LIQUID:* Combine the ingredients in a pot and add enough cool liquid to cover them by about two inches. It is important to begin with a cool liquid, to gently and thoroughly extract the flavor from your ingredients as the liquid gradually rises to a simmer. In the case of meat-based broths, this tactic also helps ensure that your finished broth will be clear. A hard boil should always be avoided because it could "cook out" the flavor of the aromatic ingredients. Furthermore, a vigorous boil could cause the fat and impurities to be mixed back into the broth, rather than collecting on the surface where you can skim them away.

➡ *SIMMER THE BROTH GENTLY AND SKIM AS NECESSARY:* Use a flat spoon, a skimmer, or a spider to lift any foam or fat that rises to the surface of the broth for the best flavor. As the broth begins to simmer, it will look cloudy and may be full of particles. After the first hour or so, and several careful skimmings, the broth should begin to clear and take on a distinct golden or brown color. If you don't skim faithfully, the broth might become cloudy and have a bitter taste. The most foam is thrown from the broth in the first hour or so of cooking time, but you should continue to skim the broth throughout cooking time.

Continue to simmer until the broth is flavorful. Once the broth has the flavor you like, it is time to stop cooking the broth and strain it. Allow the broth to cool slightly before straining. Set a colander or sieve over a large bowl or other container to collect the broth as you strain. While you could certainly just pour the contents of the entire pot through a strainer or colander, you can improve the appearance of the broth by taking the time to ladle the broth out of the pot without jostling the solid ingredients.

CHICKEN BROTH

CHICKEN BROTH IS a crucial ingredient in soup making and the flavor of home-made broth is hard to beat. You can double or even quadruple this recipe and freeze the extra so you always have some on hand. To make a double chicken broth, substitute cold chicken stock or broth for the water in this recipe.

MAKES ABOUT 2 QUARTS

1. Place the chicken and water in a large pot (below left). The water should cover the chicken by at least two inches; add more if necessary. Bring the water slowly to a boil over medium heat.

2. As the water comes to a boil, skim away any foam that rises to the surface (below center). Adjust the heat once a boil is reached so that a slow, lazy simmer is established. Cover partially and simmer for 2 hours, skimming as often as necessary.

3. Add all of the remaining ingredients. Continue to simmer, skimming the surface as necessary, until the broth is fully flavored, about 1 hour.

4. Remove the chicken pieces from the pot and cool slightly. Dice or shred the meat and use to garnish the broth or save for another use; discard the skin and bones.

5. Strain the broth through a colander or sieve into a large metal container (below right). Discard the solids.

6. If you are using the broth right away, skim off any fat on the surface. If you are not using the broth right away, cool it quickly by transferring it to a metal container (if it's not in one already) and placing the container in a sink filled with ice cold water. Stir the broth as it cools, and then transfer it to storage containers. Store in the refrigerator for up to 5 days, or in the freezer for up to 3 months. Label and date the containers clearly before putting them into the freezer.

4 lb stewing hen or chicken parts or meaty bones, such as backs and necks

3 qt cold water

1¼ cups diced onion

⅓ cup diced carrot

½ cup diced celery

5 to 6 whole black peppercorns

3 to 4 parsley stems

1 bay leaf

1 sprig fresh thyme

1½ tsp salt, or as needed

Make It Easier

Some stores sell packages of necks and backs that can be used to prepare broth. This broth can also be made with the carcasses of roasted birds. Save the bones after all of the meat has been pulled or carved away (freeze them if you will not be making the broth within a day or two). You will need the carcasses of about 3 birds for each batch of broth.

BEEF BROTH

4 lb beef (chuck, ribs, shank, or neck)

3 qt water

2 cups coarsely chopped onions

1¼ cups coarsely chopped leek (white and light green parts)

⅓ cup coarsely chopped carrot

½ cup coarsely chopped celery

¼ cup celery leaves

3 to 4 parsley stems

3 to 4 black peppercorns

1 bay leaf

2 tsp salt, or as needed

½ tsp dried thyme or 1 sprig fresh thyme

If, after straining the broth, you find the flavor to be weaker than you would like, simply put the broth back on the stove and boil it down until the flavor has concentrated to your taste.

F OR THE CLEAREST broth, be sure to skim the liquid frequently as it comes to a simmer and as often as necessary thereafter. Never let it reach a boil; this will make the broth cloudy. In describing the proper state of a broth as it simmers, the French use the verb *fremir*—to tremble. This means that there should be movement on the surface, but only a few lazy bubbles should be seen breaking the surface.

MAKES ABOUT 2 QUARTS

1. Preheat the oven to 400°F.

2. Put the beef in a roasting pan and place in the oven. Roast the beef until deep brown, about 45 minutes to 1 hour.

3. Transfer the beef to a soup pot. Pour 1 cup of the water into the hot roasting pan and scrape the bottom to loosen any drippings; pour over the beef. Add the remaining water (there should be enough to cover the beef by 2 inches; add more water if necessary) and bring to a simmer. Cover partially and simmer gently for 2 hours. Frequently skim away any scum that rises to the surface.

4. Add the remaining ingredients. Continue to simmer gently until the broth has developed a full, rich flavor, about 2 hours. Remove the meat and use to garnish the broth or reserve for another use.

5. Strain the broth through a fine sieve or cheesecloth-lined colander into a large metal container. Discard the solids.

6. If you are using the broth right away, skim off any fat on the surface. If you are not using the broth right away, cool it quickly by placing the container in a sink filled with ice cold water. Stir the broth as it cools, and then transfer it to storage containers. Store in the refrigerator for up to 5 days, or in the freezer for up to 3 months. Label and date the containers clearly before putting them into the freezer.

Make It Easier

If the broth is allowed to chill overnight in the refrigerator, the fat will harden and rise to the surface, where it is easy to lift away, leaving the broth completely fat free.

FISH BROTH

U SE ONLY THE bones from mild, lean white fish, such as halibut or sole, to make this broth. Bones from oily fish, like salmon, will make a broth that is overpowering.

MAKES ABOUT 2 QUARTS

1. Heat the oil in a soup pot over low heat. Add the fish bones, onions, leeks, celery, and mushrooms (if using). Stir until all the ingredients are evenly coated with oil. Cover the pot and cook without stirring for about 5 minutes.

2. Add the wine (if using) and simmer until the volume of wine is reduced by half. Add the water, peppercorns, parsley stems, fresh herbs, and bay leaves. Bring the broth just up to a simmer. Continue to simmer gently for 35 to 45 minutes.

3. Strain the broth through a sieve. Discard the solids. If the broth is not be used right away, cool it thoroughly before storing it in the refrigerator for up to 3 days or in the freezer for up to 6 weeks (be sure to label and date the storage containers).

Make It Easier

This recipe, as well as those for other broths, can easily be multiplied if you have a good quantity of ingredients on hand. It takes no longer to simmer a gallon of broth than it does two quarts. You can freeze any that you don't need right away. Frozen homemade broth is a "convenience food" that can help make meal preparation a snap on busy nights. If you freeze the broth in ice cube trays, then transfer the frozen cubes to freezer bags, it's easy to retrieve exactly the amount you need. Each cube is about 2 tablespoons of broth; 8 cubes equals 1 cup. Be sure to label and date your frozen broth, so that you use the oldest broth first.

2 tbsp vegetable oil

5 lb fish bones from lean, white fish

2½ cups thinly sliced onions

2½ cups thinly sliced leek (white and light green parts)

1 cup thinly sliced celery

1 cup white mushrooms or mushroom stems, thinly sliced (optional)

1 cup dry white wine (optional)

2½ qt cold water

10 black peppercorns

6 parsley stems

2 sprigs fresh thyme, tarragon, or dill

2 bay leaves

The bones must be perfectly fresh to make this broth. If you won't be able to prepare it right away, store the bones in the freezer. Shells from shrimp, crab, and lobster can be substituted for the bones to prepare a crustacean broth. They can be stored in the freezer, too, until you have enough ingredients and time to make a batch.

VEGETABLE BROTH

2 tsp olive or corn oil

1 to 2 garlic cloves, finely minced

2 tsp minced shallots

3 qt water

1¼ cups thinly sliced onion

3 cups sliced leek (white, light green, and dark
    green parts)

½ cup thinly sliced celery

⅓ cup thinly sliced carrot

⅓ cup thinly sliced parsnip

1 cup thinly sliced broccoli stems

1 cup thinly sliced fennel (with some tops)

½ cup dry white wine or vermouth (optional)

1 tbsp salt, or as needed

4 to 5 whole black peppercorns

½ tsp juniper berries

1 bay leaf

1 sprig fresh thyme or ¼ tsp dried leaves

THE FLAVOR OF this broth far exceeds that of commercially prepared vegetable broths, which always seem to taste like the can they came in. In addition to soups, vegetable broth can be used to prepare grain or bean dishes instead of water or chicken broth, and is good to use as the cooking liquid for pan-steamed vegetables.

MAKES ABOUT 2 QUARTS

1. Heat the olive oil in a soup pot over medium heat. Add the garlic and shallots and cook, stirring frequently, until they are translucent, 3 to 4 minutes.

2. Add the remaining ingredients and bring slowly up to a simmer. Cook until the broth has a good flavor, about 1 hour.

3. Strain the broth through a sieve and then allow it to cool completely before storing in the refrigerator.

Make 1t Easier

When preparing vegetables for other dishes, save any wholesome trim or peels that you want to put into the broth. Then every few days, put on a pot of broth. You will get a nutrient boost, as well as avoiding the use of canned broths that might be higher in sodium than you'd like.

LEFT TO RIGHT: *White and light green vegetables including leeks, parsnips, celery, mushrooms, celery root, and onions produce light-colored broths; roasting vegetables for your stock produces a rich, savory flavor and a deeper color.*

☼ FOCUS ON VEGETABLE BROTHS

A combination of vegetables gives a vegetable broth a well-balanced flavor. You can control the flavor and color of the broth by selecting your vegetables carefully. Beets, carrots, and tomatoes will affect a broth's color and can be used to advantage as the base for soups like Borscht (page 34) or Cold Carrot Bisque (page 207).

➡ *FOR A LIGHT COLORED BROTH* with a savory flavor, choose a variety of onions (leeks, white or yellow onions, shallots, garlic, and scallions). Add parsnips, celery (or celery root), mushrooms, pea pods, or broccoli stems, in fact, any light green or white vegetable you like (except potatoes, which will produce a cloudy, starchy broth). Cut the vegetables small or slice them thin, to encourage the best flavor extraction.

➡ *ADDING ORANGE AND RED VEGETABLES* to your broth will give the finished broth a deeper, redder color. Carrots and tomatoes are common additions. To further intensify the flavor and color of your broth, cut the vegetables and put them in a baking dish. Toss them with a little oil and roast them until the juices the vegetables release begin to turn brown.

➡ *LEARN WHAT 4 POUNDS OF CUT-UP VEGETABLES LOOKS LIKE* in your soup pot, and you can improvise easily. Just fill up the pot, add enough water to cover the vegetables by slightly less than 2 inches, and bring the broth to a simmer. Don't let the broth reach a rolling boil; some of the flavorful compounds in certain vegetables are destroyed at high temperatures. Once the broth has simmered for about 30 to 40 minutes, you can strain it. Vegetable broths don't become as clear as meat broths, so you can simply pour the broth through a strainer rather than ladling the broth away from the solids.

☼ FOCUS ON CONSOMMÉS

Consommés are richly flavored, perfectly clear broths of the best quality. They are made by gently simmering a flavorful stock or broth with a combination of lean raw ground meat (beef, chicken, or fish, depending upon the flavor you want for your consommé), egg whites, aromatic vegetables, herbs, and spices along with an acidic ingredient—tomato, lemon juice, vinegar, or dry wines, for instance.

➡ All of these ingredients, known in the professional kitchen as the clarification, should be very cold. They are stirred together with the stock or broth you have selected as your base; it must also be very cold for the best results. While the consommé simmers, the ingredients in the clarification begin to bind together into a loose mass, something you may have heard referred to as a raft since it floats on the surface of the soup.

➡ Sometimes, you may find a small break in the raft that permits you to see into the pot. If not, use the handle of a wooden spoon to make a small opening. This vents the steam away from the consommé as well as gives you a window so you can check on the color, flavor, and clarity of the consommé as it cooks. Turn the heat down as low as possible and continue to simmer very gently. You should see small bubbles rising to the surface, not too many and not too rapidly. Some chefs suggest that you baste the raft as the consommé simmers to improve flavor extraction.

➡ Most consommés should simmer 1 to 1½ hours. By that time, the color and flavor of the consommé is well developed and the raft is just starting to sink. Your next job is separate the consommé from the raft without breaking it up and spoiling your careful work. Do not pour the consommé and raft through the sieve! Widen an opening in the raft big enough to fit a ladle through and ladle the consommé out of the pot and through a very fine wire-mesh strainer (sometimes known as a bouillon strainer) or a colander or strainer that you've lined with cheesecloth or a large coffee filter.

➡ Your finished consommé should be crystal clear, highly flavored, richly colored, and full-bodied. It should also be completely fat free. If time allows, chill the consommé and remove the fat that hardens on the surface. If you don't have time, you can drag strips of coffee filter paper over the surface to blot away any droplets of fat.

➡ The range of garnish options for a consommé are legion, and runs the gamut from chopped fresh herbs to springtime vegetables, dumplings to wontons, and on. Consommés can be served cold; if you've done a good job of preparing the consommé, it may gel as it is cooled, for an unforgettable cold soup.

Oignon Brûlée

To give your consommés, broths, or stocks a rich, golden color, you can use this technique to bolster both flavor and color:

1. Cut an onion in half, put the cut side down into a very hot, dry cast iron pan.

2. Let the onion cook until it is extremely dark, almost black.

3. Add the charred onion, known in French as a *oignon brûlée*, to the pot as the consommé simmers.

CHICKEN CONSOMMÉ

Consommés require a lot of attention and patience, so when you decide to make consommé, make the biggest batch you can manage using the largest pot you have available. Consommé, like all broths, freezes beautifully.

MAKES ABOUT 2 QUARTS

1. Combine the cold broth, chicken breast, egg whites, tomato purée, onion, carrot, celery, oignon brûlé (if using), parsley, thyme, bay leaf, salt, and peppercorns in a 6-quart pot. Stir until the ingredients are evenly blended. Place the pot over low heat. Stir the consommé frequently while it begins to heat up to a simmer.

2. As soon as the solid ingredients begin to form a raft and rise to the surface, stop stirring the soup; you want the raft to stay in one piece so it won't break up and cloud the finished consommé. When the raft has risen to the surface, check it carefully.

3. Simmer the consommé until it is very flavorful and extremely clear, 1 to 1½ hours. Ladle the consommé from the pot and strain it through a wire-mesh strainer lined with a coffee filter. The consommé can be served now with the garnish of your choice. You can also cool the consommé and then store it in sealed containers in the refrigerator for up to 1 week and in the freezer for up to 2 months.

3 quarts Chicken Broth (page 15), cold

1½ lb lean ground chicken breast

5 egg whites, lightly beaten

¼ cup tomato purée (or 2 tbsp tomato paste)

½ cup minced onion

⅓ cup minced or grated carrot

⅓ cup minced celery

½ oignon brûlée, halved and charred (optional, see opposite)

2 sprigs parsley

1 sprig thyme

1 bay leaf

2 tsp kosher salt

4 or 5 black peppercorns

CHICKEN AND CORN NOODLE SOUP

Stewing hens (or fowls) are the best choice for soups; they are more full-flavored than fryers or broilers, and you will end up with a soup that has a wonderfully rich flavor and body. You can use the entire bird to prepare a gallon of broth. The saffron lends this soup a deep golden color as well as a subtle flavor, but may be omitted if you prefer.

MAKES 8 SERVINGS

1. Combine the stewing hen with the broth, onion, carrot, celery, and the saffron threads in a soup pot. Bring to a simmer and cook for about 1 hour, skimming the surface as necessary.

2. Remove the stewing hen from the broth. When cool enough to handle, pick the meat from the bones and cut into a neat dice.

3. Strain the saffron broth through a fine sieve.

4. Add the noodles, corn, finely diced celery, and parsley to the broth. Return the soup to a simmer. Season to taste with the salt and pepper. Serve in heated bowls.

½ stewing hen or fowl, quartered

2 qt Chicken Broth (page 15)

¾ cup chopped onion

½ cup chopped carrot

½ cup chopped celery

1 tsp crushed saffron threads

1 cup dry egg noodles

¾ cup corn kernels (fresh or frozen)

½ cup finely diced celery

1 tbsp chopped fresh parsley

Salt as needed

Freshly ground black pepper as needed

ROAST TURKEY BROTH

*with Caramelized Butternut Squash
and Sage Dumplings*

{PICTURED AT RIGHT}

*4 lb turkey legs or meaty turkey bones (wings,
    backs, necks) and giblets (excluding the liver)*

*3 qt Chicken or Turkey Broth (page 15), or as
    needed*

1¼ cups thinly sliced onion

⅓ cup thinly sliced carrot

½ cup thinly sliced celery

5 to 6 whole black peppercorns

3 to 4 parsley stems

1 bay leaf

1 sprig fresh thyme

Salt as needed

2 tbsp unsalted butter

2 cups diced butternut squash (about 1 pound)

Freshly ground white pepper as needed

1 recipe Sage Dumplings (page 234)

The Sage Dumplings (page 234) can be cooked
ahead and held under refrigeration until needed.

THIS DOUBLE BROTH is perfect for a cold winter's day. If you happen to have the carcass of a roast turkey on hand, chop it into large pieces and roast it instead of the fresh bones. You can add leftover roast turkey meat to the soup as well.

MAKES 8 SERVINGS

1. Preheat the oven to 400°F. Spread the turkey legs or bones in a single layer in a roasting pan and roast in the oven until deep golden brown, about 1 hour.

2. Transfer the turkey legs or bones to a large soup pot. Add 2 cups of the broth to the hot roasting pan and scrape the bottom of the pan with a wooden spoon to loosen any drippings. Pour over the turkey legs or bones.

3. Add enough broth to cover by at least 2 inches. Bring slowly to a boil over medium heat. As the liquid comes to a boil, skim away any foam that rises to the surface. Adjust the heat once a boil is reached so that a slow, lazy simmer is established. Simmer for 1 hour, skimming as often as necessary.

4. Add the onion, carrot, celery, peppercorns, parsley stems, bay leaf, thyme, and salt to taste. Continue to simmer, skimming the surface as necessary, until the broth is fully flavored, about 1 hour.

5. While the broth is simmering, heat the butter in a large ovenproof skillet over medium heat. Add the squash and cook, stirring occasionally, until brown on all sides, 15 to 20 minutes. Season the squash with the salt and pepper and place the skillet in the 400°F oven. Roast the squash until tender, about 10 minutes. Remove the squash from the oven, drain off any excess fat, and set aside.

6. When the broth is fully flavored, strain it through a fine sieve or cheesecloth-lined colander into a clean soup pot. If you used turkey legs, remove the skin, pull the meat from the bones, dice it, and return it to the broth or save for another purpose. Discard the remaining solids.

7. Add the squash and dumplings to the broth. Return to a simmer briefly to heat through. Season to taste with salt and pepper. Serve in heated bowls.

If you are not serving all the soup at once, refrigerate the broth, squash, and dumplings separately, and reheat only as much as you need.

STRACCIATELLA

{PICTURED AT LEFT}

THE NAME OF this simple soup means "rags." By whipping the soup as you add the beaten eggs and Parmesan cheese, the eggs cook into threads or "rags." Use either homemade or good-quality canned broth to prepare this soup.

MAKES 6 TO 8 SERVINGS

6 cups Chicken or Beef Broth (pages 15, 16)

2 whole eggs

¼ cup freshly grated Parmesan cheese

Salt as needed

Freshly ground white pepper as needed

6 to 8 slices French bread

Extra-virgin olive oil as needed

1 garlic clove, halved

1 tbsp chopped parsley (optional)

1. Preheat the oven to 375°F. Bring the broth to a simmer in a soup pot.

2. Whisk the eggs and Parmesan together in a small bowl. Whip the broth constantly as you add the egg mixture to the broth in a thin stream. Season the soup to taste with salt and pepper. Keep warm.

3. Brush each slice of bread with olive oil and rub with the cut side of a garlic clove half. Place on a baking sheet and toast in the oven until lightly browned and crisp, 4 to 5 minutes.

4. Place each piece of toast in the bottom of a heated soup bowl and ladle the soup over the toast. Sprinkle with parsley (if using) and serve immediately.

AVGOLEMONO

Greek Egg and Lemon Soup

AVGOLEMONO IS THE name of a soup and a sauce. Both are made with chicken broth, eggs, and lemon. The differences between the two are that the sauce is thicker than the soup, and the soup contains rice. The soup should have a definite taste of lemon, but not an overpowering one. Use only freshly squeezed lemon juice for a clean, delicate flavor.

MAKES 6 TO 8 SERVINGS

6 cups Chicken Broth (page 15)

⅓ cup long-grain white rice

4 eggs, separated

Salt as needed

Freshly ground white pepper as needed

Freshly squeezed lemon juice as needed

1. Bring the broth to a simmer in a soup pot. Add the rice and cook until the rice is tender, about 15 minutes.

2. Whip the egg yolks in a large bowl until thickened. Whip the egg whites in another bowl to soft peaks. Fold the whites into the yolks. Add the egg mixture to simmering broth, whipping constantly. The soup will become frothy and thick.

3. Season the soup to taste with the salt, pepper, and lemon juice. Serve in heated bowls.

FILLING INGREDIENTS:

3 oz chicken breast, cooked or raw

4 oz pork meat, cooked or raw

2 tbsp butter (if needed)

3 oz mortadella

3 oz prosciutto

1 large egg

6 oz Parmigiano-Reggiano cheese

Salt and nutmeg as needed

1 recipe Pasta Dough (page 233)

1½ qt Beef or Chicken Broth (page 16, 15)

TORTELLINI IN BRODO

T HIS IS A well-known dish in Italy, specially served during holidays. Tortellini are also popular accompanied by various sauces, of course, but are more typically enjoyed *in brodo*—in broth—as in this flavorful preparation.

MAKES 6 TO 8 SERVINGS

1. If you are using uncooked meats, cut them into large dice and sauté them in the butter over medium-high heat until they are golden on all sides and have cooked through, about 6 to 7 minutes total cooking time. Let the meat cool before you grind it.

2. Set up a meat grinder with a bowl to catch the meat as you grind it. Cut the cooked meats into pieces and drop them through the opening of the meat grinder while it is running. Grind the mortadella and the prosciutto with the cooked meats.

3. Add the egg, Parmigiano-Reggiano, salt, and a few grains of nutmeg to the ground meats. Stir to blend evenly. Refrigerate until needed.

4. Make the pasta dough as described on page 233 and roll it into thin sheets. Cut each sheet into 2-inch wide circles or squares. Fill the dough squares or circles with a small amount of the filling (about 1 teaspoon). Fold them in half and press the edges together to seal the tortellini. Finish shaping them by folding the two tips around your index finger and press the tips well to seal them together. Repeat with the remaining balls of pasta dough.

5. Bring the broth to a simmer in a soup pot over medium-high heat. Add the tortellini and cook until the pasta is tender, about 10 minutes.

6. Serve the soup immediately in heated soup plates or bowls. Pass additional grated Parmigiano-Reggiano cheese on the side.

Though there are an abundance of good-quality premade filled pastas available, the taste of freshly made tortellini is well worth the time and effort. Find the recipe and instructions for making the pasta dough on page 233.

PETITE MARMITE

{PICTURED AT LEFT}

WHEN IT COMES to having their own dinner, many professional chefs like nothing better than a big bowl of petite marmite, a heavenly broth full of meat, poultry, and vegetables. Though named and claimed by the French, this soup can be found in one form or another in virtually every world cuisine, although the aromatic flavorings and the presentation may vary. Some people serve the broth as a first course with the meats and vegetables following; others present the meats and vegetables as the soup's garnish (the approach suggested here). Add some crusty bread and either way you serve it, this soup makes a healthy and hearty meal.

MAKES 8 SERVINGS

1. Remove the neck and giblets from the cavity of the chicken. Rinse the cavity with cold water. Place the beef and chicken in a large soup pot and cover with the cold broth. Bring to a simmer over low heat. With a shallow flat spoon, skim the scum off as it rises to the surface and discard. Simmer until the beef and chicken are fork-tender, about 2 hours.

2. Remove the beef and chicken and cool. Strain the broth through a cheesecloth-lined strainer. Return the broth to the soup pot.

3. Add the celery, leeks, onion, carrot, turnip, cabbage, and sachet to the broth. Bring to a simmer and cook until the vegetables are tender, 15 to 20 minutes. Remove and discard the sachet.

4. When the beef and chicken have cooled, remove the gristle from the beef and dice. Remove the skin and bones from the chicken. Dice the chicken meat. Return the beef and the chicken to the broth. Simmer for an additional 5 minutes to heat thoroughly. Season to taste with the salt and pepper.

5. Serve in heated bowls, garnished with the parsley and croutons.

Preparing Marrow for a Petite Marmite

Some people do not consider a Petite Marmite to be authentic unless it contains diced marrow. To add the marrow, first soak 1 pound of marrow bones in cold water for several hours; rinse well. Place the bones in a pot, cover with cold water, and bring to a simmer. Cook until the marrow can easily be scooped out of the bone with a spoon, 45 minutes to 1 hour. Dice the marrow and add it to the broth when you add the diced meat and poultry.

---

1 chicken (about 3 pounds)

1½ lb beef bottom round

3 qt Chicken Broth (page 15), cold

2 celery stalks, diced

1 cup diced leeks, white and light green parts

1½ cups diced onion

½ cup diced carrot

1 cup diced white turnip

2 cups diced or shredded white or green cabbage

Sachet: 1 bay leaf, ¼ tsp dried thyme, 4 black peppercorns, 4 parsley stems, 1 peeled garlic clove enclosed in a large tea ball or tied in a cheesecloth pouch

Salt as needed

Freshly ground black pepper as needed

¼ cup chopped parsley

1½ cups Croutons (page 222)

You may substitute any of the following meats for, or combine them with, the beef and chicken: venison or other game meats, oxtails, pheasant or other game birds, turkey, ham hocks, pork, or lamb. The total weight should be about 4 pounds. Increase the broth as needed to cover the meats completely and follow the method appropriately.

ONION SOUP GRATINÉE

{PICTURED AT LEFT}

THE SECRET TO making a fine French onion soup is to give it lots of time to develop flavor. The onions should be cooked slowly until they become deeply caramelized. Use a heavy gauge pot and allow plenty of time to get the rich color you need; you want the onions to be about as dark as a cup of coffee. Keeping the heat low and cooking them gently gives you a rich flavor and avoids problems of scorching and bitterness. Give yourself plenty of time; it takes almost an hour to get the right color.

MAKES 8 SERVINGS

1. Heat the oil in a soup pot over medium-low heat. Add the onions and cook without stirring until the onions begin to brown on the bottom. Raise the heat to medium, stir, and continue to cook, stirring occasionally, until the onions are deeply caramelized (dark golden brown). The total cooking time will be 40 to 45 minutes. If the onions begin to scorch, add a few tablespoons of water and continue cooking.

2. Add the garlic and continue to cook for an additional minute. Add the brandy and simmer until the liquid has nearly evaporated, 2 to 3 minutes.

3. Add the broth and sachet. Bring to a simmer and cook, partially covered, for 45 minutes to 1 hour, skimming the surface as necessary and discarding the fat. Remove and discard the sachet. Season to taste with salt and pepper.

4. When ready to serve the soup, preheat the oven to 350°F and bring 2 quarts of water to a boil. Ladle the soup into individual oven-proof soup crocks. Top each crock with a slice of bread and sprinkle with the grated cheese, covering the bread completely and allowing the cheese to touch the edge of the crock.

5. Set the soup crocks in a baking dish and add enough boiling water to the baking dish to reach two-thirds up the sides of the crocks. Bake until the soup is thoroughly heated and the cheese is lightly browned, 10 to 15 minutes. Serve immediately.

Make It Authentic

For an authentic French presentation, we've suggested baking the soup along with its crouton and topping of cheese. You can skip that step if you are short on time, but try it this way at least once; your efforts will be well repaid.

¼ cup olive or vegetable oil

5 cups thinly sliced onions

1 tsp minced garlic

½ cup brandy

1½ qt Beef or Chicken Broth, heated (pages 16, 15)

Sachet: 3 to 4 parsley stems, ½ tsp each dried thyme and tarragon, 1 bay leaf enclosed in a large tea ball or tied in a cheesecloth pouch

Salt as needed

Freshly ground black pepper as needed

8 slices French bread

1 cup grated Gruyère cheese, or as needed

If this is your first time making onion soup, you may wonder if you are burning the onions. Don't panic. If a few bits of onion get too dark, immediately add a spoonful of broth or water. That will stop the scorching. Stir well to even out the color.

{PICTURED AT RIGHT}

2 medium beets

2 tbsp minced bacon

2½ cups minced onion

2 celery stalks, cut into matchsticks

2 parsnips, cut into matchsticks

1 carrot, cut into matchsticks

1 leek, white and light green parts, cut into
*   matchsticks*

½ head Savoy cabbage, shredded

2 qt Chicken or Vegetable Broth (pages 15, 18)

Sachet: 1 tsp dried marjoram, 4 to 5 parsley
*   stems, 2 cloves peeled garlic, and 1 bay leaf*
*   enclosed in a large tea ball or tied in a*
*   cheesecloth pouch*

Red wine vinegar as needed

Salt as needed

Freshly ground black pepper as needed

½ cup sour cream

¼ cup minced fresh dill

BORSCHT

BORSCHT IS ONE of those soups that has dozens of variations. This version of the classic Russian beet soup uses lots of vegetables and a touch of bacon for extra flavor. You can leave the bacon out and use vegetable broth if you prefer a vegetarian soup. Grating the beets into the soup releases maximum beet flavor. Though this recipe calls for the borscht to be served hot, it is also delicious when served cold.

MAKES 8 SERVINGS

1. Simmer the beets in enough boiling water to cover until partially cooked, 10 to 15 minutes. When cool enough to handle, peel and reserve for later use (use gloves to keep your hands from turning purple).

2. Cook the bacon in a soup pot over medium heat until crisp, 6 to 8 minutes.

3. Add the onion, celery, parsnips, carrot, leek, and cabbage. Cover and cook over low heat, stirring occasionally, until the vegetables are translucent, about 15 minutes.

4. Add the broth and sachet. Bring to a simmer and cook for 10 minutes.

5. Grate the parboiled beets (wear gloves) directly into the soup and simmer until all the vegetables are tender, about 10 minutes.

6. Remove and discard the sachet. Season to taste with the vinegar, salt, and pepper. Serve in heated bowls, garnished with the sour cream and dill.

{PICTURED AT RIGHT}

1 chayote

3 tbsp olive oil

1 poblano chile

1 tsp minced garlic

2 tbsp minced jalapeño

1 tsp ground coriander (preferably fresh ground)

*1½ lb boneless, skinless chicken breasts, cut into
    small cubes*

1½ qt Chicken Broth (page 15)

5 canned Italian plum tomatoes, chopped

1 cup diced onion

⅓ cup small-dice carrot

½ cup small-dice celery

1 cup small-dice yellow squash

1 tbsp chopped cilantro

Salt as needed

Freshly ground black pepper as needed

CHICKEN VEGETABLE SOUP AZTECA

THIS SOUP INCLUDES several important New World foods: poblano chiles, jalapeño, tomatoes, and a soft-skinned squash known as a chayote.

MAKES 8 SERVINGS

1. Preheat the oven to 350°F. Rub the chayote with 1 teaspoon of the oil and place on a baking sheet. Roast the chayote in the oven until the skin browns lightly and the flesh becomes barely tender, 25 to 30 minutes. When cool enough to handle, use a paring knife to scrape away the skin. Cut the chayote in half from top to bottom and use a spoon to scoop out the edible seed, which you can either discard or eat as a snack. Dice the flesh and set aside.

2. Increase the oven temperature to Broil. Brush the poblano with 1 teaspoon of the oil. Place the poblano under the broiler and turn as it roasts so that it blackens evenly on all sides. Put the poblano in a small bowl and cover. Let the poblano steam for 10 minutes, then remove it from the bowl and pull off the skin. Use the back of a knife to scrape away any bits that don't come away easily. Remove and discard the seeds, ribs, and stem. Dice the flesh and set aside.

3. Heat the remaining oil in a soup pot over medium heat. Add the garlic, jalapeño pepper, and coriander. Cook, stirring occasionally, until slightly softened, about 4 minutes. Add the chicken and cook, stirring occasionally, until the chicken is just cooked through, about 8 minutes.

4. Add the chayote, poblano, broth, tomatoes, onion, carrot, celery, and yellow squash. Bring to a simmer and cook until all the vegetables are tender, about 30 minutes. Add the cilantro and season to taste with the salt and pepper. Serve in heated bowls.

Preparing a Chayote Squash

Once an important food for the Aztec and Maya peoples of Central America, the chayote is a pear-shaped fruit with furrowed, pale green skin. It is also known variously as a mirliton, a christophene, and a vegetable pear. It has a rather mild flavor that has been described as a blend of cucumber, zucchini, and kohlrabi.

You can roast the chayote to blister the skin and make it easy to remove. Once roasted, cut the chayote in half from top to bottom. There is a single large seed in the center of the squash that you will be able to slice through easily. Use a spoon to scoop out the seed, which you can either discard or eat as a snack. Use a paring knife to scrape away the skin. Dice the flesh and set aside.

☀ PREPARING BELL PEPPERS AND CHILES

Peppers may be prepared in several ways for the soups and stews of Latin America, Southeast Asia, the Mediterranean, and the American Southwest.

➡ *CUTTING AND SEEDING PEPPERS:* Cut a bell pepper or chile in half or quarters lengthwise from the stem end to the root end. Using the tip of a paring knife, cut away the stem, pale membranes (also called ribs), and seeds (below right). Since the heat of chiles comes from a substance called capsaicin that is found in their seeds and membranes, you can lower a dish's heat level by removing all or most of the seeds and membranes. When working with very hot chiles, you

might choose to wear plastic gloves to protect your skin from the irritating oils they contain. Be careful not to touch your eyes, nose, and mouth after touching cut chiles. Wash your hands after working with hot chiles.

➡ *PEELING RAW PEPPERS:* The skins of peppers and chiles are thin, tough, and firmly attached to the flesh. Peppers and chiles are often peeled before they are used in a dish to improve the dish's flavor and texture. The thin but relatively tough skin can be removed using a swivel-bladed peeler or paring knife. This approach is ideal for dishes that highlight the peppers' sweet flavor or that include raw peppers, such as a salad or salsa. Cut the pepper into sections first to create edges of skin that make peeling easier.

➡ *ROASTING AND PEELING PEPPERS:* When peppers and chiles are charred over a flame, grilled, roasted, or broiled, not only are the flavors brought out, but the skins are loosened as well. If you have gas burners, hold the peppers over the flame with tongs or a large kitchen fork, turning to char them evenly. If your grill is hot, char the peppers over hot coals or high heat. To roast or broil peppers and chiles in a hot oven or under a broiler, halve them; remove their stems, seeds, and membranes; and place them cut side down on an oiled sheet pan. Broil or roast until their skin is black and blistered.

Once the entire pepper is evenly charred, transfer to a paper bag or bowl and close or cover tightly. By the time they are cool enough to handle, about 10 minutes, steam will have loosened the skin enough that it peels away easily. Peel and rub it away with your fingertips, using a paring knife if the skin clings in some places.

DOUBLE CHICKEN BROTH

with Shiitakes, Scallions and Tofu

THIS SOUP IS quick to prepare and makes a good introduction to a meal of stir-fried shrimp and vegetables. "Double broth" means simply that chicken broth is used to poach more chicken, which doubles the flavor of the broth.

MAKES 8 SERVINGS

1. Place the tofu on paper toweling and let drain while the soup is simmering. Trim any visible fat from the chicken breast and cut it into strips.

2. Bring broth to a simmer in a soup pot over high heat. Add the chicken, reduce the heat to low, and simmer for 10 minutes. Skim away any foam that rises to the surface.

3. Add the tofu, shiitakes, scallions, cilantro, and ginger. Simmer until all ingredients are heated through and the flavors are blended, 5 to 10 minutes.

4. Add the soy sauce, pepper, and lime juice to taste. Serve in heated bowls.

To serve this soup on its own as an entire meal, increase the amount of chicken breast and include as many of the following items as you like: broccoli florets, sliced celery, shredded bok choy or celery, cabbage, snow peas, green beans, chick peas, or cucumbers. Conclude the meal with a fruit-flavored sorbet or ice.

1 cup diced soft tofu

½ lb boneless, skinless chicken breast

2 qt Chicken Broth (page 15)

8 shiitake mushrooms (dry or fresh)

6 scallions, sliced diagonally

2 tbsp chopped fresh cilantro

2 tsp minced fresh ginger

4 tsp soy or tamari sauce

½ tsp freshly ground black pepper, or as needed

Freshly squeezed lime juice as needed

SOTO AYAM

Indonesian Chicken, Noodle, and Potato Soup

{PICTURED AT LEFT}

Don't let the long list of ingredients and steps deter you from making this soup. It's truly delicious and not all that much trouble to make, despite appearances. Any of the ingredients you can't find at your supermarket are available at Asian groceries. To crush the aromatic ingredients, cover with a piece of plastic wrap and smash with the bottom of a heavy pot or skillet.

MAKES 8 SERVINGS

1. Remove the giblets from the chicken; discard or save the liver for another use. Wash the chicken and rub it with ½ teaspoon of the salt. Set aside.

2. Heat the oil in a skillet over high heat. Add the chopped shallots, lemongrass, garlic, ginger, black pepper, and turmeric. Cook, stirring constantly, until the aroma is apparent, about 30 seconds. Remove from the heat.

3. Combine the broth and remaining 1½ teaspoons salt with the chicken, giblets, and shallot mixture in a soup pot. Bring to a simmer and cook until the chicken is cooked through and tender, about 45 minutes. Skim often to remove the foam that rises to the surface during simmering.

4. Remove the chicken from the broth and, when cool enough to handle, remove the bones from the chicken. Return the bones to the broth and continue to simmer for another hour, skimming as needed. Meanwhile, dice the chicken meat and set aside.

5. Place the potatoes in a saucepan, cover with cold water, and bring to a simmer. Cook until tender, about 20 minutes. Drain and spread the potatoes in a single layer to cool.

6. Soak the beans threads in hot water to cover until tender, about 5 minutes. Rinse and separate the strands under cool running water. Chop into 2-inch pieces and set aside.

7. When the broth has simmered for an hour, strain it through a fine sieve. Mix the soy sauce, chili paste, and sugar together; stir into the strained broth.

8. Add the diced chicken meat, cooked potatoes, soaked bean threads, scallions, chopped eggs, and celery to the broth. Bring to a simmer and add a squeeze of lemon to taste.

9. Serve the soup in heated bowls, garnished with the fried shallots. Pass the lemon wedges on the side.

1 small chicken (about 3 pounds)

2 tsp salt

½ tbsp vegetable oil

4 shallots, chopped

2 stalks fresh lemongrass, bottom 4 or 5 inches only, crushed

1 garlic clove, crushed

One 1-inch slice fresh ginger, crushed

½ tsp crushed black peppercorns

¼ tsp turmeric

1½ qt Chicken Broth (page 15)

1¼ cups diced yellow or white potatoes

1 oz dried mung bean threads ("cellophane noodles")

2 tbsp soy sauce

½ tbsp red chili or hot bean paste

½ tsp sugar

4 scallions, thinly sliced

2 hard boiled eggs, chopped

1½ celery stalks, diced

FOR GARNISH

Fried Shallots (page 238)

1 lemon, cut into wedges

VIETNAMESE WATER SPINACH AND BEEF SOUP

{PICTURED AT LEFT}

WATER SPINACH IS cultivated and also grows wild throughout Asia. Also known as swamp cabbage, it bears no relationship to either ordinary spinach or cabbage, though it is used in much the same way as spinach for some purposes. Water spinach leaves are tender and have a sweet, mild flavor and slightly slippery texture when cooked. The edible stems provide a crisp contrast to the leaves. Look for water spinach at Asian groceries. It wilts quickly, so buy only the freshest looking bunch. Plan to store it no longer than two days wrapped in a plastic bag in the bottom of your refrigerator. If you cannot find water spinach, ordinary spinach makes a fine substitute.

MAKES 6 TO 8 SERVINGS

1. Bring a medium pot of water to a boil. Add the water spinach or spinach leaves and cook just until wilted, 1 to 2 minutes. Remove the spinach with a slotted spoon and drain well. When cool enough to handle, squeeze the excess moisture from the spinach and chop it. Set aside.

2. Soak the beans threads in hot water to cover until tender, about 5 minutes. Rinse and separate the strands under cool running water. Chop into 2-inch pieces and set aside.

3. Heat the oil in large wok or soup pot over medium-high heat. Add the shallots, garlic, and red pepper. Stir-fry for 30 seconds. Add the beef and stir-fry for 1 minute. Add the broth, soy sauce, fish sauce, lemon juice, and sugar. Bring the soup to a simmer. Add the spinach and season to taste with the salt and black pepper.

4. Distribute the bean threads evenly between heated bowls. Ladle the soup over the bean threads and garnish with the cilantro.

2 oz fresh water spinach, tough stem parts trimmed, or 1 cup packed spinach leaves

1 oz dried mung bean threads ("cellophane noodles")

1 tbsp vegetable oil

1 tbsp sliced shallot

½ tsp minced garlic

Pinch crushed red pepper

3 oz beef flank steak, cut into thin strips

1 qt Chicken Broth (page 15)

1 tbsp soy sauce

1 tbsp Vietnamese fish sauce (nuoc mam)

1 tbsp lemon juice

½ tsp sugar

Salt as needed

Freshly ground black pepper as needed

2 tbsp chopped cilantro

1½ cups packed spinach leaves, rinsed well

2 cups Chicken Broth (page 15)

2 cups Dashi (page 62)

1 tbsp tamari

6 oz soft tofu, diced

½ cup crabmeat, picked over for shells, roughly cut if pieces are large

¼ cup dried wakame seaweed, broken into 1-inch pieces (optional)

Salt as needed

Freshly ground white pepper as needed

1 egg, beaten

1½ tsp dark (Asian) sesame oil

CRABMEAT TOFU SOUP

I F YOU WISH to use instant dashi in this soup, increase the quantity of chicken broth to 4 cups and use 1½ teaspoons of instant dashi granules.

MAKES 6 SERVINGS

1. Bring a medium pot of water to a boil. Add the spinach and cook just until wilted, 1 to 2 minutes. Remove the spinach with a slotted spoon and drain well. When cool enough to handle, squeeze the excess moisture from the spinach and chop it. Set aside.

2. Bring the broth and dashi to a simmer in a large wok or a soup pot. Add the tamari tofu, crabmeat, and seaweed (if using). Season to taste with the salt and pepper.

3. Return the soup to a simmer. While stirring gently, pour the egg into the soup and continue to stir gently until bits of egg float to the top of the soup.

4. Just before serving, add the sesame oil and chopped spinach. Serve in heated bowls.

Asian Ingredients

- **TOFU** is sold in solid blocks that usually weigh about 12 ounces. It is packed in liquid (usually water) to keep it fresh and to prevent it from drying out. Tofu is a perishable food that will be best if you prepare it within 2 days of purchase.

  Tofu is available in a variety of firmnesses: silk, which is very soft and slippery almost like a custard; medium, and firm. Drain and press the tofu as follows:

  Put 3 or 4 layers of paper towels in a plate or baking pan. Remove the tofu from the package and put it on the plate. Add 3 or 4 more layers of paper towels to cover the tofu. Next, put something flat, like a baking pan, on top of the stack. To press the tofu

for a more compact texture, set a few cans in the pan for weight. Put the whole assembly into the refrigerator and let the tofu drain for about 1 hour.

- **DASHI,** a primary ingredient in Japanese cooking, is a broth made by simmering flakes of dried bonito tuna (*katsuobushi*) with pieces of seaweed. Instant dashi (*dashi-no-moto*) is available as powdered granules or a liquid concentrate. In the U.S., it is sometimes marketed as "bonito-flavored soup stock."

- **KELP** (also sold as *kombu, konbu, laminaria*) is the best known species of seaweed. It has been cultivated in Japan for about 300 years. A rich stock (*dashi*) can be prepared from kelp because of its concentration of the flavor-enhancer, glutamic acid.

- **NORI** is an edible seaweed belonging to entirely different families of algae. It is native to Japan and also coastlines from the Atlantic to the Baltic Sea, and the Pacific coasts of North and South America to the beaches of Hawaii. In Ireland, it is called *sloke;* and, in Wales, *laver,* where it is eaten as a fresh vegetable.

  Fresh seaweed is chopped, pressed between bamboo mats, and dried either in drying rooms or in the sun. Good quality nori is mild-tasting and black with a purple-green sheen.

- **WAKAME** looks and tastes like slippery spinach, and can be used in much the same manner as *kombu* in broths and soups. When dried wakame is soaked in water it expands to at least 10 times its dried size.

MUSSEL SOUP

{PICTURED AT LEFT}

YOU CAN SUBSTITUTE a variety of seafood for the mussels if you like. Any white fish, such as flounder, halibut, or monkfish, works well, as does shelled and deveined shrimp. Freshly shucked clams or oysters are tasty in this soup, too.

MAKES 8 SERVINGS

1. In a pot large enough to accommodate the mussels, combine the wine, shallot, bay leaf, thyme sprig (if using), and enough water to raise the liquid level to about 1 inch. Bring to a boil. Add the mussels, cover, and steam until the mussels open, about 5 minutes. Use a slotted spoon to transfer the mussels to a bowl and let cool slightly. Remove the mussels from their shells and set aside (discard the shells as well as any mussels that do not open). Strain the cooking liquid through a coffee filter and set aside.

2. Heat the olive oil in a soup pot over medium heat. Add the onion, leek, celery, and garlic. Cover the pot, reduce the heat to medium-low, and cook until the vegetables are translucent, 6 to 8 minutes.

3. Combine the mussel cooking liquid with the reserved tomato juice. Add enough fish broth or water to make 1 quart. Add this mixture along with the tomatoes and the dried basil to the soup pot. Bring to a simmer and cook, partially covered, for 10 to 12 minutes.

4. Add the mussels and cover the pot. Simmer until the mussels are heated through, about 2 minutes.

5. Season to taste with the salt, pepper, and lemon zest. Serve in heated bowls, garnished with the fresh basil or parsley.

About Mussels

Mussels are both delicious and attractive. They are best when you give them appropriate care. Remember that they should be alive when you buy them and when they go into the pot. The first, and most important, step is buying them from a reliable source. The fish market, stall, or counter you visit should smell pleasantly of the sea and be very busy. Strong or unpleasant odors may be sign that the fish is not fresh. The faster the fish is sold, the fresher it is likely to be.

- Keep mussels in paper bags or wrapping in the refrigerator until you are ready to cook them. Try to buy seafood the day you want to cook it, but if you need to hold it for a day or two, it will be fine. (continues on next page)

½ cup white wine

1 shallot, minced

1 bay leaf

1 fresh thyme sprig (optional)

50 mussels (about 3 pounds), scrubbed and debearded

¼ cup olive oil

1 cup finely diced onion

1¼ cups finely diced leek, white and light green parts

½ cup finely diced celery

2 tsp minced garlic

2 cups chopped plum tomatoes, peeled and seeded, juices reserved

1 to 2 cups Fish Broth (page 17) or water, as needed

1 tsp dried basil

Salt as needed

Freshly ground black pepper as needed

½ tsp grated lemon zest

¼ cup chopped fresh basil or parsley

Try one or more of any of the following variations:

- Add ½ teaspoon of saffron with the tomatoes

- Substitute ¼ cup Pernod and ¼ cup dry vermouth for the white wine

- Add a sachet containing ½ teaspoon each of anise seeds and fennel seeds and 1 clove of peeled garlic, at the same time that the tomatoes are added

- When you are ready to cook mussels, the first step is to clean them well. Put them in a colander, set them in the sink, and turn on the cold water tap. One by one, take the shellfish in one hand and a scrub brush in the other. Clean the shells thoroughly under running cold water. You may see that some of the shellfish has opened up. As long as the shell snaps shut again when you tap it, the mussel or clam is fine. If it stays open, throw it out.

- The hairy, inedible filaments that protrude from a mussel are known as its "beard." To debeard a mussel, trap the hairy "beard" between the flat side of a paring knife blade and the pad of your thumb or pinch the filaments between thumb and forefinger, and then pull the beard away firmly. Debearding a mussel kills it, so wait until just before cooking to perform this step.

- Once the mussels are cooked, the shells will open up and the edges of the meat inside should be curled. If any of them do not open, that is a sign that they were not alive. Don't serve unopened cooked mussels; throw them out.

EGG DROP SOUP

3 tsp vegetable oil

5 tbsp thinly sliced scallion greens

1½ tsp minced fresh ginger

2 qt Chicken Broth (page 15)

1 tsp salt, or as needed

¼ tsp freshly ground white pepper, or as needed

¼ cup cornstarch dissolved in 2 tablespoons cold water

2 eggs, beaten

THIS HOMEMADE VERSION of the Chinese restaurant favorite is quick and easy to make. Adding the cornstarch gradually allows you to thicken the soup to suit your taste.

MAKES 8 SERVINGS

1. Heat the oil in a large wok or a soup pot over medium-high heat. Add 1 tablespoon of the scallion greens and the ginger. Stir-fry until softened, about 1 minute.

2. Add the broth and bring to a boil. Season to taste with the salt and pepper.

3. Stir the cornstarch mixture to recombine any starch that has settled to the bottom. While stirring the soup, add about half of the cornstarch mixture to the soup. Continue to stir until the soup comes back to a simmer and thickens. The soup should have a slightly thick consistency. If needed, add the remaining cornstarch mixture in small doses to the soup while stirring. Let the soup return to a simmer each time before adding more cornstarch. (Depending on how thick you like your soup, you may not need to use all of the cornstarch.)

4. Beat the eggs gently in a bowl. Pour them into soup while slowly stirring with a spoon, breaking the eggs into pieces.

5. Serve in heated bowls, garnished with the remaining scallion greens.

CHINESE HOT AND SOUR SOUP

COMPARE THIS SOUP to the Thai Hot and Sour Soup on page 53 and you will see that though the theme of both is the interplay of spicy-hot and sour flavors, they are completely different soups. The Thai soup derives its heat from chile peppers and its sour from citrus; the Chinese soup is hot from white and black peppercorns and sour from two kinds of vinegar. The garnishes in the two soups are also quite different.

MAKES 10 TO 12 SERVINGS

1. Soak the cloud ears and lily buds in enough warm water to cover until softened, about 10 minutes. Drain and rinse well. Cut the stems off the cloud ears and lily buds. Cut the cloud ears in small pieces and the lily buds in half. Set aside.

2. Heat the oil in a large wok or soup pot over medium-high heat. Add the scallion greens and ginger. Stir-fry briefly, about 30 seconds. Add the pork and stir-fry until cooked through, 1 to 2 minutes.

3. Add the cloud ears, lily buds, cabbage, and bamboo shoots (if using). Stir-fry until the cabbage is tender, about 2 minutes.

4. Add the broth and tofu and bring to a simmer. Add the soy sauce, white vinegar, rice vinegar, salt, white pepper, and black pepper.

5. Stir the cornstarch mixture to recombine any starch that has settled to the bottom. While stirring the soup, add about half of the cornstarch mixture to the soup. Continue to stir until the soup comes back to a simmer and thickens. The soup should have a slightly thick consistency. If needed, add the remaining cornstarch mixture in small doses to the soup while stirring. Let the soup return to a simmer each time before adding more cornstarch. (Depending on how thick you like your soup, you may not need to use all of the cornstarch.)

6. Stir the egg and sesame oil into the soup and return to a simmer. Serve in heated bowls, garnished with the cilantro.

Make It Authentic

With little flavor of their own, dried cloud ears (also known as black fungus, wood ears, or tree ears) soak up the other flavors of the soup and provide a soft, slightly rubbery textural element to this soup. Dried tiger lily buds, also known as golden needles, add texture, too, as well as a slightly sweet or musky flavor. Find these and other ingredients not available at your supermarket in an Asian grocery.

---

2 tbsp dried cloud ears

2 tbsp dried tiger lily buds

1 tbsp vegetable oil

1 tbsp chopped scallion greens

¾ tsp minced ginger

¼ lb pork butt, ground or cut into matchsticks

1½ cups shredded Napa cabbage

¼ cup drained canned bamboo shoots, thinly sliced (optional)

5 cups Chicken Broth (page 15)

1 cup diced soft tofu

1 tbsp Chinese black soy sauce

1 tbsp white vinegar

1 tbsp rice vinegar

1 tsp salt, or as needed

¾ tsp freshly ground white pepper

¾ tsp freshly ground black pepper

¼ cup cornstarch dissolved in 2 tablespoons cold water

1 egg, lightly beaten

1½ tsp dark (Asian) sesame oil

⅓ cup chopped cilantro

WONTON SOUP

WONTONS:

3 oz ground pork

½ cup finely chopped Napa cabbage

2 tbsp Chicken Broth (page 15)

1 tbsp finely chopped scallion greens

½ tsp minced fresh ginger

¾ tsp soy sauce

¾ tsp dark (Asian) sesame oil

Pinch salt

Pinch freshly ground white pepper

1 package wonton wrappers

1 egg, beaten

SOUP:

2 tsp vegetable oil

1 tsp minced scallion greens

½ tsp minced fresh ginger

5 cups Chicken Broth (page 15)

1½ tsp Chinese black soy sauce

Salt as needed

Freshly ground black pepper as needed

GARNISH:

1 egg, lightly beaten

1 oz ham, cut into thin strips

¼ cup watercress sprigs (optional)

Look for Chinese black soy sauce and any other ingredients not carried by your supermarket at an Asian grocery.

THOUGH IT'S EASY enough to order wonton soup from your neighborhood Chinese restaurant, you may find that the freshly made wonton soup you prepare with this recipe beats the restaurant version you have grown used to. Making the wontons is fun; it takes a bit of time, but your speed will increase as you get the hang of it. You can tightly wrap and freeze any leftover wrappers for next time. Once the wontons are made, the soup comes together in a snap.

MAKES 8 SERVINGS

1. Make the wontons: Combine the pork, cabbage, broth, scallion, ginger, soy sauce, sesame oil, salt, and pepper. Mix well. Place ½ teaspoon of the mixture in the center of a wonton wrapper. Brush the edges of the wrapper with beaten egg and fold into a triangle. Twist and press two triangle points together to form a wonton. Repeat with the remaining filling and wrappers to make about 32 wontons.

2. Bring a large pot of water to a boil. Cook the wontons in the boiling water until they float, about 2 minutes. Drain and rinse under cool water. Transfer to a bowl, cover, and set aside.

3. Make the soup: Heat 1 teaspoon of the oil in a large wok or a soup pot over medium-high heat. Add the scallion and ginger and stir-fry for 30 seconds. Add the broth and bring to a simmer. Add the soy sauce and the salt and pepper to taste. Keep hot.

4. Heat the remaining 1 teaspoon of oil in a nonstick omelet pan or small skillet over medium-low heat. Add the beaten egg and cook until set on the bottom, about 1 minute. Flip the omelet and cook until completely set, 1 to 2 minutes. Transfer the omelet to a cutting board and slice into thin strips.

5. Distribute the wontons evenly between heated bowls (there should be at least 4 per bowl). Ladle the soup over the wontons and garnish with the omelet strips, ham, and watercress (if using).

SALMON MISO SOUP

Miso, which is fermented soybean paste, is a principle ingredient in Japanese cooking. It comes in a variety of flavors and colors. Most miso is quite salty, though low-salt varieties are available. Containing large amounts of protein and B vitamins, it's also highly nutritious. The variety called for in this soup, yellow (shinshu) miso, is very mellow as misos go. Daikon is a large white Asian radish with a sweet flavor and crisp texture. Look for daikon and miso as well as many of the other ingredients called for here in Asian groceries and health food stores. See the sidebar on page 44 for more information on Asian ingredients, and page 62 for instructions on making your own dashi.

MAKES 8 SERVINGS

1. Heat 1 teaspoon of the oil in a nonstick omelet pan or small skillet over medium-low heat. Add the beaten egg and cook until set on the bottom, about 1 minute. Flip the omelet and cook until completely set, 1 to 2 minutes. Transfer the omelet to a cutting board, dice, and set aside.

2. Heat the remaining 2 teaspoons of oil in a large wok or soup pot. Add 1½ tablespoons of the scallion and the ginger. Stir-fry briefly, about 30 seconds. Add the carrot and daikon. Stir-fry until tender, about 3 minutes.

3. Add the broth, miso, and instant dashi. Stir to combine and dissolve. Add the seaweed (if using).

4. Bring the soup to a simmer. Add the tofu, salmon, sesame oil, and black pepper. Simmer until the salmon is just cooked, about 1 minute. Serve in heated bowls, garnished with the remaining scallions and diced omelet.

3 tsp vegetable oil

1 egg, lightly beaten

3 tbsp thinly sliced scallion greens

½ tsp minced fresh ginger

¼ cup diced carrot

¼ cup diced daikon

1½ qt Chicken Broth (page 15)

5 tbsp yellow miso

2¼ tsp instant dashi

¼ cup dried wakame seaweed, broken into 1-inch pieces (optional)

1 cup diced soft tofu

½ cup finely diced fresh boneless, skinless salmon fillet (about 3 ounces)

2¼ tsp dark (Asian) sesame oil

¼ tsp freshly ground black pepper

THAI HOT AND SOUR SOUP

{PICTURED AT LEFT}

THAI HOT AND sour soup creates a fascinating interplay of spicy hot chile and sour citrus flavor on the palate. All of the ingredients are crucial to the overall flavor, so don't leave anything out. You can find them at Asian groceries and some specialty markets. Once you have all your ingredients assembled, the soup is a snap to put together.

MAKES 8 SERVINGS

1. Bring a medium-sized pot of water to a boil. Add the shrimp and boil until cooked through, about 3 minutes. Use a slotted spoon to transfer the shrimp to colander. Rinse under cold water, drain, and set the shrimp aside. Cook the rice noodles in the same pot of boiling water until tender, 2 to 3 minutes. Drain, rinse under cold water, and drain again. Set aside.

2. Combine the broth with the lemon grass, fish sauce, chili oil, lime zest, pickled chili, lemon juice, and lime juice in a wok or soup pot. Bring to a simmer and cook for 10 minutes. Strain or use a slotted spoon to remove the lemon grass.

3. Distribute the rice noodles, shrimp, mushrooms, and cilantro between 8 heated soup bowls. Pour the broth over and serve.

¼ lb small (30-35 count) shrimp, peeled and butterflied

2 oz thin rice noodles (vermicelli)

2 qt Chicken Broth (page 15)

1 stalk fresh lemon grass, cut into 2-inch pieces, smashed

¼ cup Thai fish sauce (nam pla)

2 tbsp chili oil

2 tsp lime zest

½ pickled chili

Juice of 1 lemon

Juice of 1 lime

⅓ cup drained canned straw mushrooms

¼ cup chopped cilantro

Thai Ingredients

Thai cuisine calls for a number of ingredients that once were difficult to find unless you lived near a thriving Asian community; now many larger supermarkets carry a surprising selection of these unique ingredients:

- GALANGAL is one such ingredient. It looks and tastes a little like fresh ginger, but adds a unique flavor all its own.

- WILD LIME LEAVES add a unique sharpness to dishes. Lemon or lime zest can be substituted if you can't locate fresh wild lime leaves.

- THAI BASIL, sometimes known as anise basil or holy basil, has deep green leaves that are smaller and more pointed than Western basil leaves. They grow on purplish stems, topped with pretty, reddish purple flower buds. You can substitute other basils for Thai basil if necessary.

- CILANTRO is stocked in most grocery stores. Select bunches of cilantro that still have the roots attached, if you can find them. Many Southeast Asian dishes call for the root. Once you've thoroughly rinsed the root, chop it very fine with a chef's knife.

- COCONUT MILK, CURRY PASTES, and FISH SAUCE are ubiquitous in curries and stir fries. Taste several varieties to find a variety you like best.

Hearty Soups

MAKING A HEARTY soup is essentially no different than making a broth-style soup. You start with a good broth and then add some additional ingredients including an array of vegetables and meats. The main distinction is the quantity of ingredients that are cooked in the broth. More often than not, a hearty soup also includes some ingredient that thickens the broth a bit. Dry beans, potatoes, and pasta are added to a simmering minestrone. Potatoes, noodles, rice, and other grains—all of these ingredients will add some body to a soup, making it taste and feel more substantial. In other words, hearty. These are the soups that you can serve as a complete and satisfying meal.

While some hearty soups are thickened by the natural release of starches from vegetables, like potatoes or ingredients like pasta, others benefit from a specific thickener. Goulash Soup (page 73) calls for a bit of flour. Tortilla Soup (page 81) includes crushed toasted tortillas that simmer and "dissolve" into the soup. Some, like Leblebi (page 85), call for the soup to be served over chunks of bread.

Main Ingredients

Hearty soups are made from a combination of ingredients. Choosing and preparing your ingredients with care is the first step in making a great soup. There are virtually countless options available, from robust, chunky soups made with a combination of meats and vegetables to rib-sticking soups that include beans and pasta.

Clear broths, good-quality stocks, dashi, water, vegetable essences, or juices may all used as the liquid base for vegetable soups. Some hearty soups begin with the process of making a good broth such as Minestra Maritata (page 76). For those soups, remember to observe the same standards and guidelines as you would for a broth, opting for cuts from more exercised portions of large animals, more mature birds, and perfectly fresh fish and seafood. Other hearty soups may call for a

prepared broth. If you prefer to buy prepared broths or stocks, your soups can still have great quality and flavor. To be certain, you can conduct a broth sampling as described on the following page.

Hearty broths typically include a variety of additional ingredients. Vegetables can be employed both as major flavoring ingredients as well as for their aromatic qualities. Starchy vegetables like potatoes and squashes are also common in these soups to give the broth some body and texture. Prepare each vegetable as required by your recipe, trimming, peeling, and cutting it into neat and relatively even-sized pieces so that they cook uniformly and have an attractive appearance. You can find more information in the table on pages 6–9, Shopping for Soup Ingredients.

Other ingredients typically included in hearty soups include beans, whole grains, or pasta. For a relatively clear soup, cook these starchy ingredients separately and add them to the soup as a garnish. The more rustic approach calls for these ingredients to be cooked in the broth as part of the soup-making process. Such soups tend to have more body and are sometimes referred to as hearty vegetable soups.

Supporting Flavors

The soups in this chapter reflect a global influence. You'll find recipes that include a few strands of saffron or a spice sachet to infuse the soup with flavor as it simmers. Others may be flavored by a last minute addition of herbs or herb purées. Vegetable combinations include *mirepoix* (onions, carrots, and celery), *soffrito* (onions, celery, and garlic cooked with some bacon or pancetta), or the "Cajun Trinity" (onions, celery, and peppers).

Be sure to taste the liquid and add seasonings as necessary from the start of cooking time up to and including just before serving. Salt and pepper are virtually indispensable, but you will find that additional aromatics are also important: a squeeze of lemon juice, a dash of vinegar, or a few drops of a flavorful oil. (We've included some flavored oils in Chapter 9 on page 237.)

Fortified wines such as sherry, vinegar, or citrus juices may be used for last-minute flavor adjustments. Heavy cream is another option to give your soup a more mellow flavor.

Garnishing Hearty Soups

Croutons (page 222) are the most common type of garnish for a hearty soup. They add a bit of crunch that stands in contrast to the rest of the ingredients. Add other garnishes, such as minced scallions, chopped herbs, pesto, grated cheese, or salsa, to vegetable soups like Potage au Pistou (page 68) and Clemole con Salsa de Rabanos (page 72) just before serving.

The Soup Pantry

PREPARED BROTHS OR STOCKS

Having some good-quality prepared stocks and broths in your cupboard makes it simple to create soups. Not all brands are made the same way, however, but if you invest a little time and money, you'll find the one that you like best, as well as learn a few tricks for customizing it quickly.

To do a tasting, buy a few different brands (including low sodium versions) of the broths and stocks you use most frequently. Remember that there may be different brands located in different parts of your store, if there is a separate "natural" or "health" foods section.

Heat the broths before you taste them, and if called for, dilute them according to the package directions. The ideal temperature for the broth is 145°F—hot, but not scalding. Have some paper on hand to make some notes and to record your observations, and a few slices of bread to "clean" your palette after each taste. Taste each broth, one at a time, without adding any additional seasonings. Consider the way the broth looks, too. Does it have a distinctive and appealing color? Before moving on to the next broth, notice whether the broth is salty, sweet, and so forth, and decide how you like the taste. It might help to give each one a score, especially if you have several brands you'd like to test.

To get the most out of your favorite(s), go back to your notes. If the broth seemed a little salty, you will want to be careful about how much salt you add to your soup. If it seemed a little sweet, add a bit of vinegar or wine to temper the sweetness. If it wasn't as bright as you'd like, add seasonings like spices or fresh herbs, a slice of ginger, or a few garlic cloves for a little boost.

FROZEN OR CANNED VEGETABLES

Fresh seasonal vegetables may cry out to be made into soups, but there are plenty of times during the year when pickings are slim at the market and farm stands have been closed for weeks. Frozen vegetables are a good option, since they are typically harvested and flash frozen just hours after picking. Some of our favorite frozen vegetables to keep on hand include peas, spinach, corn, squashes, okra, and green beans. You should thaw and drain leafy vegetables like spinach or collard greens, but you can add peas, corn, or squashes directly to the soup, right from the freezer.

Improvising

One of the best things about these hearty soups is their flexibility. You can almost add a little of this and a dab of that— some cooked beans, the last few mushrooms, cooked pasta or rice, or slivers of leftover roast chicken. This means that, even if you follow our recipe, your soup will be uniquely yours. If you make a big pot of soup to enjoy over several days, you can make it different every day by introducing a few new flavors or colors or texture to each pot you reheat.

☼ BASIC METHOD FOR HEARTY SOUPS

Most hearty soups can be prepared with a small selection of basic kitchen equipment: a pot with a tight fitting lid, a spoon and a ladle, and a few knives to cut up your ingredients. Your recipe may call for a spice sachet or bouquet garni, which are described on pages 13 and 126.

➡ **CREATE A FLAVOR BASE:** Onions, carrots, leeks, scallions, celery, mushrooms, peppers, chiles, tomatoes, and parsnips are just some of the ingredients you might use to create the soup's flavor base. Typically, you will cut these ingredients up fairly fine so that they can infuse the soup's liquid with flavor. The next step is to heat a small amount of fat in your soup pot over medium heat. Add the flavoring vegetables and cook them as directed in your recipe. You may cook them until they are just starting to release some of their flavor, but haven't changed color, or you may cook them until they are more deeply colored. The extent of cooking time, indicated in your recipe, influences both the flavor and the color of your soup.

➡ **ADD INGREDIENTS IN ORDER AND SIMMER GENTLY:** Denser ingredients that require long cooking times should be added to the soup first, followed by those that are more tender. Finally, any ingredients that are fully cooked already (beans, perhaps, or diced cooked meat) are added at the very end, just long enough to get hot. Most recipes are written so that you will know when to add what, but if you are experimenting with your own additions, remember that ingredients with textures similar to squashes, turnips, and carrots will take the longest time to cook. Leafy ingredients and greens take the least.

➡ **SIMMER UNTIL THE SOUP HAS A RICH FLAVOR AND GOOD BODY:** Soups don't require a lot of attention while they simmer beyond making sure that soup isn't cooking too rapidly. The aroma should escape from the pot, since the lid is almost always left slightly ajar. If the lid were on tight, you might not be able to see that the soup is boiling too quickly. Without smelling the soup as it cooks, you might forget to come check it as it cooks. If you don't have a lid for your soup pot, the soup will cook away and you'll end up with less soup. Some soups need to be skimmed while they simmer. The test for doneness is simple: the broth should have a good flavor and all of the ingredients in the soup should be fully cooked and tender. You can serve hearty soups right away, but you may prefer to let them mellow overnight. Follow the instructions on page 5 for cooling and storing soups.

FISHERMAN'S SOUP

with Shrimp and Fresh Herbs

{PICTURED AT LEFT}

I T IS WORTH the effort to find a fresh pineapple for this soup. You may be able to find peeled and cored fresh pineapple in the produce section of your grocery store.

MAKES 6 SERVINGS

1. Heat the oil in a soup pot over medium heat. Add the chili paste and garlic, and sauté until fragrant, stirring constantly, about 20 seconds.

2. Add the chicken broth, tomatoes, pineapple, tamarind, 2 tablespoons of the fish sauce, and the sugar. Bring the broth to a boil, stirring to dissolve the tamarind paste. As soon as the soup comes to a boil, reduce the heat and simmer until flavorful, about 5 minutes.

3. Add the shrimp and taro root, and simmer just until the shrimp is barely cooked through, 5 minutes. Season the soup to taste with the lime juice, additional fish sauce, and salt and pepper.

4. Divide the shrimp, bean sprouts, cilantro, and basil equally among 6 warmed soup bowls. Ladle the warm broth over the shrimp and garnishes, top with the fried shallots, and serve at once.

2 tbsp peanut oil

2 tbsp Vietnamese chili paste

2 tsp minced garlic

10 cups Chicken Broth (page 15)

2 cups diced plum tomatoes

1 cup diced pineapple

¼ cup tamarind pulp

2 tbsp Vietnamese fish sauce, plus as needed

1 tbsp sugar

1 lb shrimp (31-35 count), peeled, deveined, and halved lengthwise

½ cup diced taro root

2 tbsp lime juice, or as needed

Salt as needed

Freshly ground black pepper as needed

¾ cup bean sprouts, trimmed

¼ cup cilantro leaves

6 Thai basil leaves, cut in halves

Fried Shallots (page 238)

LEFT TO RIGHT: *Remove the peel from the taro root (wear gloves to avoid irritation) and then cut with a sharp knife; the fried shallots are a delicious garnish for this and other soups in this book, and are easy to make. Find the recipe on page 238.*

MINESTRONE

{PICTURED AT LEFT}

MINESTRONE, LITERALLY "big soup," is an Italian classic packed with vegetables, pasta, and beans. A bowl of minestrone can be a meal all by itself. There is no one right way to make minestrone. Recipes vary from cook to cook according to individual preferences, so feel free to improvise with other vegetables, beans, or pasta shapes to suit your taste. Pancetta is a type of Italian bacon. It can usually be found in delis and butcher shops, but if it is unavailable in your area, you can omit it or substitute regular bacon.

MAKES 8 SERVINGS

1. Heat the oil in a soup pot over medium heat. Add the pancetta and cook until the fat melts, 3 to 5 minutes. Do not allow the pancetta to brown.

2. Add the cabbage, onions, carrots, celery, and garlic. Cook until the onions are translucent, 6 to 8 minutes.

3. Add the broth, potatoes, and parmesan cheese rind. Bring to a simmer and cook until the vegetables are tender, about 30 minutes. Do not overcook them.

4. Meanwhile, cook the vermicelli according to package directions until tender. Drain.

5. When the vegetables in the soup are tender, add the cooked vermicelli, tomatoes, chickpeas, and kidney beans. Remove and discard the Parmesan rind.

6. Season the soup to taste with the pesto, salt, and pepper. Serve in heated bowls, sprinkled with the cheese.

2 tbsp olive oil

1 oz pancetta, chopped (5 to 6 thin slices)

1½ cups chopped green cabbage

1 cup chopped onions

1 cup sliced carrots

¼ cup chopped celery

2 garlic cloves, minced

2 qt Chicken Broth (page 15)

½ cup peeled, diced potato

1 piece Parmesan cheese rind (about 3 inches square)

¾ cup vermicelli or angel hair pasta (broken into 2-inch pieces)

½ cup chopped plum tomatoes (peeled and seeded)

¼ cup cooked chickpeas (drained and rinsed if using canned)

⅓ cup cooked kidney beans (drained and rinsed if using canned)

⅓ cup Pesto (page 241)

½ tsp salt, or as needed

¼ tsp freshly ground black pepper, or as needed

Freshly grated Parmesan cheese as needed

DRIED BEEF SOUP

Caldo de Carne Seca

{PICTURED AT LEFT}

U SING DRIED BEEF, or carne seca, adds complexity to the richness of this dish. We've included instructions to make your own carne seca, essentially a type of beef jerky. If you use purchased dried beef, you may need to soak it in warm water to cover for 30 minutes (or more) to remove some of the salt.

MAKES 8 SERVINGS

1. Heat a soup pot over medium heat. Add the olive oil or lard. When the fat is shimmering, add the onion and sauté, stirring occasionally, until it is tender and a deep golden brown, 12 to 15 minutes. Add the garlic and continue to sauté until aromatic, 30 to 40 seconds.

2. Add the beef, tomatoes, and cilantro, stir well to coat with the oil or lard, and sauté for an additional 3 minutes. Add the broth, potatoes, and carrots, and bring the soup to a boil, skimming the surface, as needed. Reduce the heat slightly, and simmer the soup until the carrots are tender, 25 to 30 minutes. Season to taste with salt and pepper.

3. Serve the soup in heated bowls.

Making Carne Seca

To make your own carne seca, trim a 3-pound piece of boneless beef round to remove all surface fat. Use a slicer to cut the meat into thin slices, about ⅛-inch-thick. If you partially freeze the meat, it is easier to slice thinly. Blend ¼ cup each of lime juice and soy sauce, and then add 1 tablespoon kosher salt, 1 tablespoon chili powder, 2 teaspoons of onion powder, and 2 teaspoons of garlic powder in a bowl. Add the sliced beef and turn to coat it evenly. Let the meat marinate for 30 minutes.

Preheat an oven (use a convection oven if you have one) to 175°F. Arrange the meat slices in a single layer on racks set on baking sheets or pans. Dry the meat in the preheated oven until it is thoroughly dried and leathery, 1 to 2 hours (depending upon the thickness of your slices.) Let cool completely, then refrigerate until needed.

---

2 tbsp olive oil or lard

1½ cups thinly sliced onion

1 tsp minced garlic

¾ lb carne seca (dried beef), diced or cut into strips (see note)

2 cups chopped plum tomatoes, fresh or canned

½ cup chopped cilantro leaves

8 cups Beef Broth (page 16)

1 cup medium-dice potatoes

½ cup medium-dice carrots

Salt as needed

Freshly ground black pepper as needed

PARAGUAYAN DUMPLING SOUP

Bori-Bori

{PICTURED AT LEFT}

BORI-BORI IS A hearty soup from Paraguay made with meat, vegetables, and cornmeal-cheese dumplings. Just a few threads of the optional saffron will give the soup a rich golden color.

MAKES 8 SERVINGS

1. Make the dumplings: Combine the cornmeal, Parmesan, flour, baking powder, salt, pepper, egg, scallions, and oil in a mixing bowl. Cover the batter and let it rest at least 45 minutes and up to 3 hours before shaping and cooking the dumplings (see step 6).

2. Heat 1 tablespoon of the oil in a soup pot over medium-high heat. Season the beef shank with salt and pepper and add it to the hot oil. Sear the beef on all sides, turning as necessary, until browned, 7 to 8 minutes.

3. Add the chicken broth and simmer over low heat until the beef is tender, 45 to 50 minutes. Remove the beef to a plate and let cool. Strain the broth through a fine sieve and reserve.

4. Return the soup pot to medium-high heat. Add the remaining oil and heat over medium-high heat. Add the onion, carrot, celery, and garlic and sauté, stirring frequently, until the onion is tender and translucent, 8 to 10 minutes.

5. Add the strained broth to the soup pot along with additional chicken broth, if needed, to make 8 cups. Bring the broth to a simmer and add the bay leaf, clove, and saffron threads, if using. Simmer until the vegetables are tender and the broth is flavorful, 30 minutes. Remove the bay leaf and clove and discard.

6. Trim the cooled beef and cut it into medium dice. Return the beef to the soup. To form the dumplings, pinch off small pieces of dough (about 1 teaspoon) and roll them into balls. Add the dumplings to the soup and simmer until the dumplings are cooked through, 20 to 25 minutes. Stir in the parsley, and season to taste with salt and pepper. Serve immediately in warmed soup bowls sprinkled with Parmesan cheese.

PARMESAN DUMPLINGS

⅓ cup white or yellow cornmeal

⅓ cup grated Parmesan cheese

¼ cup all-purpose flour

½ tsp baking powder

½ tsp salt

Pinch of freshly ground black pepper

1 large egg, lightly beaten

2 tbsp minced scallions, white portion only

1 tbsp canola oil

2 tbsp canola oil or bacon fat

1 lb boneless beef shank

Salt as needed

Freshly ground black pepper as needed

8 cups Chicken Broth (page 15), plus as needed

1½ cups minced onion

¾ cup small-dice carrot

¾ cup small-dice celery

2 tsp minced garlic

1 bay leaf

1 whole clove

2 or 3 crushed saffron threads (optional)

3 tbsp chopped flat-leaf parsley

¼ cup grated Parmesan cheese

¾ cup dried navy beans, sorted, rinsed, and
soaked (page 157)

2 tbsp olive oil

1 cup diced carrots

2½ cups diced leeks, white and light green parts

1¼ cups diced onion

2½ quarts Chicken Broth (page 15), heated

Pinch saffron threads (optional)

1 cup green beans, cut into 1-inch lengths

1 cup diced yellow or white potato

1 cup diced zucchini

¾ cup vermicelli or angel hair pasta, broken
into 2-inch lengths

2 cups diced tomatoes, peeled and seeded

Salt to taste

Freshly ground black pepper to taste

¾ cup Pistou (page 241), or as needed

POTAGE AU PISTOU

Vegetable Soup with Garlic and Basil

PISTOU IS BOTH the name of this soup as well as the garlic and basil condiment used to season it. Pistou, the condiment, is the French version of Italy's pesto. Pistou, the soup, is the French version of Italy's minestrone. You can substitute 1½ cups of drained and rinsed canned navy beans for the dried. Simply add them to the soup in step 5. This soup is best in late summer when many of the ingredients can be purchased from your local farmstand or picked from your garden. Served with a loaf of crusty bread (with olive oil for dipping) and a bottle of chilled dry white wine, it makes a fine meal.

MAKES 8 TO 10 SERVINGS

1. Drain the beans and place them in a large saucepan. Add 1 quart of water and bring to a simmer. Cook until tender, about 1 hour, adding more water if necessary to keep the beans covered.

2. Heat the oil in a soup pot over medium heat. Add the carrots, leeks, and onion. Cook until the onion is translucent, about 10 minutes. Add the broth and saffron (if using) to the vegetables, bring to a simmer, and cook for 10 minutes.

3. Add the green beans, potato, and zucchini. Continue to simmer for 10 minutes. Add the vermicelli and simmer until tender, about 8 minutes.

4. Drain the beans of their cooking liquid and add them to the soup along with the tomatoes. Season to taste with the salt and pepper and continue to simmer for another minute.

5. Add the pistou to the soup, to taste, just before serving (see note below). Serve in heated bowls.

Using Pistou

This fragrant herb paste should not be allowed to overheat, or the basil will become bitter and the sauce will go from creamy to oily, so pistou is best added to a soup just before serving. An even better way to incorporate the intense flavor of the pistou into the soup is by spooning it into individual soup bowls before the hot soup is ladled on top. Stir to blend the pistou into the soup and serve immediately.

HAM BONE AND COLLARD GREENS SOUP {PICTURED AT LEFT}

THIS HEARTY SOUTHERN-STYLE soup is packed with vitamin- and mineral-rich collard greens. Ham bone soup was originally meant as a means to get the most meals out of a ham, but we have developed this recipe using a smoked ham hock (which should be available from your supermarket) so you don't have to purchase and eat a whole ham to make the soup. If you do happen to have a meaty ham bone, though, by all means use it instead of the ham hock. Ham hocks can be quite salty, so use salt-free homemade broth or a reduced-sodium canned variety to make this soup.

MAKES 8 SERVINGS

1 smoked ham hock

3 qt Chicken Broth (page 15)

1¼ lb collard greens

1 tbsp vegetable oil

¼ cup minced salt pork (about 3 ounces)

1¼ cups minced onion

½ cup minced celery

½ cup all-purpose flour

Sachet: 5 to 6 black peppercorns, 4 parsley stems, 1 fresh thyme sprig or ½ tsp dried enclosed in a large tea ball or tied in a cheesecloth pouch

½ cup heavy cream

4 tsp malt vinegar, or as needed

Tabasco sauce to taste

1. Place the ham hock and broth in a pot large enough to accommodate both. Bring to a simmer and cook, partially covered, for 1½ hours. Remove the ham hock from the broth and allow both to cool slightly.

2. Meanwhile, bring a large pot of salted water to a boil. Cut the tough ribs and stems away from the collard greens. Plunge the greens into the boiling water and cook for 10 minutes. Drain and cool slightly. Chop the greens coarsely and set aside.

3. Heat the oil in a soup pot over medium heat. Add the salt pork and cook until crisp, 3 to 5 minutes. Add the onion and celery; cook, stirring occasionally, until tender, about 5 minutes.

4. Add the flour and cook, stirring frequently, for 5 minutes. Gradually add the broth, whisking constantly to work out any lump of flour. Bring to a simmer and add the collard greens, ham hock, and sachet. Cook for 1 hour.

5. Remove and discard the sachet. Remove the ham hock and cool slightly. Trim away the skin and fat and dice the lean meat. Add the meat back to the soup.

6. Add the cream and season to taste with the vinegar and Tabasco. Serve in heated bowls.

Simmering the ham hock in both the broth and the completed soup adds an intense smoky flavor to this dish, after which the meat is diced and added back to the soup as garnish.

CLEMOLE CON SALSA DE RABANOS

Vegetable Soup with Radish Salsa

SALSA DE RABANOS

1 cup water

4 tsp salt

1 tbsp red wine vinegar

1 cup finely chopped radishes

½ cup minced onion

¾ cup orange juice

½ cup lime juice

1½ lb tomatillos, husks removed, quartered

1 cup chopped cilantro

3 serrano chiles, stem and seeds removed, chopped

1½ lb boneless pork loin

10 cups water

1½ cups minced onion

2 tsp minced garlic

Salt as needed

Freshly ground black pepper as needed

3 ears of corn, husked and cut into 3 pieces

1½ cups sliced zucchini

1½ cups green beans, trimmed and cut into ½-inch-long pieces

THE RADISH SALSA in this dish is a traditional offering in parts of Mexico and South America. In Oaxaca, Mexico, elaborate sculptures carved from radishes are displayed each year on December 23rd, The Night of the Radishes.

MAKES 6 SERVINGS

1. To make the salsa, combine 1 cup of water, salt, and vinegar in a bowl. Add the radishes, onion, orange, and lime juice. Cover tightly and let the salsa rest in the refrigerator at least 1 and up to 3 hours before serving.

2. Purée the tomatillos, cilantro, and serranos to a coarse paste in a food processor or blender. Set aside.

3. Trim the pork loin and cut it into large cubes. Place it in a large soup pot, and add the water (there should be enough to cover the pork by at least 2 inches), the onion, and garlic. Bring to a boil over high heat, skimming any foam that rises to the surface. As soon as a full boil is reached, reduce the heat and simmer the pork, covered, until the pork is tender, about 45 minutes. Season to taste with salt and pepper.

4. Add the corn, zucchini, and green beans to the soup. Continue to simmer until all the vegetables are tender, 10 to 15 minutes.

5. Just before serving, remove the soup from the heat, and stir in the tomatillo mixture. Season to taste with salt and pepper. Serve the soup in heated bowls topped with the salsa.

GOULASH SOUP

REMINISCENT OF THE paprika-flavored Hungarian stew of the same name (spelled *gulyás* in Hungarian), this thick soup is robust enough to be a meal by itself. Serve it with a dab of sour cream, if you wish, and accompany it with lots of dark pumpernickel bread and dark beer.

MAKES 8 SERVINGS

1. Sauté the salt pork in a soup pot over medium heat until the bits of pork are crisp and the fat has rendered, 4 to 5 minutes.

2. Add the cubed beef or veal and sauté in the fat until the meat begins to brown, 3 to 4 minutes. Add the onions and cook, covered, over medium-low heat until the onions are translucent, 8 to 10 minutes.

3. Add the vinegar and boil over high heat until the liquid begins to reduce, about 2 minutes. Reduce the heat to medium, add the flour, and stir with a wooden spoon and cook for 1 more minute. Stir in the paprika, then the tomato purée, and mix thoroughly. Cook for 2 to 3 minutes.

4. Add the broth and the sachet. Bring the soup to a simmer and cook until the meat is almost tender, about 30 minutes. Add the diced potatoes and simmer until tender, about 20 minutes. Remove and discard any fat on the surface of the soup with a shallow spoon.

5. Season to taste with the salt and pepper. Serve in heated bowls, garnished with the sliced scallions or chives.

Make It Different

Replace the beef broth with 1 quart of dark beer. Add 1 finely diced red bell pepper at the same time as the onions. Substitute sweet paprika for the hot paprika, and garnish with chopped dill or scallions.

6 tbsp minced salt pork, slab bacon, or fat back

1 lb beef or veal chuck, cut into ½-inch cubes

2½ cups minced onions

2 tbsp red wine vinegar

2 tbsp all-purpose flour

1 tbsp hot paprika

¾ cup tomato purée

1 qt Beef Broth (page 16)

Sachet: 1 tsp each caraway seeds, dried marjoram, and thyme, 4 fresh parsley stems, 2 cloves peeled garlic, and 1 bay leaf enclosed in a large tea ball or tied in a cheesecloth pouch

2½ cups cubed or diced yellow or white potatoes

Salt to taste

Freshly ground black pepper to taste

¼ cup finely sliced scallion greens or chives

CIOPPINO

{PICTURED AT LEFT}

A SAVORY TOMATO BROTH full of seafood and vegetables, cioppino is an American original created in San Francisco by Italian immigrants. It's a meal in and of itself. Although not traditional, you can substitute 1 cup of lump crab meat for the crabs. If you purchase fennel with the tops still attached, save some of the nicest looking sprigs for a garnish. Serve the cioppino with large garlic toasts or crusty sourdough bread.

MAKES 8 TO 10 SERVINGS

1. Heat the oil in a soup pot over medium heat. Add the scallions, peppers, onion, and fennel. Cook, stirring occasionally, until the onion is translucent, 6 to 8 minutes.

2. Add the garlic and cook for another minute.

3. Add the white wine, bring to a boil, and cook until the volume of wine is reduced by about half, 4 to 6 minutes.

4. Add the fish broth, tomatoes, tomato purée, and bay leaves. Cover the pot and simmer the mixture slowly for about 45 minutes. Add a small amount of water, if necessary. Cioppino should be more of a broth than a stew.

5. Season to taste with the salt and pepper. Remove and discard the bay leaves. Add the clams and simmer for about 10 minutes. Discard any clams that do not open.

6. Separate the claws from the crabs and cut the bodies in half. Add the crab pieces, shrimp, and swordfish to the soup. Simmer until the fish is just cooked through, about 5 minutes.

7. Add the basil and adjust the seasoning to taste, if necessary. Serve in heated bowls or soup plates.

2 tbsp olive oil

1½ cups sliced scallions, white portion only

2 cups diced green peppers

1½ cups diced onion

1¼ cups diced fennel

1 tbsp minced garlic

1 cup dry white wine

1 qt Fish Broth (page 17)

8 cups chopped plum tomatoes (peeled and seeded)

½ cup tomato purée

2 bay leaves

½ tsp salt, or as needed

Freshly ground black pepper

20 littleneck clams, scrubbed well

3 steamed hardshell crabs

20 medium shrimp, peeled and deveined

1¼ lb swordfish or halibut steaks, diced

3 tbsp shredded basil

½ small head Savoy cabbage (about 1 pound)

½ bunch broccoli rabe

½ head Bibb lettuce

¼ lb chicory

2 oz pancetta

2 oz prosciutto skin

1 medium Spanish onion, peeled and left whole

2 garlic cloves, peeled

¾ lb pork ribs

¼ bunch parsley

1 bay leaf

2 sprigs thyme

2 qt water

5 oz fresh Italian sausage, cooked, casings re-moved, and sliced

2 oz caciocavallo cheese, cut into small pieces

¼ tsp chopped fresh hot pepper, or as needed

12 slices of bread, toasted or grilled

¼ cup extra-virgin olive oil

MINESTRA MARITATA

"Italian Wedding Soup" from Campania

THIS SOUP MIGHT come as a surprise to Americans used to thinking of Italian wedding soup as a broth garnished with tiny little meatballs served at a wedding reception. This soup gets its name from an Italian expression used to describe two things that go well together. They say that they are *maritati* (married). The combination of greens and meat in a clear broth certainly does work well and deserves to be called *maritata*, even if it isn't served as part of a wedding celebration.

MAKES 6 SERVINGS

1. Clean and wash the cabbage, broccoli rabe, lettuce, and chicory. Cut the greens in big pieces and mix them together; set aside.

2. Cut the pancetta into small pieces and place in a stock pot with the prosciutto skin, whole onion, whole garlic, pork ribs, herbs, and about 2 quarts of cold water with a little salt. Bring to a simmer over low heat, and let cook for about 1½ to 2 hours, depending on the ribs. Remove the ribs, pick off the meat, and cut it in coarse pieces.

3. Strain the broth, add back the cooked meat and the sausage, and bring the soup back to a simmer over low heat. Add the greens and cook for 8 to 10 minutes; the greens should still be hard. Add the caciocavallo and the hot pepper. Simmer for another 10 minutes. Remove and discard whatever is left of the prosciutto skin, and serve each bowl with the toasted or grilled bread and topped with a drizzle of a good extra-virgin olive oil.

SHIITAKE MUSHROOM AND YUKON GOLD POTATO SOUP WITH BACON

One ¼-inch thick piece pancetta, finely chopped
(about 1 ounce)

⅓ cup diced carrot

½ cup diced celery

¾ cup diced onion

1½ cups diced yellow turnip

2 cups sliced fresh shiitake mushrooms

2½ cups diced Yukon Gold potatoes

6 cups Vegetable Broth (page 18)

2 tbsp chopped fresh flat-leaf parsley

2 tbsp chopped fresh marjoram

Salt to taste

Freshly ground black pepper to taste

THIS HEARTY YET low-fat soup is guaranteed to satisfy hunger during the chilly fall and winter months. Pancetta is an Italian bacon that is tied in a roll as it is cured, causing it to have a spiral appearance when it is sliced. Unlike most American bacon, it is not smoked. Pancetta is available from specialty and butcher shops as well as many supermarket delis. If you cannot find it, substitute 1 slice of regular bacon.

MAKES 8 SERVINGS

1. Cook the pancetta in a soup pot over low heat until all the fat is melted and the meat begins to crisp, 6 to 8 minutes.

2. Add the carrot, celery, onion, and turnip. Cover and cook until softened, about 3 minutes. Add the mushrooms, potatoes, and broth. Bring to a simmer and cook until the potatoes are tender, 10 to 12 minutes.

3. Add the herbs and season to taste with the salt and pepper. Serve in heated bowls.

MUSHROOM BARLEY SOUP

1 tbsp vegetable oil

1¼ cups small-dice onion

⅓ cup small-dice carrot

½ cup small-dice celery

⅓ cup small-dice parsnip (optional)

3 cups sliced white mushrooms

2 qt Chicken Broth (page 15)

¾ cup pearl barley

½ tsp salt, or as needed

½ tsp freshly ground black pepper, or as needed

1 tbsp chopped parsley

2 tbsp dry sherry or sherry wine vinegar
(optional)

FRESH WHITE MUSHROOMS are used in this version of a traditional winter soup, but feel free to bolster the flavor by incorporating your favorite fresh or dried wild mushrooms. A splash of sherry added at the last moment brings this humble dish up to a whole new level. This soup will mellow and deepen in flavor if it is prepared a day ahead. Adjust the consistency with a little water or additional broth.

MAKES 8 SERVINGS

1. Heat the oil in a soup pot over medium heat. Add the onion and cook, stirring frequently, until golden brown, about 10 minutes.

2. Add the carrot, celery, parsnip (if using), and mushrooms. Stir well to combine with the onion. Cover the pot and cook over low heat for 3 to 4 minutes.

3. Remove the cover and add the broth and barley. Bring to a simmer and cook until the barley is tender, about 30 minutes.

4. Season the soup to taste with salt and pepper. Stir in the parsley. Stir in the sherry or vinegar (if using) just before serving. Serve in heated bowls.

CORNED BEEF, BARLEY, AND CABBAGE SOUP

CORNED BEEF IS beef that has been cured in a seasoned brine (salt and water solution). Try serving this soup with the Rye Rusks on page 221.

MAKES 8 SERVINGS

1. Combine the brisket and broth in a soup pot. Bring to a simmer and cook until the meat is fork-tender, about 2 hours. If necessary, turn the meat occasionally during simmering to keep all surfaces evenly moist.

2. Add the onions, cabbage, celery, barley, and spice sachet. Continue to simmer for 1 hour.

3. Remove the brisket and let cool slightly. Trim away any excess fat, dice the meat, and set aside.

4. Use a shallow spoon to skim excess fat from the surface of the soup. Add the tomatoes and parsley. Simmer 15 minutes more.

5. Add the diced meat to the soup. Season to taste with the salt. Serve in heated bowls.

1¼ lb corned beef brisket

4 qt Chicken Broth (page 15)

2 cups diced onions

6½ cups chopped Savoy cabbage (about ½ head)

¼ cup diced celery

¼ cup pearl barley

Sachet: 3 crushed garlic cloves, 3 parsley stems, 1 bay leaf, 1 tsp dry thyme, and 1 tsp cracked black peppercorns enclosed in a large tea ball or tied in a cheesecloth pouch

1¼ cups diced tomatoes (peeled and seeded)

⅓ cup coarsely chopped flat-leaf parsley

Salt to taste

MINNESOTA WILD RICE SOUP

CLEAN WILD RICE before cooking by placing it in a bowl with plenty of cold water. Give the rice a stir, then set the bowl aside for a few minutes to let any debris float to the surface. Pour off the water and proceed with the recipe.

MAKES 8 SERVINGS

1. Heat the butter in a soup pot over medium heat. Add the carrots, leeks, and celery. Cook until softened, about 5 minutes.

2. Reduce the heat to low, add the flour, and stir well. Cook gently for about 3 minutes, stirring constantly.

3. Add the broth gradually, whisking well with each addition to eliminate lumps. Bring to a simmer.

4. Add the wild rice and salt. Continue to simmer the soup until the rice is tender but still chewy, about 45 minutes.

5. Stir in the heated cream and sherry. Season to taste with salt. Serve in heated bowls, garnished with the chives and parsley.

2 tbsp unsalted butter

1 cup finely chopped carrots

2½ cups finely diced leeks (white and light green parts)

1 cup finely diced celery

¼ cup all-purpose flour

2 qt Chicken Broth (page 15)

¾ cup wild rice

½ tsp salt, or as needed

¾ cup heavy cream, hot

3 tbsp dry sherry

¼ cup minced chives

3 tbsp chopped parsley

TORTILLA SOUP

{PICTURED AT LEFT}

THIS SOUP, FRAGRANT with the aromas of cilantro, chili powder, and cumin, is both flavored and thickened with corn tortillas. Toasting the tortillas before grinding them helps develop the fullest flavor. Garnished with avocado, cheese, chicken, and toasted tortilla strips, this soup can be the center of a light meal, rounded out with a green salad.

MAKES 6 SERVINGS

1. Preheat the oven to 300°F. Cut the tortillas into matchsticks. Place them in an even layer on a baking sheet and toast in the oven for about 15 minutes. Or, toast the strips by sautéing them in a dry skillet over medium heat, tossing frequently. Reserve about ½ cup of the strips for a garnish. Crush the remainder in a food processor or blender.

2. Heat the oil in a soup pot over medium heat. Add the onion and garlic and cook, stirring frequently, until they have a sweet aroma, 5 to 6 minutes.

3. Add the tomato purée and continue to cook for another 3 minutes. Add the cilantro, chili powder, and cumin and cook for another 2 minutes.

4. Add the broth, crushed tortillas, and bay leaf. Stir well, bring the soup to a simmer, and cook for about 25 to 30 minutes.

5. Serve the soup in heated bowls, garnished with the shredded chicken, cheddar cheese, reserved tortilla strips, and diced avocado.

Make It Different

As an alternative to using tortilla strips for a garnish, cut one of the tortillas into wedges and toast them in the oven. Mash the avocado with a little lime juice and some diced tomato to make a guacamole. When ready to serve, place a dollop of the guacamole on the tortilla wedges and float these "croutons" on top of the soup. Scatter grated cheese over all, and garnish with the shredded chicken, if desired. You could also substitute vegetable broth for the chicken broth, omitting the shredded chicken garnish, for a vegetarian version of this soup.

4 corn tortillas

2 tsp vegetable oil

¾ cup finely grated or puréed onion

1 garlic clove, finely minced

¾ cup tomato purée

1 tbsp chopped fresh cilantro leaves

1½ tsp mild chili powder

1 tsp ground cumin

6 cups Chicken Broth (page 15)

1 bay leaf

½ cup shredded cooked chicken breast (from about ½ breast)

2 tbsp grated cheddar cheese

½ cup diced avocado (see note below)

Handling Avocados

Avocado will turn brown if it is cut very far in advance. Avoid cutting the avocado more than 1 hour before you will need it. Once you cut it, sprinkle the diced flesh with a little lemon or lime juice and toss gently to coat all the pieces. Cover the avocado and keep refrigerated. If avocados are not in season or unavailable, substitute peeled, seeded, and diced tomatoes or cucumbers.

2 poblano chiles

4 tsp corn oil

1 ancho chile

10 oz smoked pork, diced (about 2½ cups)

Salt to taste

Freshly ground black pepper to taste

1¼ cups diced onion

2 garlic cloves, minced

1 jalapeño pepper, seeded and minced

3 tbsp masa harina (optional)

2 tbsp tomato paste

1½ quarts Chicken Broth (page 15)

1 tsp dried oregano

1 tsp dried thyme

¾ cup canned hominy, rinsed and drained

Juice of 1 lime, or as needed

½ cup grated jalapeño jack cheese

2 tbsp chopped fresh cilantro

½ cup diced jícama (optional)

*1 tomatillo, papery hull removed, washed, and
diced (optional)*

*2 to 3 radishes, diced or cut into matchsticks
(optional)*

POSOLE-POBLANO SOUP

with Smoked Pork and Jalapeño Jack Cheese

TRADITIONALLY SERVED AT Christmas, this thick Mexican soup is full of deep, complex flavors. Some of the ingredients may be unfamiliar to you, but they should not be difficult to find either at your supermarket or a Latin American grocery. Poblanos are dark green fresh chiles that range from mild to quite spicy. Anchos are dried, ripe poblanos. Roasting (for the poblanos) and toasting (for the ancho) intensifies their flavors. Hominy (corn from which the hull and germ have been removed) is available canned in either gold or yellow varieties. If you have a good butcher or smokehouse nearby, you might be able to acquire some smoked pork shoulder. Otherwise, most supermarkets sell smoked pork chops. *Masa harina* ("dough flour") is made from the dried dough used to make corn tortillas. It provides flavor and a slight thickening effect, but you can omit it and still have a delicious soup. Quaker makes masa harina, or purchase a Mexican brand, such as Maseca, if available.

MAKES 6 SERVINGS

1. Preheat the broiler. Brush the poblanos with 1 teaspoon of the oil. Place the poblanos under the broiler and turn as they roast so that they blacken evenly on all sides. Put the poblanos in a bowl and cover. Let the poblanos steam for 10 minutes, then remove them from the bowl and pull off the skin. Use the back of a knife to scrape away any bits that don't come away easily. Remove the seeds, ribs, and stem from the poblanos. Chop the flesh coarsely. Set aside.

2. Heat a cast iron or other very heavy skillet over high heat. Remove the stem and seeds from the ancho and straighten it into a single layer. Toast the ancho by placing it in the hot skillet and pressing down hard with a metal spatula until it crackles and a wisp of smoke rises, 3 to 5 seconds. Flip over and repeat with the other side. Chop the ancho coarsely and set aside.

3. Heat the remaining oil in a soup pot over medium heat. Season the pork cubes with the salt and pepper and add to the pot. Cook until the pork is well browned, about 5 minutes. Add the onion and continue to cook another 5 minutes. Add the garlic and jalapeno pepper and cook 1 minute more. Add the masa harina (if using) and cook for 1 minute. Add the tomato paste and cook for 1 minute.

4. Add 4½ cups of the broth along with the oregano and thyme. Bring to a simmer and cook for at least 20 minutes.

5. Meanwhile, place the remaining 1½ cups of broth and the ancho chile in a saucepan. Bring to a simmer and cook until the chile is quite tender, about 15 minutes. Purée the ancho and broth in a blender. *(recipe continues)*

6. When the soup has simmered for at least 20 minutes, add the ancho purée. Continue to simmer another 15 minutes. Add the poblanos and the hominy. Simmer the soup 10 minutes more.

7. Just before serving, season to taste with the lime juice, salt, and pepper. Serve in heated bowls, garnished with the cheese, cilantro, and jícama, tomatillo, and radish (if using). Or, put the garnishes in small bowls and pass them on the side.

MULLIGATAWNY SOUP

MULLIGATAWNY SOUP IS a product of the British colonization of India. The British required a separate soup course with their meals, but the Indian custom was to serve all the foods in a meal at one time. Furthermore, the closest dishes to soup in Indian cuisine at that time were used as thin sauces poured over rice or dry curries. They were never drunk by themselves. Mulligatawny was born of this need. The name, which is a corruption of "milagu-tannir," comes from the Tamil people of southern India. It means "pepper water," hence the large amount of black pepper in the recipe. For the best flavor, grind the spices fresh yourself. If you like, you can substitute chicken for the lamb without sacrificing authenticity.

MAKES 8 SERVINGS

1 to 2 jalapeño peppers

4 tsp ground black pepper

1 tbsp ground coriander

2 tsp ground turmeric

¾ tsp ground cumin

½ tsp ground nutmeg

¼ tsp ground cloves

5 garlic cloves

2 tsp grated or minced fresh ginger

2 tbsp butter

2½ cups diced onions

1 lb lamb stew meat, cut into ½-inch cubes

2 qt Chicken Broth (page 15)

⅓ cup tomato paste

1½ tsp salt

⅔ cup diced carrot

1½ cups diced apples (peeled and cored)

¾ cup diced potato

½ cup frozen peas

Lemon slices as needed (optional)

1. Remove the stem from the jalapeño. If you prefer a milder spice level, remove the seeds as well. Grind the jalapeño, black pepper, coriander, turmeric, cumin, nutmeg, cloves, garlic, and ginger to a paste in a blender or with a mortar and pestle.

2. Heat the butter in a soup pot over medium heat. Cook the onions, stirring occasionally, until golden brown, about 10 minutes. Add the spice paste and cubed lamb and cook for 5 minutes.

3. Add the broth, tomato paste, and salt. Bring to a simmer and cook for 20 minutes. Add the carrot, apples, and potato. Continue to simmer the soup until everything is tender, about 20 minutes more.

4. Add the peas and simmer just until heated through, about 5 minutes. Serve the soup in heated bowls, garnished with lemon slices (if using).

LEBLEBI

Tunisian Chickpea Soup

CHICKPEAS (GARBANZO BEANS) are an important food in many parts of the world, particularly the band of countries that stretches from India through the Middle East to the Mediterranean. Buy dried chickpeas from a store that is likely to turn over its stock quickly, because chickpeas that are extremely dry will not soften properly no matter how long you cook them. Middle Eastern or Indian groceries and health food stores are good bets. You can also substitute 3½ cups of drained and rinsed canned chickpeas for the dried (skip the cooking in step 2 and go directly to adding the spice paste in step 3). This recipe calls for a mortar and pestle, but if you don't have them, you can mince the garlic by hand, sprinkle it with the salt, and mash it to a paste with the side of a large knife. You can use a spice grinder to grind the cumin seeds, or you can substitute ½ teaspoon of toasted ground cumin.

MAKES 6 SERVINGS

1. Heat the oil in a skillet over medium heat. Add the onion and cook until translucent, 6 to 8 minutes. Set aside.

2. Drain the soaking liquid from the chickpeas and place them in a large saucepan or a soup pot. Add the broth and bring to a simmer. Cover and simmer gently for 20 minutes.

3. Crush the whole cumin seeds with the ½ teaspoon salt in a mortar. Add the garlic and crush to a paste. Add this garlic-spice paste and the harissa to the soup. Continue to simmer until the chickpeas are barely tender, 15 to 20 minutes.

4. Add the onions and the olive oil they were cooked in and simmer until the chickpeas are fully tender, about 15 minutes. Season to taste with salt and pepper.

5. To serve, place the bread chunks in the bottoms of heated soup bowls and ladle about ½ cup of broth into each bowl. Arrange the remaining garnishes in small bowls or on a tray along with the olive oil and additional salt and pepper. Once the bread has softened, add the chickpeas to the soup bowls. Serve immediately with choice of garnishes.

1½ cups dried chickpeas, soaked overnight in 1 quart of water

2 tbsp olive oil

⅔ cup diced onion

8 cups Vegetable or Chicken Broth (pages 18, 15)

1 tsp toasted cumin seeds

½ tsp salt, plus more to taste

5 garlic cloves, coarsely chopped

1 tsp Harissa (page 236)

Freshly ground black pepper to taste

GARNISHES:

Three 1-inch-thick slices of day old French bread, cut into 1-inch cubes

2 hard-boiled eggs, coarsely chopped

2 lemons, quartered

One 6-oz can tuna, drained and flaked

½ cup thinly sliced scallion (white and green parts)

¼ cup coarsely chopped capers, drained

⅓ cup Harissa (page 236)

Ground cumin to taste

Cruet of extra-virgin olive oil

HLELEM

Tunisian Vegetable and Bean Soup

{PICTURED AT LEFT}

PACKED WITH BEANS and greens, this slightly spicy vegetable soup is both tasty and good for you. Harissa is a Tunisian hot sauce or paste usually made with hot chiles, garlic, cumin, coriander, caraway, and olive oil. It's available in cans, jars, or tubes from Middle Eastern markets and specialty stores. Or, make your own using the recipe on page 236.

MAKES 8 SERVINGS

1. Soak the dried lima beans and chickpeas separately overnight in three times their volume of water. Drain and cook them separately in two times their volume of fresh water until they are tender, about 45 minutes. Drain and reserve the cooking water from both the lima beans and chickpeas. Combine the lima beans and chickpeas; set aside. Combine the cooking waters and set aside.

2. Heat the olive oil in a soup pot over medium heat. Add the garlic, celery, and onion. Cook, stirring occasionally, until the onion is translucent, 4 to 6 minutes.

3. Add the broth, reserved bean cooking liquid, and the tomato paste. Mix together until well blended and bring to a simmer for 10 minutes.

4. Approximately 10 minutes before serving, add the cooked beans and chick peas, the Swiss chard, and the pasta. Simmer until the pasta and chard stems are tender, about 10 minutes.

5. Add the harissa and stir until blended. Season to taste with the salt and pepper. Serve in heated bowls, garnished with the chopped parsley.

½ cup dried lima or butter beans

½ cup dried chickpeas

2 tbsp olive oil

1 tsp garlic minced

½ cup diced celery

¾ cup minced onion

1 qt Chicken Broth (page 15)

⅓ cup tomato paste

4 large Swiss chard leaves, stems removed and cut into 1-inch pieces, leaves shredded

⅓ cup angel hair pasta, broken into bite-sized pieces

2 tbsp Harissa (page 236)

Salt to taste

Freshly ground black pepper to taste

½ cup chopped parsley

{PICTURED AT RIGHT}

2 tbsp butter

¼ cup all-purpose flour

2 cups diced onion

1 cup diced celery

1 cup diced green bell pepper

3 tbsp vegetable oil

4 garlic cloves, minced

2 tbsp tomato paste

¼ cup white wine

1 qt Chicken Broth (page 15)

1 cup tomato purée

1 ham hock

¾ cup sliced okra

½ lb Andouille sausage, sliced into
    ¼-inch pieces

2 duck breasts (preferably smoked), skinless

2 tsp salt, or as needed

1 tsp freshly ground black pepper, or as needed

½ lb shrimp, peeled and deveined

3 plum tomatoes, seeded, diced

½ tsp hot sauce

DUCK, SHRIMP, AND ANDOUILLE GUMBO

GUMBO IS A stew-like dish that was created in Louisiana and is now recognized and enjoyed in many varieties. Originally, it combined meat and shellfish, okra, tomatoes, bay leaf, and hot pepper. Make and eat it the same day, or enjoy it a day later, as the taste improves after the flavors have had time to marry.

MAKES 6 TO 8 SERVINGS

1. In a small saucepan, combine the butter and flour to form a roux, and cook over medium heat until dark brown, stirring frequently, about 8 to 10 minutes.

2. While the roux is cooking, sauté the onions, celery, and bell pepper in 2 tablespoons of the vegetable oil over medium to medium-high heat until golden brown, about 12 to 15 minutes.

3. Add the garlic and cook for 2 more minutes, or until the aroma of the garlic is noticeable. Add the tomato paste and cook to a rich red-brown color, stirring constantly, about 3 to 4 minutes. Deglaze the pan with the white wine and allow the wine to reduce by half.

4. Bring the chicken broth to a simmer. Whisk the roux into the hot broth, making sure there are no lumps, and then add the vegetable mixture. Add the tomato purée, ham hock, and the okra and simmer for 15 to 20 minutes.

5. While the gumbo is simmering, cook the andouille in a sauté pan over medium-high heat until browned and cooked through, about 4 to 5 minutes. Remove the andouille from the pan and reserve the fat. Season the duck breasts with ½ teaspoon salt and ¼ teaspoon pepper, and sauté in the andouille fat over medium-high heat until cooked thoroughly, about 4 to 5 minutes on each side. Once cool enough to handle, cut into medium dice; set aside.

6. Season the shrimp with ½ teaspoon salt and ¼ teaspoon pepper. Heat a skillet over high heat, add the remaining tablespoon of oil, and sear the shrimp in the oil until brightly colored and just cooked through, about 2 to 3 minutes. Add the shrimp, andouille, and duck to the gumbo along with the tomatoes. Continue to simmer until all the ingredients are heated through, about 5 minutes. Season with the remaining salt and pepper, and hot sauce to taste.

SEAFOOD GUMBO

IN ADDITION TO a small amount of roux, this gumbo is thickened with filé powder, which is the ground, dried leaves of the sassafras tree. It has a woodsy, root beer-like flavor. Filé powder is usually added to the gumbo after it is removed from the heat, as excessive heat can make the filé stringy. Some people do not care for the texture of filé, so you might prefer to serve it on the side and allow individuals to add it to their liking. You can find filé powder in the spice section of most large supermarkets.

MAKES 8 SERVINGS

1. Combine the seasoning mix ingredients. Set aside.

2. Heat the oil in a soup pot over low heat. Add the flour and cook, stirring frequently, until the flour turns dark brown and has an intensely nutty aroma, about 10 minutes.

3. Increase the heat to high and add the onion, celery, and green pepper. Cook until the vegetables are softened, about 5 minutes. Add the garlic, Tabasco, and seasoning mix. Stir well and cook for 1 minute longer. Stir in the tomato sauce and bring to a simmer. Cook for 10 minutes.

4. Add the broth, return to a simmer, and cook for 45 minutes.

5. Meanwhile, cook the sausage in a nonstick skillet over medium heat until browned on both sides, 5 to 7 minutes. Drain on paper towels.

6. Add the sausage, oysters, tomatoes, crab, shrimp, and rice to the gumbo. Bring to a boil, stir in the filé, and cover. Remove from the heat, and let stand 10 to 12 minutes. Season to taste with the salt and pepper. Serve in heated bowls.

OPPOSITE, CLOCKWISE FROM UPPER LEFT: The roux for the gumbo should cook long enough to achieve a dark, golden brown color; onion, green pepper, and celery are often referred to as the "holy trinity" of Cajun cooking; remove the pot from the heat before adding the file powder.

SEASONING MIX:

¼ tsp garlic powder

¼ tsp freshly ground white pepper

Pinch freshly ground black pepper

Pinch cayenne

Pinch hot paprika

Pinch dried thyme

Pinch dried oregano

1 tbsp canola oil or unsalted butter

2 tbsp all-purpose flour

2½ cups diced onion

1½ cups diced celery stalks

¾ cup diced green bell pepper

1 garlic clove, minced

¾ tsp Tabasco sauce

1 cup tomato sauce

3½ cups Fish Broth (page 17)

1 link andouille sausage, sliced

8 fresh oysters, shucked

¾ diced plum tomatoes (peeled and seeded)

¾ cup crab meat, picked over for shells

⅔ cup small shrimp, peeled and deveined

⅔ cup cooked white rice

1 to 2 tsp filé powder

Salt to taste

Freshly ground black pepper to taste

{ PICTURED AT RIGHT }

*5 oz slab bacon, rind removed, cut into
    small dice*

¾ cup minced onion

2 garlic cloves, minced

2 qt Chicken Broth (page 15)

4 cups sliced okra

1½ cups coarsely chopped taro greens

*1 Scotch bonnet chile, pricked with a fork and
    left whole*

*4 tsp fresh thyme leaves, coarsely chopped,
    or 2 tsp dried*

Salt to taste

Freshly ground black pepper to taste

10 oz crabmeat, picked over for shells

3 scallions, sliced

¾ cup coconut milk

Juice of 2 limes, or more to taste

CALLALOO

CALLALOO IS THE greens of the taro root. It is popular in the Caribbean, where it is cooked and eaten in much the same way as collard or turnip greens are in the Southeastern United States. It is also used to make a wonderful soup of the same name. Callaloo can be purchased at Caribbean markets, but if you cannot find it in your area, fresh spinach makes a fine substitute. Whatever greens you use, be sure to wash them thoroughly to remove any grit.

MAKES 8 SERVINGS

1. Cook the bacon in a soup pot over medium heat until crisp, about 8 minutes. Add the onion and garlic and cook, stirring occasionally, until softened, about 3 minutes.

2. Add the broth, okra, greens, chile, and thyme along with a pinch of salt and pepper. Bring to a simmer and cook for 30 minutes.

3. Just before serving, remove the chile and add the crabmeat, scallions, coconut milk, and lime juice. Season to taste with salt and pepper. Serve in heated bowls.

Stews

F IT IS hard to tell when a soup goes from being a broth to a hearty soup, it is just as difficult to determine when a hearty soup turns into a stew. Stews are made from a variety of ingredients, from traditional long-simmered beef stews (like Catalan Beef Stew, page 117) to quick-cooking stews (like our Italian-Style Summer Vegetable Stew, page 98), made from a selection of seasonal greens.

CHOOSE THE BEST INGREDIENTS

Stewing is a gentle, slow cooking technique that transforms all manner of foods into tender morsels in a rich, flavorful sauce. This often means ingredients that are more mature and flavorful. If you are planning a beef stew, choose cuts from the shoulder or the shank for a deep, rich taste. For poultry stews, you may need to use a stewing hen or fowl, or perhaps feature leg or thigh meat instead of breast. You can find more information in the table on pages 6–9, Shopping for Soup Ingredients.

COOK THE STEW PROPERLY

A good stew is never cooked at a hard boil. Cooking a stew that hard and fast would result in a disappointing dish. For tender, melting textures and big, bold flavors, keep the stew at a bare simmer with just a few lazy bubbles bursting on the surface. If you wish, you can opt to finish stews in the oven. This has the effect of maintaining a slow, steady, even, and very gentle heat. The only caveat is that you need to be more vigilant about checking the dish as it stews. Once you move something from the stovetop into the oven, it is a little easier to forget about it. Use your kitchen timer to keep track of the stew as it cooks.

FLAVOR, SEASON, AND GARNISH THE STEW JUDICIOUSLY

You nearly always can add other ingredients to a stew as it simmers. If the ingredients you want to add are already cooked (beans, pasta, rice, potatoes, meats, and so forth), add them in the last few minutes of cooking time, just long enough for them to reheat. Other ingredients may need to be added earlier on, as the stew simmers, so that they finish cooking at the same time as the main ingredients. Add seasonings a little at a time throughout the cooking process. Adding just a little bit at a time gives you more control.

If you are simmering dry beans in the stew, don't add any salt or acidic ingredients like wine or vinegar until the beans are beginning to turn tender. Remember that the flavor of your stew will deepen as it cooks, but if you don't add seasonings throughout, the flavor may not have the depth you intended.

☀ BASIC METHOD FOR STEWS

A delicate stew of tender springtime vegetables may not seem to share many similarities with a robust stew made from oxtail, and yet there are certain culinary principles they both share. The basic ingredients are cut into pieces, and then gently cooked in a flavorful liquid. Italian-style Summer Vegetable Stew (page 98) shows the bright, fresh results you can achieve when the main ingredients are cooked as is, with no initial searing or blanching. Oxtail Stew in Red Wine (page 114) takes advantage of the flavor intensification you get from browning the ingredients before the actual stewing begins.

➡ *PREPARE THE INGREDIENTS:* Choose a heavy-gauge ovenproof pan with a lid, such as a Dutch oven, that is just large enough to hold all the ingredients. The first step in all stews is to cut the food into appropriately-sized pieces. Once you've done that, you are ready to incorporate them into the stew at the correct point. For some dishes, you will brown the ingredients quickly in fat over high heat, and then continue with aromatics; for others, you will add them along with the stewing liquid.

➡ *COOK THE AROMATIC INGREDIENTS:* The degree to which the aromatic ingredients—onions, garlic, carrots, tomatoes, or mushrooms, for instance—are cooked will influence the flavor and color of the finished stew. Sweating or smothering the aromatics releases their flavor into the stew without any additional browning. If the aromatics are cooked until browned, the stew will have a deeper color. If you have browned the main ingredients, remove them from the pot and add the aromatics to the same fat (adding more oil or butter if needed).

➡ *ADD THE STEWING LIQUID:* Once all the ingredients are sautéed, add the stewing liquid. This may be something as simple as a bit of water to let the flavors of the ingredients shine through, or a more complex mixture of broth and wine. Spices and herbs may be added as well. If they are not edible, wrap them in cheesecloth to make a spice sachet for easy retrieval later. Stews usually call for enough liquid to cover the food completely. You can adjust the level throughout cooking time.

➡ *COOK THE STEW:* Low heat is suggested for all stews, never a hard boil. Reduce the heat as low as possible. Placing a lid slightly ajar on the pot traps the escaping steam and allows it to condense and fall back onto the stew. You can also cook stews in a 350°F oven. Cooking in the oven rather than on the stovetop is a reliable way to stew, since cooking over a flame can lead to overly rapid cooking and scorching. In either case, check the stew periodically to maintain a slow and gentle cooking speed in order to extract as much flavor as possible without drying out the food. Use a spoon or skimmer to degrease the stew, spooning off as much of the floating fat as possible, in order to give the final sauce a better consistency.

➡ *FINISH THE STEW:* When all the ingredients are tender to the bite, it is time to make final seasoning adjustments. You can add salt and pepper to taste as well as other options: a splash of citrus juice or a fortified wine, chopped fresh herbs, some pesto, and so forth. Some stews benefit from 24 hours of rest. If time permits, let your stew cool and refrigerate it in a covered container overnight. As a side benefit, any fat will harden on the surface so you can lift it off easily and completely.

ITALIAN-STYLE SUMMER VEGETABLE STEW

{PICTURED AT RIGHT}

4 cups water, or as needed

2 slices pancetta

1 large carrot, cut into medium dice

1 Idaho potato, cut into medium dice

3 small yellow onions, cut into medium dice

1 cup cooked or canned cannelini beans, drained

1 cup green beans

1 cup medium-dice zucchini

*2 scallions, green and white portions, cut into
⅓-inch lengths*

*¾ cup small dried pasta (shells, bow ties,
or orrechietti)*

Salt as needed

Freshly ground black pepper as needed

PESTO

½ cup diced plum tomatoes

⅓ cup chopped basil

2 tsp minced garlic

1 tbsp extra-virgin olive oil

SERVE THIS QUICK-COOKING vegetable stew with a hearty red wine to stand up to the bold flavors of the pancetta and the pesto of basil, garlic, and tomato. Letting the stew rest briefly before serving gives the pesto's flavors a chance to open up.

MAKES 4 SERVINGS

1. Combine the water and pancetta in a large soup pot. Bring to a boil, reduce the heat to a low simmer, and add the carrot, potato, onions, and cannelini beans. Simmer slowly over low heat until the potatoes are tender, 30 to 35 minutes. Add the greens beans, zucchini, scallions, and pasta; simmer until all the vegetables are flavorful and the pasta is tender, 20 to 25 minutes. Season to taste with salt and pepper.

2. While the stew cooks, make the pesto: Chop together the tomatoes, basil, and garlic with a chef's knife or in a food processor to make a relatively smooth paste. Transfer to a bowl and stir in the extra-virgin olive oil.

3. Stir the pesto into the stew and let rest off the heat, covered, for a few minutes before serving. Serve immediately in warmed soup plates.

MOROCCAN-STYLE VEGETABLE STEW

{PICTURED AT LEFT}

THIS HEARTY AND warming stew can be doubled and leftovers will freeze well. Cool the stew to room temperature and store in an airtight container; the stew can be stored in the freezer for up to 2 weeks. Thaw in the refrigerator or microwave. Serve the stew over a bed of couscous, as shown here.

MAKES 4 SERVINGS

1. Combine the ginger, paprika, cumin, turmeric, mustard, coriander, cinnamon, cardamom, and cayenne. Toast the spice blend in a dry, nonstick skillet over low heat until fragrant, about 2 minutes.

2. Heat the oil in a in a large pot over medium-high heat until it shimmers. Add the onion, leek, and garlic; sauté, stirring frequently, until translucent, about 3 to 5 minutes. Add the spice blend and sauté until fragrant, about 1 to 2 minutes. Stir in the pumpkin, squash, and zucchini. Add enough broth to cover the vegetables; simmer for 10 minutes. Add the remaining broth, the eggplant, carrots, celery, currants, and tomato purée. Simmer until the vegetables are tender, about 25 minutes.

3. Stir the chick peas and fava beans into the simmering vegetables; add the lemon juice and salt. Cover the pot and cook until heated through, about 5 minutes. Divide the stew among 4 bowls and sprinkle with the grated lemon zest.

1½ tsp minced ginger

½ tsp paprika

¼ tsp ground cumin

¼ tsp turmeric

¼ tsp dry mustard

¼ tsp ground coriander

¼ tsp ground cinnamon

¼ tsp ground cardamom

⅛ tsp cayenne

1 tbsp olive oil

1 large yellow onion, diced

1 medium leek, cleaned and sliced thin

2 tsp minced garlic

½ cup diced pumpkin

½ cup diced butternut squash

½ cup diced zucchini

3 cups Vegetable Broth (page 18)

1½ cups diced eggplant

2 carrots, diced

1 celery stalk, diced

⅓ cup currants

3 tbsp tomato purée

⅓ cup cooked or canned chick peas, rinsed

⅓ cup cooked fava beans

2 tsp fresh lemon juice

¼ tsp salt

1½ tsp grated lemon zest

CRAWFISH ÉTOUFFÉ

{PICTURED AT LEFT}

CRAWFISH, OR CRAYFISH, are sold live or as cooked meat. If you buy crawfish meat, look for the words "fat-on." Crawfish fat is an integral part of a good étouffé.

MAKES 5 SERVINGS

1. Heat the bacon fat or oil in a casserole or Dutch oven over medium heat until it shimmers. Add the onion to the tagine or casserole and sauté over medium heat, stirring frequently, until the onion is translucent, about 6 minutes. Add the celery, bell pepper, and garlic; cover the pan and cook over low heat, stirring occasionally, until the vegetables are tender and translucent, about 10 minutes. Add the paprika, white and black pepper, cayenne, and ½ teaspoon salt. Sauté, stirring constantly, until aromatic, about 1 minute.

2. Sprinkle the flour over the vegetables and continue to cook, stirring constantly, until the mixture is thick and pasty, about 3 minutes. Add the broth and stir well to work out any lumps. Bring to a simmer over medium heat. Add the crayfish tails and their fat. Cover the pot and cook over very low heat, stirring frequently, until the crayfish is cooked through and very hot, 8 to 10 minutes. Add a little more broth as needed throughout the cooking time if the étouffé is getting too thick. Season to taste with additional salt and pepper.

3. Add the butter, scallions, basil, and parsley and stir to combine. Serve the étouffé in heated bowls.

3 tbsp bacon fat or canola oil

1½ cups minced onion

1 cup minced celery

¾ cup minced green bell pepper

2 tsp minced garlic

1 tbsp mild paprika

¼ tsp ground white pepper

¼ tsp freshly ground black pepper, or as needed

⅛ tsp ground cayenne

Salt as needed

¼ cup all-purpose flour

2 cups Fish or Chicken Broth (pages 17, 15) or as needed

1¼ lb crawfish tail meat with fat

3 tbsp butter

1 cup thinly sliced scallions, white and green parts

¼ cup basil chiffonade

2 tbsp chopped flat-leaf parsley

OYSTER STEW

THIS STEW IS a quick, elegant dish that is traditionally served on New Year's Eve throughout various parts of the country. If you don't want to shuck the oysters yourself, use 1 pint of shucked oysters.

MAKES 8 SERVINGS

1. Drain the oysters in a colander over a bowl. Reserve the juice.

2. Heat a soup pot over medium heat. Add the bacon and cook until crisp, about 6 to 8 minutes. Use a slotted spoon to transfer the bacon to a paper towel-lined plate and set aside.

3. Add the onion to the bacon fat and cook until translucent, about 6 minutes. Do not brown. *(recipe continues)*

24 fresh oysters, shucked, juices reserved

4 bacon slices, minced

1 onion, minced

¼ cup all-purpose flour

1½ qt milk

1 bay leaf

1 cup heavy cream, heated

½ tsp salt, or as needed

¼ tsp freshly ground black pepper, or as needed

Oyster crackers as needed

4. Reduce the heat to low, add the flour, and cook for 3 to 4 minutes, stirring constantly with a wooden spoon. Add the milk and reserved oyster juice gradually, using a whisk to work out any lumps between each addition. Add the bay leaf and simmer the soup for 20 minutes, skimming as necessary.

5. Add the whole oysters and continue to simmer until oysters are barely cooked, about 5 minutes. Remove the soup from the heat.

6. Add the hot cream and season to taste with the salt and pepper. Serve in heated bowls, garnished with the reserved bacon and oyster crackers.

{PICTURED AT RIGHT}

3 tbsp canola oil

1½ lb chicken, meat, sliced ½-inch thick

Salt as needed

Freshly ground black pepper as needed

1 lb Andouille sausage, sliced ½-inch thick

2 cups minced yellow onion

2 cups diced green bell pepper

1½ cups diced celery

2 tsp minced garlic

2 tbsp paprika

¼ tsp ground cayenne

¼ tsp ground white pepper

2 cups chopped plum tomatoes, peeled and seeded, juices reserved

3 cups Chicken Broth (page 15) or as needed

1 bay leaf

¼ cup basil chiffonade

2 tsp chopped fresh thyme

1 tsp Tabasco

30 shrimp, 21–25 count, peeled and deveined

4 cups cooked short-grain rice

1 cup sliced scallions, white and green parts

SHRIMP AND CHICKEN JAMBALAYA

ANDOUILLE SAUSAGE IS an important part of this jambalaya because it adds a rich, smoky flavor along with plenty of garlic and spice. If Andouille sausage isn't easy to find in your area, substitute other available spicy sausages such as chorizo or linguiça.

MAKES 8 SERVINGS

1. Heat the oil in a Dutch oven over high heat until it shimmers. Season the chicken with salt and pepper and then sear in the hot oil, turning as necessary, until golden on all sides, about 8 minutes. Transfer to a warm plate or pan. Add the sausage to the pan and continue to sauté until it is lightly browned on both sides, about 6 minutes. Transfer to the same plate or pan as the chicken and reserve.

2. Add the onion, bell pepper, celery, garlic, paprika, cayenne, and white pepper to the Dutch oven and cook over medium-low heat, stirring frequently, until the vegetables start to release some of their juices and are beginning to soften, about 10 minutes. Add the tomatoes with their juices and simmer briefly, about 1 to 2 minutes. Add the broth and bay leaf and bring the jambalaya to a simmer. Cover the Dutch oven and simmer, stirring occasionally, until the vegetables are almost completely tender, about 15 minutes.

3. Return the browned chicken and sausage to the Dutch oven, along with any juices they may have released. Add the basil, thyme, and Tabasco, and return to a simmer over low heat until flavorful, about 10 minutes. Add the shrimp to the jambalaya and simmer until the shrimp are cooked all the way through, about 5 minutes.

4. Add the cooked rice and mix well. Serve the jambalaya in heated bowls, topped with the sliced scallions.

3½ lb boneless lamb leg, cut into 1½-inch cubes

Salt as needed

Ground white pepper as needed

1½ cups plain yogurt

2 tbsp minced ginger root

1 tbsp minced garlic

2 tsp ground cardamom

12 oz cashew nuts

¼ cup ghee (see sidebar) or canola oil

3 cups small-dice yellow onion

1 tsp ground cumin

1 tsp ground cardamom

1 tsp ground fennel

2 tbsp ground coriander

6 Thai bird chiles, chopped, or to taste

⅓ cup chopped cilantro stems

Water as needed

1 cup heavy cream

Salt to taste

½ cup chopped cilantro leaves

1 cup pan-roasted cashews (see page 241)

LAMB KHORMA

LAMB KHORMA IS a sensuous curry made by simmering lamb with yogurt and cream and thickening the sauce with a cashew paste. If you can find goat's milk yogurt or sheep's milk yogurt, it will make a discernable difference in this dish.

MAKES 8 SERVINGS

1. Trim the lamb and cut it into large pieces. Season with salt and pepper and put in a bowl. Add the yogurt, 1 tablespoon of ginger, the garlic, and cardamom. Stir or toss until the ingredients are evenly distributed and the lamb is coated. Cover and refrigerate for at least 30 minutes and up to 3 hours.

2. Put the cashews in a small bowl and add enough hot water to cover them. Let the cashews soak for 30 minutes and then drain. Grind the drained cashews to a coarse paste in a food processor. Set aside.

3. Heat the ghee or oil in a casserole or Dutch oven over medium heat until it shimmers. Add the onion and sauté until transparent, 6 to 8 minutes. Add the cumin, cardamom, fennel, the remaining ginger, and the coriander. Cook until aromatic, stirring often, about 2 minutes. Add the chiles, cilantro stalks, and cashew paste; stir well to be sure that nothing is sticking. Sauté, stirring frequently and adding water a tablespoon at a time if necessary, until the mixture is very aromatic, about 2 minutes.

4. Add the lamb and the yogurt marinade, increase the heat, and stir until the pieces are evenly coated. Once the meat's juices begin to flow, reduce heat to low, cover, and simmer very slowly, stirring occasionally, until the meat is nearly tender, about 45 minutes.

5. Add the cream and continue to simmer until the curry is flavorful and thickened and the lamb is tender, 10 to 15 minutes. Season to taste with additional salt, pepper, or chopped bird chile. Serve garnished with the cilantro leaves and cashews.

Making Ghee

Ghee, a type of cooking butter used in Indian cooking, can be purchased in jars at Asian or Indian markets, but it is easy to make yourself.

Cube 1 pound of cold unsalted butter, place in a saucepan, and set over low heat. Once the butter has melted, increase the heat slightly. The pure butterfat will become very clear. Some foam will rise to the top; skim it away. Increase the heat slightly and continue to cook the butter until the milk solids that have fallen to the bottom of the pan turn a deep golden color. Immediately remove the pan from the heat. Ladle the clear butterfat, or ghee, into a clean container; discard the liquid at the bottom of the pan. You can keep ghee in the refrigerator for up to 2 weeks.

GREEN CHILE AND PORK STEW
WITH POTATOES

{PICTURED AT LEFT}

P OBLANO CHILES AND jalapeños give this dish its color and flavor. Whenever you work with hot chiles, wear gloves to protect your hands and be diligent about washing your hands, your tools, and the cutting board when you are done. Serve warm flour tortillas and a little grated Monterey Jack cheese to accompany this stew.

MAKES 6 SERVINGS

1. Heat the oil in a casserole or Dutch oven over medium heat until it shimmers. Season the pork with salt and pepper and sauté until lightly colored on all sides. Transfer the pork to a plate or dish using a slotted spoon, allowing most of the oil to drain back into the casserole. Return the casserole to the heat, add the onions and garlic and sauté, stirring frequently, until translucent, 6 to 8 minutes.

2. Return the pork and any juices it may have released to the casserole. Add the broth, tomato purée, poblanos, chile powder, cumin, and oregano; bring the liquid to a boil. Immediately adjust the heat for a gentle simmer. Simmer the stew, covered, for 1 hour, stirring occasionally.

3. Add the jalapeños, Tabasco, vinegar, and potatoes. Continue to simmer, covered, until the potatoes and pork are very tender, about 20 minutes. Season to taste with additional salt and pepper.

4. Serve in heated bowls.

2 tbsp canola oil

3 lb boneless pork shoulder, cut into 1-inch cubes

Salt as needed

Freshly ground black pepper as needed

2 large yellow onions, cut into ¾-inch dice

1 tbsp minced garlic

4 cups Chicken Broth (page 15)

¼ cup tomato purée

3 to 4 fresh poblano chiles, roasted, seeded, peeled, and cut into ½-inch pieces (page 38)

2 tbsp mild red chili powder

1 tbsp ground cumin

2 tsp ground Mexican oregano

2 fresh jalapeño peppers, seeded, finely minced

2 tbsp green Tabasco sauce

1 tsp white vinegar

3 cups cubed red-skinned potatoes, unpeeled

VEAL STEW WITH POLENTA

{PICTURED AT LEFT}

THIS DISH IS a variation on a shepherd's pie, with polenta to replace the potato topping and a vegetable-laden stew that features tender veal.

MAKES 6 SERVINGS

1. Season the veal generously with salt and pepper. Pour some flour into a shallow plate and dust the veal pieces in the flour. Shake off any excess flour.

2. Heat the oil in a Dutch oven or casserole over medium high heat until it shimmers. Sauté the veal in the oil, stirring frequently, until the veal is a light golden color on all sides, 8 to 10 minutes. Transfer the veal to a plate and keep warm.

3. Return the pan to the heat. Add the onion, carrot, and celery root. Sauté, stirring frequently, until the onion is lightly browned, 8 to 10 minutes. Add the tomato paste and continue to sauté until there is a sweet aroma and the tomato paste darkens in color, about 5 minutes. Add the wine and stir well to dissolve all of the drippings.

4. Return the veal and any juices it may have released to the casserole. Add enough broth to cover the veal by about 1 inch and bring to a boil. Tie the rosemary, thyme, and bay leaf together into a bouquet garni, add to the stew, and reduce the heat to low. Simmer, covered, stirring occasionally, until the veal is almost tender, about 45 minutes. Season to taste with salt and pepper. Remove the bouquet garni and discard.

5. Add the Brussels sprouts and pearl onions to the stew. Simmer, covered, until the vegetables are nearly tender, about 20 minutes. Add the green beans and simmer until they are very hot, another 5 minutes. Season to taste with additional salt and pepper if necessary.

6. Preheat the oven to 375°F. Transfer the stew to a casserole or baking dish. Top with an even layer of polenta. Bake until the stew and polenta are very hot and the crust is lightly browned, about 20 minutes. Divide among heated bowls and serve.

Polenta

SOFT POLENTA, fresh from the pot, makes a perfect topping for this stew or as a side dish to serve along with braised dishes or stews. You can add fresh herbs, butter, or cheese to the polenta while it is still hot for a little additional flavor.

MAKES 6 SERVINGS

Bring the broth or water to a rolling boil. Add the salt and cornmeal very gradually while stirring constantly. Simmer over low heat, stirring frequently, until it thickens and starts to pull away from the sides of the pot, 35 to 40 minutes. Serve hot.

Ingredients (first recipe)

3 lb boneless veal stew meat, cut into 1-inch cubes

Salt as needed

Freshly ground black pepper as needed

All-purpose flour for dusting as needed

2 tbsp olive oil, or as needed

¾ cup minced onion

1 cup large-dice carrot

1 cup large-dice celery root (celeriac)

2 tbsp tomato paste

1½ cups dry red wine

6 cups Beef Broth (page 16), or as needed

2 sprigs rosemary

2 sprigs thyme

1 bay leaf

1½ cups Brussels sprouts, trimmed and halved

1 cup pearl onions, peeled and blanched

1 cup green beans, blanched

3 cups cooked polenta (recipe follows)

Ingredients (Polenta)

3½ cups chicken broth or water

1 tsp salt, or to taste

1 cup coarse yellow cornmeal

⅓ cup canola oil

3 lbs boneless lean beef chuck, cut into small dice

Salt as needed

Freshly ground black pepper as needed

2 cups small-dice yellow onions

2 tsp minced garlic

3 cups Beef Broth (page 16)

1 cup tomato purée

1 cup diced green chiles

2 fresh jalapeños, minced

10 tbsp mild pure chile powder

3 tbsp ground cumin or to taste

2 tbsp dried oregano

Korean chile pepper as needed

A REALLY BIG CHILI

YOU MAY THINK of chilis as stews of meat and beans, but in this instance the beef is the star in a vegetable and chile-laced sauce. The Korean chile pepper is worth seeking out, but don't worry if you can't find it.

MAKES 8 SERVINGS

1. Heat the oil in a casserole or Dutch oven over high heat until it shimmers. Season the beef generously with salt and pepper. Add the beef to the hot oil, working in batches if necessary, and sauté, turning as necessary, until browned on all sides, 6 to 8 minutes. Transfer to a bowl and reserve.

2. Add the onions and garlic to the casserole and sauté, stirring frequently, until the onions are translucent, 6 to 8 minutes.

3. Add the broth, tomato purée, chiles, jalapeños, and the browned beef along with any juices it may have released to the casserole. Stir well and bring to a boil. Immediately reduce the heat to establish a gentle simmer.

4. Stir in half of chile powder, half of the cumin, and half of the oregano. Continue to simmer, adjusting the seasoning with additional chile powder, cumin, oregano, salt, and pepper, until the beef is fork tender, 1½ to 2 hours. Serve in heated bowls.

{PICTURED AT RIGHT}

¼ cup olive oil

2¾ lb oxtail pieces

Salt as needed

Freshly ground black pepper as needed

2 cups chopped yellow onion

*1½ cups chopped leek, white and
    ight green parts*

1 tsp minced garlic

½ cup diced plum tomato

1 tbsp sherry vinegar or as needed

1 tbsp honey

*2 cups dry red wine, such as a good-quality
    Rioja*

3 cups Beef Broth (page 16) or as needed

4 parsley sprigs

4 thyme sprigs

1 bay leaf

OXTAIL STEW IN RED WINE

O XTAIL STEWS HAVE incredible body and flavor. We recommend that you make this a day or two before you plan to eat it—the flavor deepens as it rests. Boiled, mashed, or pan-fried potatoes (as shown here) are good accompaniments to this dish, along with a glass of the wine you used to make the stew.

MAKES 6 SERVINGS

1. Heat the oil in a casserole or Dutch oven over high heat until it shimmers. Season the oxtail pieces generously with salt and pepper; add in a single layer to the hot oil. (Work in batches, if necessary, to avoid crowding the pieces.) Sauté the oxtail, turning as necessary, until browned on all sides, about 10 minutes. Transfer to a plate, letting the oil drain back into the casserole. Cover the oxtail loosely and set aside.

2. Return the casserole to high heat until the oil shimmers. Add the onion, leek, and garlic and sauté, stirring occasionally, until golden brown, about 15 minutes. Add the tomato and cook until it deepens in color and smells sweet, about 2 minutes.

3. Add the sherry vinegar and honey. Stir until the honey is dissolved. Return the oxtail pieces and any juices they may have released to the casserole and fold the oxtail into the vegetables gently with a wooden spoon.

4. Add the red wine and enough of the broth to cover the oxtail. Bring to a simmer over low heat. Tie the parsley, thyme, and bay leaf together into a bouquet garni and add to the stew. Cover the casserole and simmer very gently over low heat until the meat on the oxtail is nearly falling from the bone, 2 to 3 hours.

5. Transfer the oxtail pieces to a heated serving bowl and keep warm. Remove and discard the bouquet garni. Return the casserole to the heat. Skim the fat and oil from the surface and bring to a simmer over medium-high heat. Simmer rapidly until the sauce thickens slightly, about 5 minutes. Season to taste with additional sherry vinegar, salt, and pepper. Pour the sauce over the oxtail pieces and serve immediately.

CATALAN BEEF STEW

{PICTURED AT LEFT}

THE CUISINE OF Spain is rapidly becoming more familiar to cooks and restaurant-goers. This dish marries a flavorful cut of beef from the shoulder with some typical Catalonian ingredients: oranges, olives, red wine, and bacon. Bitter oranges are traditional, but if you don't have access to a bitter orange, use a Valencia (juice) orange and a touch of lime juice for nearly the same flavor profile.

MAKES 4 SERVINGS

1. Heat the oil in a casserole or Dutch oven over medium high heat until it shimmers. Add the bacon, and sauté until the bacon is crisped and browned, 5 minutes. Transfer the bacon to a bowl with a slotted spoon, letting the oil drain back into the casserole.

2. Return the casserole to the heat and heat the oil until it shimmers. Season the beef generously with salt and pepper. Add the beef (working in batches to avoid crowding the pan) and sear on all sides until brown, about 8 minutes. Transfer the beef to the bowl with the bacon using a slotted spoon and letting the oil drain back into the casserole. Add the onion and sauté, stirring occasionally, until deeply caramelized, 25 to 30 minutes.

3. Return the beef and bacon to the casserole, add the red wine, orange peel, bay leaves, garlic, and parsley; bring the liquid to a boil. Immediately adjust the heat for a gentle simmer. Season the stew to taste with salt and pepper throughout cooking time. Simmer the stew, covered, until the beef is nearly tender, about 2 hours. Add the olives and continue to simmer until the beef is fork tender, 1 to 1 ½ hours. Serve in heated bowls.

1 tbsp olive oil

5 slices bacon, thick-cut, diced

2 lb boneless beef chuck or bottom round, cut into 2-inch pieces

Salt as needed

Freshly ground black pepper as needed

2 cups chopped yellow onion

2 cups red wine

2 tbsp orange peel julienne

2 bay leaves

2 tsp minced garlic

2 parsley sprigs, minced

1 cup Spanish black olives, pitted

BOLIVIAN BEEF STEW

{PICTURED AT LEFT}

THERE ARE MANY variations of this spicy, slow cooking, one-pot meal. Serve it with warm corn bread and salad greens dressed with lemon juice. Adjust the amount of jalapeño pepper to suit your family and friends.

MAKES 4 SERVINGS

1. Season the beef generously with salt and pepper.

2. Heat the oil in a Dutch oven or casserole over medium-high heat until it shimmers. Sauté the beef in the oil, stirring frequently, until the beef is browned on all sides, 8 to 10 minutes. Transfer the beef to a plate and keep warm.

3. Return the same pan to the heat. Add the onion, bell pepper, and jalapeño. Sauté, stirring frequently, until the onion is lightly browned, 8 to 10 minutes. Add the tomatoes and broth. Bring the liquid to a boil, and reduce the heat to low. Return the beef and any juices it may have released to the casserole. Simmer, covered, stirring occasionally, until the beef is tender, 1 to 1 ½ hours. Season to taste as the stew simmers with additional salt and pepper.

4. Add the squash, potatoes, and corn to the stew. Simmer, covered, until the vegetables are tender, about 20 minutes. Season to taste with additional salt and pepper. Divide the stew evenly among 4 heated bowls, sprinkle each serving with some of the cilantro, and serve.

1 lb boneless lean beef round, cut into 2-inch cubes

Salt to taste

Freshly ground black pepper to taste

1 tbsp canola oil

2 cups diced yellow onion

½ cup chopped red or green bell pepper

1 jalapeño pepper, seeded, deveined, and chopped

2 cups chopped plum tomatoes, fresh or canned

1 cup Beef Broth (page 16)

2 cups diced acorn or winter squash

2 red potatoes, diced

2 small ears of corn, sliced into 1-inch-thick rounds

2 tbsp minced cilantro

5 cups coconut milk

2 lb boneless beef chuck, cut in 2-inch chunks

⅓ cup Mussaman curry paste (or substitute red curry)

4 cups large-dice potatoes

3 tbsp fish sauce plus as needed

3 tbsp tamarind pulp

2 tbsp palm sugar, plus as needed

6 cinnamon sticks

1 tsp ground cardamom

¾ cup large-dice yellow onion

½ cup pan-roasted peanuts (see page 241)

2 tsp lime juice or as needed

Palm sugar is made by cooking down the sugary sap of the palmyra (or date) palm. You may also find it sold as coconut sugar; most agree that the two are interchangeable.

BEEF IN MUSSAMAN CURRY SAUCE

YOU CAN FIND prepared curry pastes in large grocery stores or shops that specialize in Asian products, or you can make your own—see the sidebar below.

MAKES 4 SERVINGS

1. Heat the coconut milk in a large saucepot over medium heat until it comes to a gentle boil, about 10 minutes. Skim off any cream that rises to the surface and transfer it to a small, heavy bottomed saucepan or skillet.

2. Add the beef chunks to the coconut milk in the saucepot and continue to simmer until the beef is tender, about 1 hour.

3. Bring the coconut cream to a gentle boil over medium heat. Adjust the heat to maintain a gentle boil and cook, stirring occasionally, until the coconut cream becomes thick and fragrant and tiny pools of oil glisten on the surface, 6 to 8 minutes. Add the curry paste and stir to dissolve it in the coconut cream. Simmer the mixture until it has a rich aroma, 3 to 4 minutes.

4. Add the curry paste mixture to the beef and coconut milk; stir well. Add the potatoes, fish sauce, tamarind, palm sugar, cinnamon, and cardamom, and simmer until the potatoes are par-cooked, about 10 minutes. Add the onion and peanuts and simmer until the potatoes are tender, about 5 minutes more. Season to taste with additional fish sauce, palm sugar, and lime juice. It should have a pleasing, sweet, sour, and salty balance.

Mussaman Curry Paste

Mussaman curry paste, or *phrik kang mussaman*, has a distinct aroma due to the number of spices it contains. It is usually based on dried chiles and contains coriander and cumin. The measurements given here are just a starting point.

Toast 1 tablespoon of coriander seeds and 1 teaspoon each of cumin seeds, fennel seeds, and cloves in a dry skillet or wok over moderate heat until very fragrant, about 2 minutes. Immediately transfer the spices to a plate or bowl and set aside.

Remove the stems and seeds from 2 dried red chiles. Soak the chiles and 2 pieces of dried galangal in ½ cup warm water for 20 minutes. Transfer the chiles and galangal to a mortar or a blender. Discard the soaking water.

Chop the tender inner portion of one stalk of lemongrass. Scrape the roots from a bunch of cilantro and add them to the chiles. Mince 6 or 7 garlic cloves and ¼ of a small yellow onion. Add the garlic and onion to the chiles, along with the spice mixture, 1 teaspoon of shrimp paste, and ½ teaspoon each of freshly ground black pepper and nutmeg. Grind to a smooth

paste. (If you are using a blender, you might have to add a few teaspoons of water.) Use the curry paste immediately or store it in a closed container in the refrigerator for up to 2 weeks or in the freezer for up to 6 months.

To make a marked difference in the flavor of your curry, toast the curry paste before adding it to the curry: Let a saucepan get very hot over high heat. Add the curry paste to the pan and stir it constantly. The aromas will open up and deepen dramatically. Add the coconut cream and stir well to blend the curry into the cream. It's now ready to add to your simmering curry.

FEIJOADA

1½ cups dry black beans, rinsed and sorted

1 lb corned beef

2 lb smoked pork spareribs or smoked pork chops

¾ lb slab bacon

1½ lb boneless beef chuck or eye round

1 ham hock

1 pig's foot, split

*10 to 12 cups Chicken Broth (page 15)
    or water*

1 bay leaf

2 tbsp peanut or olive oil

1½ cups minced onion

¼ lb chorizo, sliced ¼ inch thick

2 tsp minced garlic

½ cup thinly sliced scallions, cut on the diagonal

1 jalapeño, seeded and minced

Salt as needed

Freshly ground black pepper as needed

P LAN ON SPENDING two or three days putting this magnificent dish together. You can always cut back on the variety of meats we suggest here—the dish still will be delicious, it just won't be a traditional *feijoada*. Feijoada is typically served with steamed white rice, collard greens, and sliced oranges, as shown here.

MAKES 8 TO 10 SERVINGS

1. Soak the black beans in enough cold water to cover generously for at least 6 and up to 12 hours in the refrigerator. In a separate container, soak the corned beef in enough cold water to cover overnight in the refrigerator.

2. Drain the corned beef and place it in large Dutch oven along with the smoked spareribs or chops, bacon, beef, ham hock, and pig's foot. Add enough broth or water to cover the meats. Add the bay leaf, cover the Dutch oven, and bring the broth to a simmer over low heat, skimming as necessary. Simmer until the meats are all tender, removing them from the broth as they become fork-tender (20 to 30 minutes for the spareribs or chops; 45 minutes to 1 hour for the other meats), and transfer them to a bowl. When all of the meat has been removed from the Dutch oven, strain the broth, and discard the solids. (You can cool the meats and broth now and continue the cooking the next day.)

3. Drain the soaked beans and rinse well. Place them in the Dutch oven and add enough of the strained broth to cover the beans. Bring the broth to a boil over medium-high heat and then immediately reduce the heat for a slow simmer, skimming as necessary, until the beans are tender and creamy to the bite, 1½ to 2 hours. Season to taste with salt. Drain the beans, reserving their cooking liquid separately.

4. Heat the oil the Dutch oven over medium heat until it shimmers. Sauté the onion in the oil, stirring frequently, until golden, about 10 minutes. Add the chorizo, garlic, scallions, and jalapeño; sauté, stirring frequently, until very hot and aromatic, about 5 minutes. Return the drained beans to the Dutch oven along with enough of the strained liquid from the beans to make a stew-like consistency. Simmer until the feijoada is very flavorful, 10 to 15 minutes. Lightly mash some of the beans with the back of a spoon to thicken the sauce, if desired. Season to taste with salt and pepper.

5. Remove the meat from the ham hocks and cut it into medium dice. Remove the rind from the bacon and cut it into a medium dice. Add the diced ham and bacon to the beans and simmer 15 minutes. Slice the corned beef, beef, and separate the spareribs into portions. Add them to the beans and continue to simmer until the feijoada is very flavorful and thickened, about 15 minutes.

{PICTURED AT RIGHT}

12 cups Chicken Broth (page 15)

3 cups dry navy beans, pre-soaked

1 lb slab bacon, sliced ¼-inch thick

1 lb garlic sausage

2 small yellow onions, peeled and left whole

3 garlic cloves

2 Bouquets Garnis (page 126)

Salt as needed

1½ lb boneless pork loin, cut into large cubes

1½ lb boneless lamb shoulder or leg, cut into large cubes

Freshly ground black pepper as needed

6 tbsp olive oil

1 cup diced leeks

1 cup sliced carrots

1 cup sliced parsnips

1 tsp minced garlic

¼ cup all-purpose flour

⅓ cup dry white wine

6 cups Beef Broth (page 16)

1 cup chopped plum tomatoes

1¾ lb duck confit

1½ cups bread crumbs

2 tbsp chopped flat-leaf parsley

CASSOULET

C ASSOULET IS A robust dish of cured and smoked meats and sausages, baked in a stew of beans until a rich crust forms. Originating in southwestern France (it's name derives from the earthenware *cassole* in which it is traditionally cooked), the dish has several regional variations, all of which claim to be the "authentic" version. According to tradition, the cook repeatedly breaks the crust and pushes it down into the stew as it bakes.

MAKES 12 SERVINGS

1. Bring the chicken stock to a boil in a large saucepot; add the beans and bacon. Return the mixture to a simmer and cook, stirring occasionally, until the beans are nearly tender, about 40 minutes.

2. Add the sausage, onions, garlic, and 1 bouquet garni. Return the mixture to a simmer and cook until the sausage is cooked through and the bacon is fork tender, about 30 minutes. Remove and reserve the sausage and bacon. Remove and discard the onions, garlic, and bouquet garni.

3. Season the beans with salt to taste continue to simmer until the beans are tender, about 20 to 25 minutes. Strain the beans, reserve them, and return the cooking liquid to the pot. Continue to simmer until the liquid reduces by half and is beginning to thicken, about 30 minutes. Reserve the sauce for later use.

4. Season the pork and lamb with salt and pepper. Heat the oil in a casserole or Dutch oven over medium-high heat until it starts to shimmer. Sear the pork and lamb in the oil on all sides, turning as necessary, until deep brown. Transfer the meat to a pan and keep warm.

5. Add the leeks, carrots, and parsnips to the casserole and sauté, stirring occasionally, until the leeks are golden brown, about 15 minutes. Add the garlic and cook until aromatic, about 1 minute. Add the flour and cook, stirring frequently, until the mixture is pasty, about 5 minutes.

6. Add the wine and 3 cups of broth to the casserole, whisking or stirring until smooth. Stir in the tomatoes and the remaining bouquet garni. Return the seared meats to the casserole, along with any juices they may have released. Add more broth if necessary to keep the meat completely moistened. Bring to a slow simmer over medium-low heat.

7. Preheat the oven to 350°F. Cover the casserole and braise the meat in the oven, skimming the surface as necessary, until the meats are fork tender, about 1 hour. *(recipe continues)*

8. Add the sliced sausage and bacon to the casserole. Cover with a layer of the reserved beans. Add the duck confit in a layer and top with the second half of the beans. Pour the sauce from the beans over the cassoulet. Toss together the bread crumbs and parsley and sprinkle in an even layer on top.

9. Turn the oven down to 300°F and bake the cassoulet, uncovered, periodically basting the crust with the juices that bubble up at the sides of the casserole, until it is very hot, the beans are very tender, and a good crust has formed, 1½ to 2 hours. Let the cassoulet rest for 15 minutes before serving. Serve in heated bowls.

Making a Bouquet Garni

The *bouquet garni* is a basic aromatic preparation called for in many soups and stews. A bouquet garni is made up of fresh herbs and vegetables tied into a bundle. You can add the herbs directly to the pot, but making them into a bouquet gives you a little more control over how much flavor they add to your dish. A basic bouquet garni includes:

- 1 sprig of thyme

- 3 or 4 parsley stems

- 1 bay leaf

- 2 or 3 leek leaves and/or 1 celery stalk, cut crosswise in half

The bouquet garni ingredients are enclosed between two halves of celery, or can be wrapped in leek leaves (if using leek leaves, be sure to rinse them thoroughly to remove any grit). Enclose the herbs in the leek leaves or celery. Cut a piece of string long enough to leave a tail to tie the bouquet to the pot handle. This makes it easy to pull out the bouquet when it is time to remove it.

FAVA BEAN STEW

IF YOU CAN find fresh fava beans, buy about 3 pounds of beans and shell them to yield about 3 cups of beans. Fresh fava beans don't require soaking, so the stew will finish cooking in about 30 minutes, instead of the 2 hours needed when using the dry beans.

MAKES 4 SERVINGS

1. Soak the beans in enough cold water to cover for at least 24 and up to 36 hours.

2. Heat the oil in a casserole or Dutch oven over medium-high heat until it shimmers. Add the onion and garlic; sauté, stirring occasionally, until the onion is browned, about 10 minutes. Add the morcilla, chorizo, and slab bacon; sauté in the hot oil until browned, about 6 to 8 minutes.

3. Add the drained soaked beans to the casserole, and then add enough cold water to cover them by about 2 inches. Bring the water to a boil over high heat. Immediately reduce the heat to establish a gentle simmer. Add the saffron. Season to taste with salt and pepper. Simmer, covered, until the beans are tender, about 2 hours. Adjust the consistency with a little cold water if the stew is getting too thick.

4. Season to taste with additional salt and pepper. Serve the stew in warm bowls garnished with chopped parsley.

2 cups dry fava beans

Cold water, as needed

2 tbsp olive oil

1 medium yellow onion, quartered

1 tsp minced garlic

4 oz morcilla (blood sausage), sliced into ¼-inch-thick slices

6 oz chorizo, sliced into ¼-inch-thick slices

4 oz slab bacon, sliced into ¼-inch-thick slices

1 pinch saffron threads, lightly crushed

Salt, as needed

Freshly ground black pepper, as needed

¼ cup chopped parsley

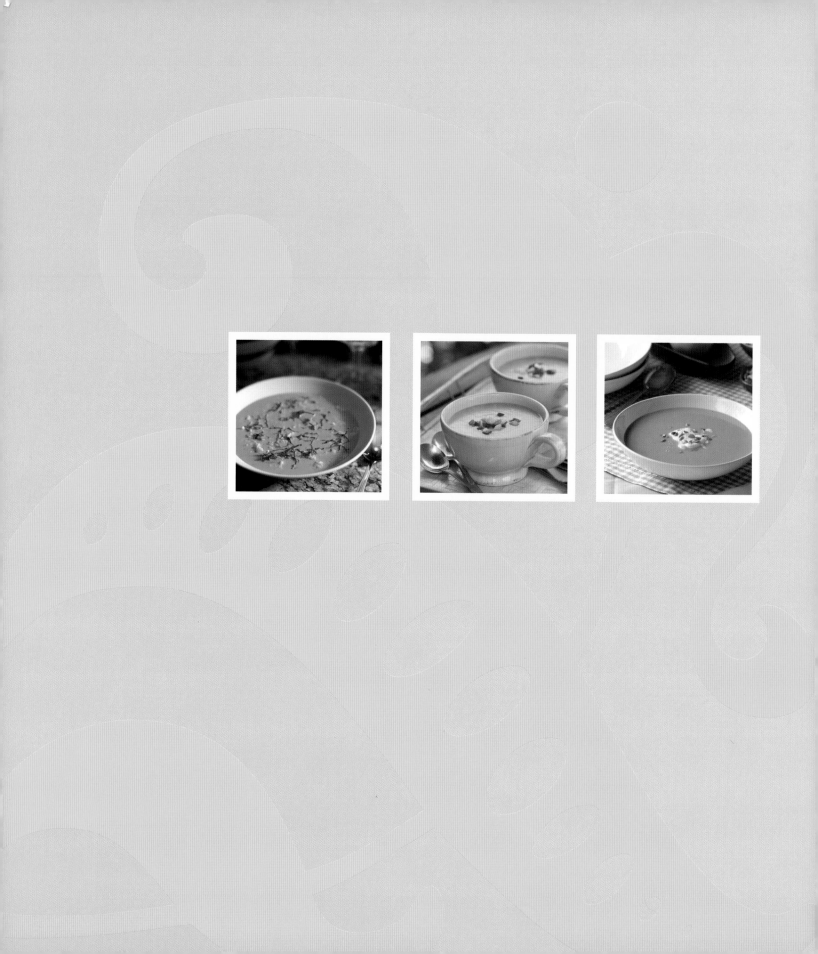

Cream Soups

ACCORDING TO CLASSICAL definitions, a cream soup is based on a béchamel sauce—milk thickened with roux—and is finished with heavy cream. A velouté soup is based on a light velouté sauce—stock thickened with roux—and is finished with a liaison of heavy cream and egg yolks. Contemporary chefs no longer draw a distinction between the two; they frequently substitute a velouté base for the béchamel in cream soups or even use the term cream to refer to a purée soup that has simply been finished with cream.

Main Ingredients

The main flavoring for some cream soups is often a single ingredient, such as broccoli, asparagus, chicken, or fish. When simmering poultry or fish in the soup to give flavor and body, be sure to trim, truss, or cut those ingredients as appropriate. Vegetables, whether used as main flavoring ingredients or as aromatics, should be well rinsed, then peeled, trimmed, and cut into small and uniform pieces so they cook evenly. (For more information, see pages 6–9, Shopping for Soup Ingredients.)

A well-seasoned, full-bodied broth, stock, or light velouté should be on hand. Milk or a light béchamel is sometimes appropriate. Bring the liquid up to a simmer, along with seasonings, aromatics, or other ingredients meant to provide flavor. Refer to specific recipes for guidance.

Thickeners, including prepared roux, flour, potatoes, or the natural thickening of the puréed main ingredient, give cream soups their texture. However, added thickeners are unnecessary if the base liquid is a prepared velouté. Assemble finishing ingredients, final flavoring and seasonings, and garnishes ahead of time to be ready to add at the proper time. Bring cream to a simmer before adding it to simmering soup. Blend liaisons and temper them just before serving the soup.

Troubleshooting Purée and Cream Soups

Cream soups and purées are best when they are intensely flavored and lightly thickened with a good color and an appealing aroma.

Soups should be made with quality ingredients, from the aromatics through to the main ingredient, and on to the finishing ingredients. Be sure that the vegetables, meats, and cream are fresh and flavorful. Trimming and cutting them properly before you add them to the soup pot allows them to release their flavors quickly, without overcooking or turning a muddy or grayish color.

TOO THICK: These soups should pour easily from the ladle or spoon; a soup thick enough to hold the spoon upright is too thick. And because they contain starchy ingredients, these soups may keep getting thicker as they simmer, or during storage. If your soup is too thick, use additional broth or water to thin it and adjust the seasoning again once the texture is right.

BURNT OR SCORCHED FLAVOR OR AROMA: Stir soups as they simmer so that they don't scorch. As you stir, check the way the spoon feels against the bottom of the pot. If the soup has started to thicken and stick, transfer it to a clean pot to prevent it from burning.

HARSH FLAVOR: If the flavor is too harsh, the ratio of ingredients used was incorrect. The vegetables may not have been properly sweated or the soup might not have been cooked long enough. Taste the soup as it simmers to determine when the flavor is best.

☼ BASIC METHOD FOR CREAM SOUPS

Cream soups are made by simmering a flavorful ingredient such as tomatoes, broccoli, or chicken in a liquid—most often broth, but sometimes milk or cream, and occasionally, water. The soup should be pleasantly thick—an effect achieved by adding flour, potatoes, or rice, or by puréeing the main flavoring ingredient.

➡ *PREPARE THE AROMATIC INGREDIENTS:* Onions and garlic are two of the most popular aromatics in any soup; you'll find them in most soups, along with additions like carrots, celery, mushrooms, tomatoes, leeks, herbs, or spices. Cook this flavor base gently in a little oil or butter over low to medium heat until they are tender, but without any noticeable browning to keep the soup's color light and appealing. Some recipes call for the main flavoring ingredient to be added at this stage to start developing the flavor. Others call for the main ingredient to be added along with the liquid.

➡ *ADD THE LIQUID AND ANY ADDITIONAL INGREDIENTS AND SIMMER:* When you are preparing large quantities of soup, it can be helpful to bring the liquid to a simmer over low heat while preparing the other ingredients. This will help reduce overall cooking time, since the soup will come to the correct cooking speed more quickly. Simmer the soup, stirring frequently and tasting as you go, until everything is tender enough to purée.

➡ *STRAIN THE LIQUID AND PURÉE THE SOLIDS:* Strain the soup through a colander or wire-mesh sieve, catching the liquid in a bowl or a clean pot. Remove and discard any bay leaves or cheesecloth pouches. Purée the solids in a food processor or blender, adding just enough of the liquid so they purée easily. Then, put the purée in a clean pot and add the liquid until you achieve a good texture and flavor.

➡ *FINISH THE SOUP WITH CREAM:* Hot cream soups are finished by adding a good quality cream. For the best results, bring the cream to a simmer before you add it to the hot soup. For a cold cream soup, let the hot soup cool completely before stirring in cold cream. Use enough cream to mellow and enrich the soup, but not so much that the taste of the cream overpowers the main ingredient. Adjust the final consistency of the soup with the reserved liquid, if necessary.

2 lb broccoli

¼ cup vegetable or olive oil

1¼ cups chopped onion

½ cup chopped celery

1¼ cups chopped leek (white and light green parts)

¼ cup all-purpose flour

1½ qt Chicken Broth (page 15)

½ cup heavy cream, heated

Fresh lemon juice to taste

Salt to taste

Freshly ground black pepper to taste

CREAM OF BROCCOLI SOUP

T HIS VELVETY SOUP is the essence of broccoli. It's relatively simple to make, yet tastes very elegant and refined. Try serving this as a first course for company.

MAKES 8 SERVINGS

1. Separate the broccoli into stems and florets. Trim away the tough outer parts of the stems. Set aside 1 cup of the nicest looking small florets to use as a garnish. Coarsely chop the remaining broccoli florets and the stems.

2. Heat the oil in a soup pot over medium heat. Add the onion, celery, leek, and chopped broccoli. Cook, stirring frequently, until the onion is translucent, about 6 to 8 minutes.

3. Add the flour and blend well. Continue to cook, stirring frequently, for 3 to 4 minutes.

4. Add the broth to the pot gradually, whisking to work out any lumps of flour. Bring the soup to a simmer and cook for 45 minutes. Stir frequently and skim the soup as needed.

5. Strain the solids, reserving the liquid. Purée the solids, adding liquid as necessary to facilitate puréeing.

6. Combine the purée with enough of the reserved liquid to achieve the consistency of heavy cream. If you wish, strain the soup through a fine sieve. Return the soup to a simmer.

7. Meanwhile, steam or boil the reserved broccoli florets until just tender.

8. Remove the soup from the heat and add the heated cream. Season to taste with the lemon juice, salt, and pepper. Serve in heated bowls, garnished with the florets.

Making a Puff Pastry Dome

Frozen puff pastry sheets can be used for an elegant presentation of cream soups or bisques. Look for an all-butter brand for the best flavor and texture. You will get 2 domes from 1 sheet.

Let the sheets thaw in the refrigerator; they should be cool but pliable. Roll them out on a lightly floured surface until they are ¼ inch thick. Use a soup plate as a template and cut around the edge, adding a ½-inch border. Make an egg wash of 1 egg mixed with 2 tablespoons of water. (You can cut the circles and make the egg wash ahead of time.)

To finish, preheat the oven to 400°F. Heat the soup and fill each bowl. Brush the rim of each pastry circle with a little egg wash, and then press the pastry onto the rim of each bowl. Pierce the pastry with the tip of a pairing knife; brush lightly with egg wash. Place the bowls on baking sheets and bake until the pastry is golden and flaky, about 10 minutes.

CREAM OF TOMATO SOUP

with Rice and Basil

{PICTURED AT LEFT}

THIS SOUP VIES with chicken noodle for the title of ultimate comfort soup. It's full of tomato flavor and tastes much better than the version that many of us grew up on—the one that comes in a red and white can. If you have really flavorful, ripe tomatoes, use them in place of the canned tomatoes. Otherwise, canned tomatoes offer the best flavor and consistency.

MAKES 8 SERVINGS

1. Heat the oil in a soup pot over medium heat. Add the carrots, celery, onion, and garlic. Cook, stirring occasionally, until softened, 6 to 8 minutes.

2. Add the flour and blend well. Continue to cook, stirring frequently, for 3 to 4 minutes.

3. Add the broth and blend well. Add the chopped tomatoes, tomato purée, and pepper. Bring to a simmer and cook for 30 minutes. Add the parsley stems and bay leaf and continue to simmer another 30 minutes.

4. Pass the soup through a strainer, pressing hard on the solids to recover as much liquid as possible. Discard the solids.

5. Blend the hot cream into the strained soup. Adjust the consistency with more broth, if necessary. Stir in the cooked rice. Season to taste with salt and more pepper if desired. Serve in heated bowls garnished with the basil.

3 tbsp vegetable oil

⅔ cup diced carrot

⅔ cup diced celery

1 cup diced onion

1 garlic clove, minced

½ cup all-purpose flour

1 qt Chicken Broth (page 15), plus more as needed

2⅓ cups diced plum tomatoes (peeled and seeded)

2 cups tomato purée

¼ tsp freshly ground black pepper, or to taste

2 parsley stems

½ bay leaf

1 cup heavy cream, hot

2 cups cooked short-grain rice, hot

Salt to taste

⅓ cup basil chiffonade

WATERCRESS SOUP

THIS THICK, RICH soup is tangy with the flavors of watercress and sour cream. Watercress grows wild in streams and brooks, but it can also be found in most supermarkets, sold in bunches or bags. Look for fresh, firm leaves with no sign of yellowing. Store in the refrigerator stems-down in a container of water covered with a plastic bag (this works well for other leafy herbs like parsley and cilantro, too).

MAKES 8 SERVINGS

1. Bring a large pot of water to a boil. Reserve 8 of the nicest looking watercress sprigs for a garnish. Remove the stems from the remaining watercress and add the leaves to the boiling water. Boil until just wilted, about 2 minutes. Drain and squeeze out any excess moisture. Purée the watercress and set aside. *(recipe continues)*

4 cups watercress, rinsed

2 tbsp butter

1¼ cups chopped leek (white and light green part)

1 cup chopped onion

1 qt Chicken Broth (page 15)

2 cups thinly sliced yellow or white potatoes (peeled)

½ tsp salt, or to taste

¼ tsp freshly ground white pepper, or to taste

1 cup sour cream

2. Heat the butter in a soup pot over medium heat. Add the leek and onion. Cook, stirring occasionally, until the onion is translucent, about 7 minutes.

3. Add the broth and bring it to a simmer. Add the potatoes and simmer until tender, about 25 minutes.

4. Purée the soup and add the watercress purée. Return the soup to a simmer.

5. Stir in the sour cream and heat through, but do not allow the soup to reach a simmer again. Season to taste with the salt and pepper. Serve in heated bowls, garnished with the watercress sprigs.

CREAM OF MUSHROOM

{PICTURED AT LEFT}

MORE "EXOTIC" VARIETIES of mushrooms, such as cremini and oyster, work well in this soup, as do regular white mushrooms. Use a combination or a single variety, depending on your taste and what's available. You may also opt to season the soup with a touch of sherry instead of the lemon juice. For an extra-special presentation, ladle the soup into oven-proof bowls, and top with a puff pastry dome as described on page 132.

MAKES 8 SERVINGS

7 tbsp butter

8 cups chopped mushrooms (about 1¼ pounds)

⅔ cup finely chopped celery

1¼ cups thinly sliced leek (white part only)

½ cup all-purpose flour

5 cups Chicken Broth (page 15)

1 fresh thyme sprig

1 cup sliced mushrooms

1½ cups heavy cream, heated

Fresh lemon juice to taste

Salt to taste

Freshly ground white pepper to taste

1. Melt 6 tablespoons of the butter in a soup pot over medium heat. Add the chopped mushrooms, celery, and leek. Cook, stirring frequently, until softened, 6 to 8 minutes.

2. Add the flour and cook, stirring constantly, for 3 to 4 minutes.

3. Whisk in the broth gradually. Add the thyme sprig, bring to a simmer, and cook for 30 minutes.

4. Meanwhile, melt the remaining butter in a skillet. Add the sliced mushrooms and sauté until cooked through, about 5 minutes. Remove from the heat and reserve.

5. Remove and discard the thyme. Purée the soup, then strain through cheesecloth or a fine sieve. Return the soup to the soup pot and place over low heat. Add the heavy cream and season to taste with the lemon juice, salt, and pepper. Heat the soup, but do not boil.

6. Serve in heated bowls, garnished with the reserved cooked mushrooms.

ROASTED RED PEPPER, LEEK, AND POTATO CREAM SOUP

{PICTURED AT RIGHT}

2 red bell peppers

4 tbsp butter

3 cups diced leeks (white and light green parts from 2 to 3 leeks)

6 cups diced russet potatoes (peeled)

6 cups Chicken Broth (page 15)

1 sprig fresh thyme, or ½ teaspoon dried enclosed in a large tea ball or tied in a cheesecloth pouch

1 cup heavy cream or half and half, heated

Salt to taste

Freshly ground white pepper to taste

½ cup finely sliced scallion greens or chives

THIS SILKY SMOOTH cream soup derives its thickness and most of its texture from potatoes rather than roux. The sweetness of the leek and red peppers make a wonderful combination. If you wish, substitute 1 cup of drained, bottled roasted red peppers for the freshly roasted peppers.

MAKES 8 SERVINGS

1. Preheat the broiler. Place the red peppers under the broiler and turn as they roast so that they blacken evenly on all sides. Put the peppers in a small bowl and cover the bowl. Let the peppers steam for 10 minutes, then remove them from the bowl and pull off the skin. Use the back of a knife to scrape away any bits that don't come away easily. Remove the seeds, ribs, and stems from the peppers. Chop the flesh coarsely.

2. Melt the butter in a soup pot over medium heat. Add the roasted peppers and leeks. Stir them in the butter to coat well. Reduce the heat to low, cover the pot, and cook until the leeks are tender and translucent, 5 to 7 minutes.

3. Add the potatoes, broth, and thyme. Bring to a simmer and cook, partially covered, until the potatoes are soft enough to mash, 25 to 30 minutes. During cooking, skim away and discard any foam that rises to the surface. Keep the liquid level constant by adding additional broth as necessary.

4. Remove and discard the thyme. Strain the solids, reserving the liquid. Purée the solids with a small amount of the liquid. Return the purée to the remaining liquid and strain through a fine sieve.

5. Bring the soup back to a simmer. Remove from the heat and add the heated cream. Season to taste with the salt and pepper. Serve in heated bowls, garnished with the scallions or chives.

½ cup butter

2½ cups finely diced leek (white and light green parts)

1¼ cups minced onion

½ cup minced celery

¼ cup flour

2 tsp dry mustard

1 cup ale or white wine

6 cups Chicken or Vegetable broth (pages 15, 18)

3 cups grated cheddar or Monterey Jack cheese

Tabasco sauce to taste

Salt to taste

Freshly ground white pepper to taste

¼ cup finely diced canned green chiles

2 tbsp minced cilantro or parsley

2 tbsp finely diced pickled jalapeños (optional)

Popcorn is a traditional garnish for this soup—here, we've dusted it with chili powder for extra flavor.

CHEDDAR CHEESE SOUP

IF YOU MAKE this soup in advance, reheat it in a double boiler over simmering water so that the cheese doesn't separate from the soup, giving it a curdled appearance. Try other cheeses such as Brie, Camembert, or even goat cheese.

MAKES 6 SERVINGS

1. Melt the butter in a soup pot over medium heat. Add the leeks, onion, and celery. Stir to coat evenly with butter. Cover the pot and cook until the vegetables are tender, 4 to 5 minutes.

2. Add the flour and stir well with a wooden spoon. Cook for 4 to 5 minutes, stirring almost constantly. Add the dry mustard and ale or wine, stirring to make a thick paste. Add the broth gradually, using a whisk to work out any lumps between each addition.

3. Bring the soup to a simmer and continue to simmer gently for 1 hour. Stir the soup occasionally and skim the surface as necessary.

4. Strain the soup through a sieve, reserving the liquid. Purée the solids and return to the soup pot. Add enough of the reserved liquid to achieve a soup consistency and strain once more.

5. Return the soup to a simmer. Whisk in the cheese and simmer until the cheese melts, about 1 minute. Season to taste with Tabasco sauce, salt, and white pepper. Serve in heated bowls, garnished with the chiles, cilantro, and jalapeños (if using).

BILLI BI

Cream of Mussel Soup

THERE ARE SEVERAL stories surrounding the origin of this suave French soup, the most popular being that a chef at the famed Maxim's of Paris named it after American tin tycoon William B. (Billy B.) Leeds, a regular customer—and huge fan of this soup. Don't pull the beards from the mussels until you are ready to cook them, as this step kills the mussels; find more information on mussels on page 47.

MAKES 6 TO 8 SERVINGS

{PICTURED AT LEFT}

2 lb mussels

1 tbsp minced shallots

1 cup white wine

1 tsp saffron threads

4 tsp butter

1 onion, minced

5 tbsp flour

5 cups Fish Broth (page 17)

Sachet: 5 to 6 parsley stems, 6 to 8 black peppercorns, 1 sprig fresh thyme or ½ teaspoon dried thyme, 1 bay leaf enclosed in a large tea ball or tied in a cheesecloth pouch

1 egg yolk

1 cup heavy cream or half and half

Salt to taste

Freshly ground white pepper to taste

1. Pull the beards off the mussels. Scrub the mussels well under cold running water. Set aside. Combine the shallots, wine, and saffron threads in a pot large enough to hold the mussels. Place over medium-high heat and bring to a boil. Add the mussels, cover the pot tightly, and reduce the heat to medium-low. Cook the mussels for 5 to 6 minutes, shaking the pot occasionally. Remove the mussels from the pot as their shells open. Discard any mussels that do not open. Separate the meat from the shells; reserve the meat and discard the shells. Strain the cooking liquid and reserve.

2. Heat the butter in a 3-quart pot over medium heat. Add the onion and stir to coat evenly. Cover the pot and cook the onion until translucent, 3 to 4 minutes. Add the flour and cook for 3 to 4 minutes, stirring almost constantly with a wooden spoon.

3. Gradually add the mussel cooking liquid and fish broth, using a whisk to work out any lumps after each addition. Add the sachet, bring to a simmer, and simmer gently for 45 minutes, stirring occasionally and skimming the surface as necessary.

4. Discard the sachet. Strain the soup through cheesecloth or a fine sieve. Return the soup to the stove and bring to a simmer.

5. Make a liaison by blending the egg yolk with the cream in a bowl. Stir in about 1 cup of the hot soup, and then stir the heated liaison mixture into the soup. Simmer for 3 minutes.

6. Add the mussel meat to the soup and simmer until the mussels are heated through. Adjust the seasoning to taste with salt and white pepper. Serve in heated bowls.

Slowly tempering in a liaison will keep the eggs and cream from curdling in the hot soup.

OYSTER AND FENNEL SOUP

1 fennel bulb, preferably with tops still intact

1 qt Chicken Broth (page 15)

2 cups Fish Broth (page 17)

2 tbsp butter

1 cup diced leek (white part only)

24 fresh oysters, shucked, juices reserved

6 cups diced white or yellow potatoes (peeled)

¼ cup white wine

2 tsp fresh thyme leaves, chopped

½ tbsp fennel seeds, toasted and crushed

1 cup heavy cream, heated

1 cup milk, heated

Salt to taste

Freshly ground white pepper to taste

I F YOUR GROCERY store only sells fennel with the tops removed, try requesting one with the tops still intact from the produce department. The feathery fronds not only assure you that the fennel you bought is still fresh, but they also make a wonderful garnish for the soup. If you can only find topped fennel, all is not lost— try some delicate fronds of dill or some snipped chives instead.

MAKES 8 SERVINGS

1. Cut the tops from the fennel bulb. Chop 2 tablespoons of the feathery leaves and set aside for a garnish. Chop the remaining stems and leaves. Core and dice the bulb. Reserve separately.

2. Bring the chicken and fish broths to a simmer in a large saucepan. Add the chopped fennel stems and leaves. Simmer for 20 minutes, then strain and reserve the broth. Discard the fennel stems and leaves.

3. Heat the butter in a soup pot over medium heat. Add the diced fennel bulb and the leek. Cook, stirring occasionally, until softened, 5 to 7 minutes.

4. Add the fennel broth, 6 of the oysters, and the potatoes, white wine, thyme, and fennel seeds. Bring to a simmer and cook until the potatoes are tender, about 25 minutes.

5. Purée the soup. Strain through a fine sieve for an extra smooth consistency, if you wish.

6. Return the soup to a simmer. Remove from the heat and add the remaining oysters with their juices, the chopped fennel leaves, and the hot cream and milk. Season to taste with the salt and pepper. Serve in heated bowls.

CHESTNUT SOUP WITH FRESH GINGER

CHESTNUTS WERE AN important part of the Native American diet, furnishing an excellent source of protein and carbohydrates. Today, chestnuts are favored not only for their wonderful flavor, but also for their low fat content, a rarity in all other nuts. Fresh chestnuts are generally available from September through February. Select firm nuts with unblemished shells and store in a cool, dry place until you make the soup.

MAKES 4 TO 6 SERVINGS

1. Preheat the oven to 400°F or bring a large pot of water to a rolling boil. Score an "X" on the flat side of each chestnut with the tip of a paring knife. Roast them on a baking sheet in the oven or boil them until the outer skin begins to curl away, about 10 minutes in the oven or 8 minutes on the stovetop. Peel away both the outer and inner layers of skin from the chestnut. Reserve 4 to 6 whole chestnuts to garnish each bowl of soup, if desired. Chop the remaining chestnuts and set aside.

2. Heat the butter in a soup pot over medium heat. Add the celery, carrot, leek, and onion. Cook, stirring frequently, until the onion is light golden brown, 8 to 10 minutes.

3. Add the broth, chopped chestnuts, and ginger. Bring the soup to a simmer and cook, stirring occasionally, until the ingredients are very tender, 35 to 40 minutes.

4. Purée the soup and return to medium heat. Add the orange juice and simmer for 2 minutes.

5. Add the cream to the soup. Season to taste with the salt, pepper, and more orange juice, if desired. Serve in heated bowls, garnished with whole chestnuts, if using.

10 oz chestnuts

1 tbsp butter

½ cup diced celery

⅓ cup diced carrot

1¼ cups chopped leek (white and light green parts)

¾ cup chopped onion

1 qt Chicken Broth (page 15)

2 tbsp grated fresh ginger

2 tbsp freshly squeezed orange juice, plus more to taste

¾ cup heavy cream, heated

½ tsp salt, or to taste

¼ tsp freshly ground black pepper, or to taste

It is easiest to peel chestnuts while they are still warm. If you are experiencing difficulties, then rewarm the nuts by dropping them back into simmering water or returning them to a warm oven.

PUMPKIN SOUP WITH GINGER CREAM

{PICTURED AT LEFT}

Look for plain pumpkin pieces in the frozen foods section of your market. Canned pumpkin will not work quite as well in this recipe, although it can be substituted if fresh or frozen pumpkin is unavailable. This soup could be garnished with a scattering of toasted pumpkin seeds, or for an elegant presentation, add a tablespoon of diced, cooked lobster meat to each portion as well.

MAKES 8 SERVINGS

1. Heat the butter in a soup pot over medium heat. Add the garlic, leek, celery, and half of the ginger. Cook, stirring occasionally, until the leek and celery are softened, 8 to 10 minutes.

2. Add the broth, pumpkin, sweet potato, cinnamon stick, and nutmeg. Bring to a simmer and cook until the pumpkin is very tender, about 30 minutes.

3. Remove and discard the cinnamon stick. Purée the soup until quite smooth. Strain through a fine sieve for an exceptionally smooth texture, if you wish.

4. Return the soup to medium heat. Add the wine, milk, lime juice, and the salt to taste. Stir to combine well and reheat the soup to just below a simmer.

5. Whip the chilled heavy cream to medium peaks and fold in the remaining ginger. Serve the soup in heated bowls, garnished with a swirl or dollop of ginger-flavored cream.

---

2 tsp butter

2 garlic cloves, minced

1¼ cups chopped leek

½ cup diced celery

2 tsp minced fresh ginger

5 cups Vegetable or Chicken Broth (pages 18, 15) or water

3 cups diced pumpkin (fresh or frozen)

1 cup sliced sweet potato

1 small piece cinnamon stick

¼ tsp freshly ground nutmeg, or to taste

½ cup dry white wine

½ cup evaporated skim milk or whole milk

2 tsp freshly squeezed lime juice

½ tsp salt, or to taste

½ cup whipped heavy cream, chilled

{PICTURED AT RIGHT}

3 tbsp butter

½ cup chopped celery

1¼ cups chopped onion

1 garlic clove, minced

¾ cup chopped leek (white and light green parts)

3 cups sliced sweet potatoes (peeled)

1 qt Chicken Broth (page 15)

3 tbsp creamy peanut butter

¼ cinnamon stick

¾ cup peanuts

1¼ cups heavy cream

Salt to taste

¾ cup heavy cream

2 tbsp molasses

Freshly grated nutmeg to taste

Chopped peanuts for garnish

SWEET POTATO AND PEANUT SOUP

S WEET POTATOES COMBINE with peanut butter and chopped peanuts to become a unique, slightly sweet soup.

MAKES 8 SERVINGS

1. Preheat the oven to 325°F. Melt the butter in a soup pot over medium heat. Add the celery, onion, garlic, and leek. Stir to coat evenly with butter. Cook, stirring frequently, until the vegetables are softened, 4 to 6 minutes.

2. Add the sweet potatoes, broth, peanut butter, and cinnamon stick. Bring to a simmer and cook until the potatoes are fully tender, about 25 minutes.

3. Meanwhile, spread the peanuts in a single layer in a pie pan. Toast the peanuts in the oven until light brown, 3 to 5 minutes. Shake the pan occasionally and watch carefully, as nuts can burn quickly. Let the peanuts cool, chop coarsely, and set aside.

4. Remove and discard the cinnamon stick. Purée the soup and strain it. Return the soup to the soup pot and place over low heat. Add ½ cup of the cream. Season to taste with salt. Keep warm but do not boil.

5. Combine the remaining ¾ cup cream with the molasses, nutmeg, and a pinch of salt. Whip until stiff peaks form. Serve the soup in heated bowls, garnished with the whipped cream and chopped peanuts.

4 tbsp butter or vegetable oil

5 cups thinly sliced onions

4 cups diced Granny Smith apples (peeled and cored)

¼ cup all-purpose flour

1 qt Vegetable Broth (page 18) or water

3 cups apple cider or juice

Sachet: 3 to 4 parsley stems, 2 whole cloves, and 1 garlic clove enclosed in a tea ball or tied up in a cheesecloth pouch

½ cup heavy cream, heated

Salt to taste

Freshly ground white pepper to taste

8 thin slices Red Delicious apple

APPLE SOUP

T HIS SOUP IS a delicate blend of tart Granny Smith apples and sweet caramelized onion. Hold the apple slices in a small bowl of water with half a lemon squeezed into it; pat the apple slices dry before garnishing the soup.

MAKES 8 SERVINGS

1. Melt the butter in a soup pot over medium heat. Add the onions and cook until golden brown, 5 to 8 minutes. Add the apples and continue to cook for 2 more minutes.

2. Add the flour and stir well with a wooden spoon. Cook over medium heat for 1 minute. Add the broth gradually, using a whisk to work out any lumps between each addition. Add the apple cider and sachet. Bring the soup to a simmer and continue to simmer gently for 30 minutes. Stir the soup occasionally and skim the surface as necessary. *(recipe continues)*

3. Discard the sachet and strain the soup through a sieve, reserving the liquid. Purée the solids and return to the soup pot. Add enough of the reserved liquid to achieve a soup consistency. Add the cream and blend well. Return to a simmer. Season to taste with salt and white pepper. Serve in heated bowls, garnished with a slice of red apple.

CREAM OF CHICKEN SOUP

1 stewing hen (about 3 pounds)

3 qt Chicken Broth (page 15)

¼ cup butter

1¼ cups thinly sliced leek (white and light green parts)

1¼ cups thinly sliced onion

¼ cup thinly sliced celery

2 tbsp minced shallots

¼ cup all-purpose flour

Sachet: 4 to 5 black peppercorns, 1 bay leaf, 4 to 5 parsley stems, 1 garlic clove, 1 sprig fresh thyme or ½ teaspoon dried thyme enclosed in a large tea ball or tied in a cheesecloth pouch

1 cup heavy cream, heated

Salt to taste

Freshly ground white pepper to taste

T HE SUCCESS OF this velvety soup relies on a rich broth made by simmering a full-flavored stewing hen in chicken broth, known as a double broth. If you already have a rich broth, use it to poach two chicken breasts. Cool and dice or shred the meat for the soup garnish, and begin the recipe by cooking the vegetables in step 3.

MAKES 8 TO 10 SERVINGS

1. Place the hen and giblets (discard or reserve liver for another use) in a tall soup pot. Cover with cold broth. Bring to a simmer, skimming away any scum as necessary. Simmer gently until the hen is fork-tender, about 1 hour (continue to skim during simmering as needed).

2. Remove the hen from the broth and let cool. Dice or shred the breast meat for a garnish; reserve the remaining meat for another use. Strain the broth through a fine sieve and set aside.

3. Clean the soup pot and place it over medium heat. Melt the butter, and then add the leek, onion, celery, and shallots. Stir to coat evenly with butter. Cover the pot and cook the vegetables, stirring occasionally, until tender and translucent, 4 to 6 minutes.

4. Add the flour and cook over low heat for 6 to 7 minutes, stirring almost constantly. Gradually add 8 cups of the broth, using a whisk to work out any lumps after each addition (refrigerate or freeze any remaining broth for another use). Add the sachet and bring to a simmer. Simmer gently for 45 minutes, stirring occasionally and skimming the surface as necessary.

5. Remove and discard the sachet. Strain the soup through a fine sieve, reserving the liquid. Purée the solids and return to the liquid. Strain the soup once more.

6. Return the soup to a simmer. Remove from the heat and add the hot cream. Add the diced or shredded breast meat. Season to taste with the salt and white pepper. Serve in heated bowls.

WATERZOOI

Belgian Cream of Chicken Soup

WATERZOOI IS RICHER and slightly thicker than the preceding Cream of Chicken Soup, due to the presence of a "liaison." A liaison is a mixture of egg yolks and cream that is used to enrich soups and stews. Liaisons are added to hot liquid using a process known as "tempering." This simply means that the temperature of the liaison must be raised gently to keep the yolks from instantly scrambling as might happen if the liaison were added directly to simmering liquid.

MAKES 8 SERVINGS

1. Place the hen and giblets (discard or reserve liver for another use) or chicken breast in a tall soup pot. Cover with the broth. Bring to a simmer, skimming away any scum as necessary. Simmer gently until the hen is fork-tender, about 1 hour (continue to skim during simmering as needed).

2. Remove the hen from the broth and let cool. Dice or shred the breast meat for a garnish; reserve the remaining meat for another use. Strain the broth through a fine sieve and set aside.

3. Clean the soup pot and place it over low heat. Melt 3 tablespoons of the butter in the pot. Add the flour and stir well with a wooden spoon. Cook for 3 to 4 minutes, stirring almost constantly. Gradually add 8 cups of the broth, using a whisk to work out any lumps after each addition. Add the sachet and bring to a simmer. Simmer gently for 45 minutes, stirring occasionally and skimming the surface as necessary. Discard the sachet.

4. Meanwhile, heat the remaining butter in a pot over low heat. Add the shallots, leeks, carrot, celery, turnip, and potatoes. Stir to coat evenly with butter. Add ½ cup of the remaining broth (refrigerate or freeze any remaining broth for another use). Cover the pot and cook the vegetables until tender, about 10 minutes. Remove from the heat.

5. Make a liaison by blending the egg yolks with the cream in a bowl. Temper the liaison by stirring in about 1 cup of the hot soup, and then stir the tempered liaison mixture into the soup.

6. Add the breast meat and cooked vegetables to the soup. Season to taste with the salt and white pepper. Serve in heated bowls, sprinkled with parsley or chives (if using).

1 stewing hen (about 3 pounds) or 1 whole roasting chicken breast

3 qt Chicken Broth (page 15)

5 tbsp butter

3 tbsp flour

Sachet: 4 to 5 peppercorns, 1 bay leaf, 4 to 5 parsley stems, 1 clove garlic, 1 sprig fresh thyme or ½ tsp dried thyme enclosed in a large tea ball or tied in a cheesecloth pouch

2 tbsp minced shallots

2½ cups diced leeks (white and light green parts)

⅓ cup diced carrot

½ cup diced celery

1½ cups diced yellow turnip

2 cups diced white or yellow potatoes (peeled)

2 egg yolks

1½ cups heavy cream or half and half

Salt to taste

Freshly ground white pepper to taste

¼ cup minced parsley or chives (optional)

MINGUICHI

Chile and Cheese Soup

{PICTURED AT LEFT}

THIS SOUP IS perfect at the end of summer when the tomatoes and corn are at their best, but it's just as flavorful in the winter, and even quicker to make from canned tomatoes and frozen corn. If you wish, you can stir the cheese into the entire pot of soup just before you serve it, but we like the way the heat of the soup melts the cheese while you eat it.

MAKES 6 SERVINGS

1. Purée the tomatoes through a food mill or in a blender and reserve.

2. Heat the oil in a soup pot over medium heat. Add the butter and melt it. Add the onion and garlic and sauté, stirring occasionally, until the onion is tender and translucent, 8 to 10 minutes. Add the corn and sauté until heated through, 5 to 6 minutes.

3. Add the puréed tomatoes and simmer for 5 minutes. Season to taste with salt and pepper. Add the broth and continue to simmer until the corn is tender and the soup is flavorful, 10 to 12 minutes. Add the roasted poblano strips and simmer until they flavor the soup, about 5 minutes. Add the milk and cream and simmer until heated through, about 5 minutes.

4. Remove the soup from the heat. Divide the cheese equally between 6 warmed soup bowls. Ladle the hot soup over the cheese and serve at once.

Poblano chiles can be easily roasted over a grill or a gas burner, or under the broiler. You can find complete instructions for roasting and seeding chiles on page 38.

3 cups seeded and quartered plum tomatoes

1 tbsp canola oil

2 tsp butter

2 cups minced onion

2 tsp minced garlic

4 cups corn kernels, thawed if frozen

2 tsp salt

½ tsp freshly ground black pepper

4 cups Chicken Broth (page 15)

2 roasted poblano chiles, peeled, seeded, cut into strips (see page 38)

½ cup milk

½ cup cream

5 oz queso manchego or Muenster

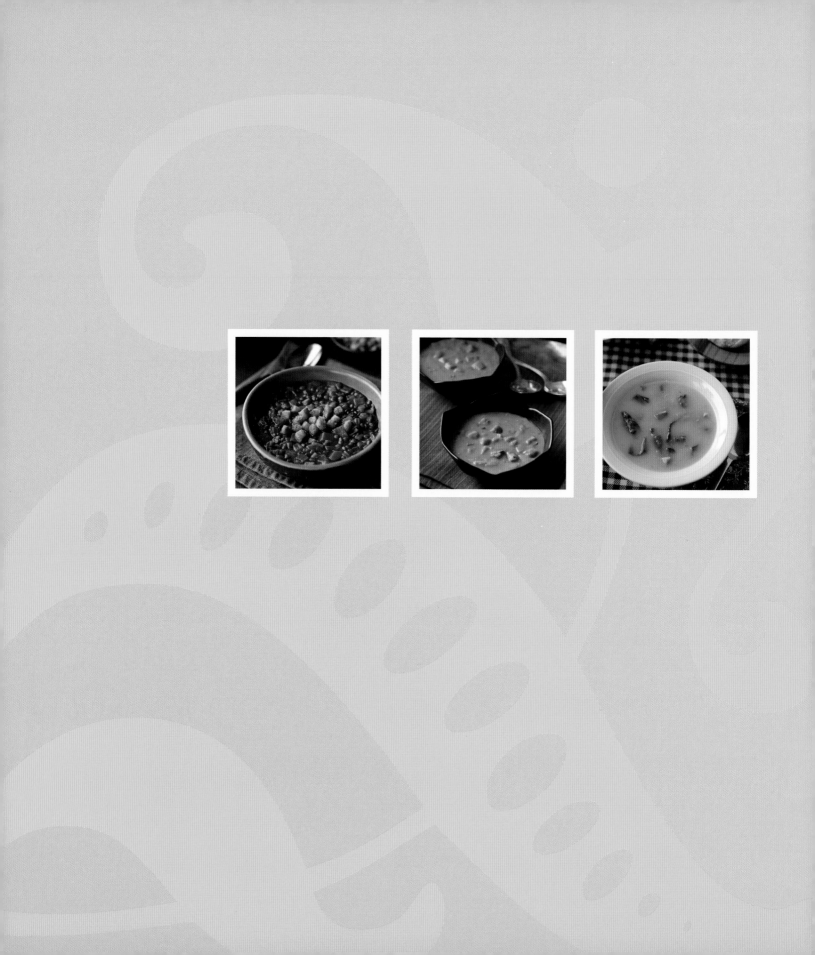

Puréed Soups

PURÉED SOUPS ARE thick soups. They get their texture from their main ingredients. After they have simmered in the soup long enough, they become so tender that they almost fall apart on their own. Dried peas, lentils, beans, or vegetables such as potatoes, carrots, and squashes can all form the basis of a hearty purée soup. Puréed soups rarely call for a specific thickener like roux or a cornstarch slurry, although some cream soups do.

You can choose how coarsely textured or smooth you want your soup to be. Some soups are puréed until they are so smooth, they are virtually indistinguishable from cream soups; these soups are often strained after puréeing for a truly silky texture (for instance, Butternut and Acorn Squash Soup (page 167). Others are intentionally left just slightly coarser; Red Lentil Soup (page 159) is a good example. Some may call for the base to be puréed and then garnished with additional ingredients like cooking greens, dice ham, or mushrooms (for instance, Caldo Verde, page 169). A third type calls for just some of the soup (approximately half) to be puréed and then blended into the unpuréed soup; classic soups like Senate Bean Soup (page 164), in fact, suggest that you just "mash" some of the ingredients by pressing them against the side of the soup pot with the back of your wooden spoon.

Main Ingredients

Root vegetables, dried beans, and hard-skinned squashes are some of the most popular ingredients for making puréed soups. (For more information about specific ingredients, see pages 6–9, Shopping for Soup Ingredients.) These ingredients are usually good keepers. Beans, for instance, can last several weeks or months in your cupboard, as long as they are kept dry and are stored in sealed containers. You can certainly substitute canned beans if you are short on time. For more information on selecting and preparing beans for soups, see opposite.

Root vegetables (potatoes, sweet potatoes, carrots, turnips, and parsnips, for instance) are typically good keepers as well, although they will start to lose quality in a few weeks. Look for firm, heavy specimens at the market with no gouges or soft spots. Store potatoes and sweet potatoes at room temperature in a cupboard that is dark and dry. If your potatoes begin to turn wrinkly or grow sprouts, or their skin and flesh turns green, you can trim away these blemishes by cutting deeply enough into the flesh to cut it completely out. However, if there is a big soft spot or any evidence of molding, don't use them.

Squashes make great puréed soups, whether you are using acorn squash, pumpkins, or butternut squash. Peeling and cutting a squash calls for a heavy, sharp knife; for more information, see page 167. If you prefer, you can substitute cubed frozen squashes for any of the fresh hard-skinned varieties we call for in our recipes. You can add them to the soup directly from the freezer.

The liquid you choose for a puréed soup can easily be plain water, as long as you include the appropriate amount of seasonings and aromatics while the soup is cooking. Broths and stocks add flavor and some body. For a rich, savory flavor in bean soups, you can make a ham bone broth by simmering a ham bone or hock in some broth or water for about 30 minutes. Taste it carefully; some ham hocks are very salty, so you will want to cut back on the quantity of salt you add to the soup.

Aromatics in the form of vegetable combinations (page 13), spice sachets (page 13), and bouquet garnis (page 126) are common. Soups in this chapter are also flavored with ginger, curry power, cumin, chiles, and citrus zest, to name just a few options. We've included information and instruction for handling less familiar ingredients throughout the chapter.

Croutons or small dices of a complementary vegetable or meat are common garnishes. Although it is not necessary, finishing ingredients such as cream or milk are used at times. For added richness, you may even include a liaison, especially in soups that have a puréed potato base.

FOCUS ON SELECTING AND PREPARING BEANS

At one time, dried beans, lentils, and peas had all but disappeared from many kitchens across our nation—with the exception of the baked beans that almost invariably accompanied a baked ham supper or hamburgers and hot dogs at summer barbecues. When Tex-Mex and Southwestern cooking became popular, beans came back into their own. Soups are a natural vehicle for dry beans of all sorts. Any country or region with a rich peasant tradition has one or two (or more) bean soups in its repertoire.

Try to choose dried legumes from a store with high turnover. Beans, lentils, and dried peas can be stored in plastic bags or other airtight storage containers for a few months and don't require refrigeration.

Preparing Beans

Although it is usually fine to substitute one legume for another in many recipes, there is a noticeable difference in taste between favas and limas, black beans and kidney beans, and navy beans and black-eyed peas. Different types of beans require different cooking times. Lentils and split peas cook in about 30 to 45 minutes. Garbanzo beans (chickpeas) and lima beans can take up to 2 hours. If time is short, use canned beans instead of cooking dried beans from scratch. Drain the beans and rinse them to remove the flavor of the canning liquid. This will also help reduce the sodium level, allowing you to season the dish to suit your own taste.

➡ **SORT AND RINSE THE BEANS:** Pour the beans onto a baking sheet and, working methodically from one end to the other, carefully sort through them, removing discolored or misshapen pieces. Submerge in cold water, removing and discarding any beans that float to the surface. Drain the beans and rinse them well with running water.

➡ **SOAK THE BEANS:** Place the sorted and rinsed beans in a container and add enough cool water to cover them by a few inches—about 4 times the volume of water to beans. Let the beans soak in the refrigerator for at least 4 hours or overnight. For a quicker soak, place the sorted beans in a pot and add enough water to cover them by a few inches. Bring the water to a simmer. Remove the pot from the heat, cover, and let steep for 1 hour.

➡ **COOK THE BEANS:** Drain the soaked beans, put them in a large pot, and add enough water to cover the beans by about 2 inches. Bring the liquid to a full boil, and then reduce the heat to maintain a simmer. Stir the beans occasionally as they cook and add more liquid if the level starts to drop.

Most recipes tell you when to add various seasonings and flavorings, but the general rule is to add salt and any acidic flavoring ingredients, such as tomatoes, vinegar, or citrus juices, only after the beans are nearly tender, to give them a smooth consistency.

Suggested Soaking and Cooking Times for Beans

LEGUME	LONG METHOD	SHORT METHOD	COOKING TIME	LEGUME	LONG METHOD	SHORT METHOD	COOKING TIME
Black Beans	12 hrs.	3 hrs.	1½–2 hrs.	Fagioli Beans	12 hrs.	2–3 hrs.	1–1½ hrs.
Black-eyed Peas	12 hrs.	2 hrs.	1–1½ hrs.	Flageolets	12 hrs.	2–3 hrs.	1–1½ hrs.
Fava Beans	12 hrs.	4 hrs.	1½–2 hrs.	Great Northern	12 hrs.	2–3 hrs.	1½–2 hrs.
Butter Beans	12 hrs.	4 hrs.	1½–2 hrs.	Lentils	No soaking		20–30 min.
Chick Peas	12 hrs.	3 hrs.	1½–2 hrs.	Navy Beans	12 hrs.	2–3 hrs.	1–1½ hrs.
Red Kidney Beans	12 hrs.	2–3 hrs.	1–1½ hrs.	Pidgeon Peas	12 hrs.	2 hrs.	1 hr.
Borlotti Beans	12 hrs.	2–3 hrs.	1–1½ hrs.	Pink Beans	12 hrs.	2–3 hrs.	1–1½ hrs.
Cannellini	12 hrs.	2–3 hrs.	1–1½ hrs.	Pinto Beans	12 hrs.	2–3 hrs.	1–1½ hrs.
Dutch Brown Beans	12 hrs.	2–3 hrs.	1½–2 hrs.	Split Peas	No soaking		20–30 min.
Egyptian Brown	12 hrs.	2–3 hrs.	1½–2 hrs.	White Bean	12 hrs.	2–3 hrs.	1–1½ hrs.

☼ BASIC METHOD FOR PURÉED SOUPS

Hearty, robust puréed soups are made from filling foods that are easy to keep on hand in cupboards all year-round: beans, dried peas, lentils, potatoes, and other root vegetables. Like all soups, you can build flavor into them every step of the way. Cooking onions and garlic in a little oil or a bit of bacon fat infuses the soup with savory richness. The way you purée your soup can have almost as much influence on the way the soup tastes as the ingredients you choose. The instructions we offer here give you all the options from chunky to coarse to silky smooth.

➡ **SWEAT THE AROMATICS AND ADD LIQUID:** Sweat the aromatic vegetables and, if appropriate, the main flavoring ingredient. Add the liquid and bring to a full boil; establish a gentle simmer. Add the main flavoring ingredient, if it was not added with the aromatics, and continue to simmer.

➡ **SIMMER GENTLY UNTIL INGREDIENTS WILL PURÉE EASILY:** Simmer until all the ingredients are soft enough to purée easily. Because most puréed soups are fairly starchy, they should be stirred frequently during cooking to prevent scorching. A gentle cooking speed and a heavy-gauge pot will also help to prevent scorching. If the soup does begin to scorch, it should be immediately transferred to a cool, clean pot and the flavor should be checked. If the soup does not taste scorched, the process may be continued.

➡ **ADD THE SPICE SACHET:** Add the spice sachet or bouquet garni approximately 1 hour before the end of the cooking time. Check the flavor as the soup develops; remove and discard the sachet or bouquet garni when the proper flavor extraction is reached.

➡ **PURÉE THE SOUP:** Purée the soup using one of the methods described below, garnish as desired, and serve. Soups that have become too thick during cooking, or if you have made them ahead, can be thinned with stock or water after they have returned to a boil. It is rare for puréed soups to be too thin.

Puréeing the Soup

You can purée soups by a variety of means: using a handheld blender directly in the soup pot, with a sieve or a food mill, or in a countertop blender food processor. Follow these guidelines to avoid scalds and burns.

➡ **FOR ALL SOUPS:** The first step, regardless of what piece of equipment you intend to use, is to pull the pot off the heat and let the soup cool for at least 10 minutes.

➡ **USING A HANDHELD BLENDER:** Be sure that the soup pot is not too full. You should have at least 4 inches of space between the top of the soup and the top of the pot. If the soup fills the pot more than that, transfer some of the soup to another bowl or pot. Put the head of the blender under the surface of the soup before you turn it on. Then, run the blender until the soup is smooth. You can strain the soup through a fine sieve after you purée it this way to remove any strings or fibers from the vegetables, if necessary.

➡ **USING A COUNTERTOP BLENDER OR FOOD PROCESSOR:** Fill the blender jar or the bowl of the food processor by about half. Remove the "funnel" from the lid of the blender or feed tube of a food processor; this allows the steam from the hot soup to escape. If you don't, some pressure will build up in the blender and the soup might fly out when you remove the lid. Turn the blender on at a low setting—typically grind. You can increase the blender's speed once the soup has become a coarse purée. After the soup is smooth, transfer it to a clean pot. Continue to purée the soup until all of it is puréed and combined in the clean pot. You can continue on to finish and garnish the soup now, or you may opt to cool it down and store it to serve later (page 5).

PURÉE OF SPLIT PEA

OR A MEATLESS version of this delicious purée, omit the bacon and ham hock, substituting Vegetable Broth (page 18) for the chicken broth, and replacing the bacon fat with vegetable oil.

MAKES 8 SERVINGS

1. Cook the bacon in a soup pot over medium-high heat until crisp and brown. Remove the bacon with a slotted spoon; drain on paper towels and set aside. Pour off all but 3 tablespoons of the bacon fat. Add the onion, carrot, celery, and leek; stir to evenly coat with fat. Cover the pot and cook the vegetables over medium-low heat, stirring occasionally, until the onion is tender and translucent, 6 to 8 minutes.

2. Add the broth, potatoes, peas, and ham hock. Bring to a simmer over medium-low heat and cook 20 minutes, stirring occasionally. Add the sachet and simmer until the split peas are soft, about 30 minutes, skimming away any scum as needed.

3. Remove and discard the sachet. Remove the ham hock and set aside to cool. When cool enough to handle, cut the ham off the bone, dice, and set aside.

4. Purée the soup (opposite) and return it to the soup pot. Stir in the diced ham and bacon. Season to taste with salt and pepper. Serve in heated bowls, garnished with croutons.

3 strips bacon, minced

1¼ cups diced onion

⅓ cup diced carrot

½ cup diced celery

1¼ cups diced leek (white and light green parts)

6 cups Chicken Broth (page 15)

2 cups diced yellow or white potatoes (peeled)

1 cup dry split green or yellow peas

1 smoked ham hock, split in half

Sachet: 1 bay leaf, 1 whole clove, 1 garlic clove, 4 to 5 peppercorns enclosed in a large tea ball or tied in a cheesecloth pouch

Salt to taste

Freshly ground black pepper to taste

1 cup Croutons (page 222)

RED LENTIL SOUP

F ALL VEGETABLES, lentils (at approximately 25%) are second only to soybeans in protein content. They have been cultivated by humans for millennia, as evidenced by their presence at ancient Egyptian and prehistoric European sites. Today, lentils are available in several varieties, such as the yellow lentil and the green (French) lentil. The red (Egyptian) lentil is the quickest cooking of all lentils and lends itself well to soup making because as it cooks, it tends to fall apart and practically purées itself.

MAKES 8 SERVINGS

1. Melt the butter in a soup pot over medium heat and add the garlic, onion, and celery. Cook until the onion is translucent, 4 to 6 minutes.

2. Reduce the heat to low, add the lentils and cumin, and stir to coat evenly with butter. Cook the lentils for 4 to 5 minutes. *(recipe continues)*

3 tbsp butter

2 garlic cloves, minced

1 cup minced onion

¼ cup diced celery

1 lb red lentils

1 tsp ground cumin

2 tbsp long grain white rice

2½ quarts Chicken Broth (page 15), plus as needed

Juice of ½ lemon

Salt to taste

Freshly ground white pepper to taste

3. Add the rice and 5 cups of the chicken broth. Bring to a simmer and cook, stirring often to avoid scorching, until the lentils dissolve and begin to look like a puréed soup, 30 to 45 minutes. Add the remaining broth as needed to adjust the consistency and heat through.

4. Season to taste with the lemon juice, salt, and pepper. Serve in heated bowls.

{PICTURED AT RIGHT}

2 tbsp vegetable oil

1¼ cups minced onion

1 garlic clove, minced

⅔ cup minced carrots

1¼ cups minced leek (white and light green parts)

½ cup minced celery stalk

1 tbsp tomato paste

7 cups Chicken or Vegetable Broth (pages 15, 18)

1¾ cups French (green) lentils

¼ cup Riesling or other slightly sweet white wine

2 tbsp sherry wine vinegar

½ lemon

Sachet: 2 sprigs fresh thyme or 1 tsp dried, 1 bay leaf, and ¼ tsp caraway seeds enclosed in a large tea ball or tied in a cheesecloth pouch

½ tsp salt, or as needed

¼ tsp ground white pepper, or as needed

1 cup Croutons (page 222)

CLASSIC LENTIL SOUP

THE EARTHY FLAVOR of lentils is brightened by Riesling and sherry wine vinegar in this refined lentil soup. It is a brothy soup, but if you'd like it to be thicker, you can purée half of the soup, then recombine with the unpuréed half. If you store this soup in the refrigerator, it may become thicker. Adjust the consistency as necessary by adding more broth, and be sure to recheck the seasoning. A garnish of fresh croutons (page 222) will add a dimension of texture and flavor to the finished soup.

MAKES 8 SERVINGS

1. Heat the oil in a soup pot over medium heat. Add the onion and garlic. Cook, stirring occasionally, until the onion is translucent, 4 to 6 minutes.

2. Add the carrots, leek, and celery. Cook, stirring occasionally, until softened, 5 to 7 minutes.

3. Add the tomato paste, stir well, and cook for 2 more minutes.

4. Add the remaining ingredients and bring to a simmer over medium-low heat. Cook until the lentils are tender, about 40 minutes. Remove and discard the sachet and lemon half. Purée the soup (page 158) if desired (the lentils may have already turned into a purée by this time).

5. Adjust the seasoning to taste with salt and pepper. Serve in heated bowls, garnished with the croutons.

CURRIED EGGPLANT AND LENTIL SOUP

{PICTURED AT LEFT}

THE COMBINATION OF eggplant, lentils, curry, and lemon is subtle yet complex and exotic. Curry powder is an Indian spice blend of up to 20 different ground ingredients. In India, where the exact ingredients vary from region to region and even from cook to cook, it is usually ground fresh daily. Commercial curry powders bear little resemblance to fresh ground versions, but they are perfectly adequate for this soup. Choose either the standard mild curry powder or the slightly hotter Madras curry powder. Cooking curry powder in fat before introducing liquid, as is done here, allows the fat to "open up" the fat-soluble flavor compounds in the curry powder, resulting in a more flavorful soup.

MAKES 8 SERVINGS

1. Simmer the broth, lentils, and potatoes in a soup pot over medium-low heat until tender, about 45 minutes.

2. Purée the soup (page 158) and return to the soup pot. Add the cream and blend well. Season to taste with the salt and pepper. Keep warm.

3. Heat the oil in a skillet over medium heat. Add the eggplant, onion, and garlic. Cook for 5 minutes, stirring occasionally. Stir in the curry powder and cook 1 minute more. Add the lemon juice and simmer over medium-low heat gently until the eggplant is tender and the lemon juice has evaporated, 2 to 3 minutes. Season to taste with salt and pepper.

4. Add the eggplant mixture to the soup and simmer over medium-low heat for 5 to 10 minutes to blend the flavors. Stir in the parsley and serve in heated bowls.

Stir the curry powder into the eggplant mixture and allow to cook for an additional minute, which will expand and intensify the flavors in the curry powder.

2 qt Chicken or Vegetable Broth (pages 15, 18)

1 cup green or yellow lentils

3 cups diced yellow potatoes (peeled)

1 cup heavy cream

Salt to taste

Freshly ground black pepper to taste

3 tbsp olive oil

6 cups cubed eggplant (peeled)

1¼ cups finely diced onion

½ tsp minced garlic

2 tbsp curry powder, or as needed

¼ cup fresh lemon juice

¼ cup chopped parsley

SENATE BEAN SOUP

1¼ cups dry navy beans

2 tbsp olive oil

¾ cup finely diced carrot

1 cup finely diced celery

1 garlic clove, finely minced

¾ cup finely diced onion

1 qt Chicken or Vegetable Broth (pages 15, 18)

1 smoked ham hock

1 cup diced yellow or white potato (peeled)

Sachet: 3 to 4 whole black peppercorns and 1 whole clove enclosed in a large tea ball or tied in a cheesecloth pouch

Salt to taste

Freshly ground white pepper to taste

Tabasco sauce to taste

1 cup Garlic Croutons (page 222)

Accs. CCORDING TO LEGEND, this soup was frequently found on the menu at the U.S. Senate dining room. When the weather became hot, it was discontinued. There was such an outcry, however, that it soon reappeared. Just to be certain that they would never be without their favorite soup again, the senate actually passed a bill requiring that it be offered every day that the dining hall was open.

MAKES 8 SERVINGS

1. Sort through the beans, discarding any stones or bad beans. Place the beans in a large pot and pour in enough water to cover by at least 3 inches. Bring to a boil, and then remove from the heat. Cover and soak for 1 hour. Drain the beans, rinse them in cold water, and set aside.

2. Heat the oil in a soup pot over moderate heat. Add the carrot, celery, garlic, and onion. Cook over low to medium heat until the garlic has a sweet aroma and the onions are a light golden brown, about 5 minutes.

3. Add the beans, broth, and ham hock. If necessary, add enough water to cover the beans by about 1 inch. Bring to a simmer over medium-low heat, cover, and cook for 1 hour.

4. Add the potato and sachet. Continue to simmer the soup over low heat until the beans and potatoes are tender enough to mash easily, about 30 minutes.

5. Remove the ham hock from the soup. When it is cool enough to handle easily, pull the lean meat away from the bone and dice it. Reserve this meat to add to the soup as a garnish.

6. Purée about half of the soup until smooth. Add this back to the remainder of the soup. If necessary, thin the soup with additional broth. Season to taste with salt, pepper, and Tabasco sauce.

7. Serve the soup in heated bowls or cups, garnished with the diced ham and croutons.

PURÉE OF WHITE BEAN SOUP

THIS RUSTIC WHITE bean soup has a sweet and gentle flavor, less exotic than the Purée of Black Bean (page 166). If you'd like more texture in the soup, purée only half the beans, as is done in the Senate Bean Soup recipe, opposite.

MAKES 8 SERVINGS

1. Sort through the beans, discarding any stones or bad beans. Place the beans in a large pot and pour in enough water to cover by at least 3 inches. Bring to a boil, then remove from the heat. Cover and soak for 1 hour. Drain the beans, rinse them in cold water, and set aside.

2. Heat ⅓ cup of the olive oil in a soup pot over medium heat. Add the leeks, onion, carrot, celery, and minced garlic. Cover the pot and cook, stirring occasionally, until the vegetables are translucent and tender, about 10 minutes.

3. Add the beans, broth, and sachet. Bring to a simmer over medium-low heat and cook, covered, until the beans are tender, 1 to 1½ hours. Stir down to the bottom of the pot from time to time with a wooden spoon to prevent the beans from sticking.

4. Meanwhile, heat the remaining ¼ cup olive oil in a small saucepan over medium heat. Add the whole garlic cloves and sauté until deep brown, about 5 minutes. Be careful not to burn them. Discard the garlic cloves and set the oil aside to cool.

5. Remove and discard the sachet. Purée the soup (page 158). Return the purée to the remaining soup and bring it back to a simmer over medium-low heat. If the soup is too thick, add additional broth.

6. Just before serving, season the soup to taste with salt and pepper. Place the toasted bread in the bottoms of heated soup bowls and top with half of the grated Parmesan. Ladle the soup over the toast and sprinkle with the garlic oil and thyme. Pass the remaining grated Parmesan on the side.

1 lb dry white beans

⅓ cup plus ¼ cup olive oil

2½ cups finely diced leeks (white and light green parts)

1¼ cups finely diced onion

⅓ cup finely diced carrot

½ cup finely diced celery

2 garlic cloves, minced

2 qt Chicken or Vegetable Broth (pages 15, 18)

Sachet: 1 sprig fresh rosemary or 1 teaspoon dried, 1 bay leaf, 4 to 5 parsley stems enclosed in a large tea ball or tied in a cheesecloth pouch

2 cloves garlic, peeled and left whole

Salt to taste

Freshly ground white pepper to taste

8 Italian bread slices, toasted

1 cup grated Parmesan cheese

1 tbsp minced fresh thyme

PURÉE OF BLACK BEAN SOUP

1 lb dry black beans

⅓ cup extra virgin olive oil

4 garlic cloves, minced

2½ cups finely diced leeks (white and light green parts)

1¼ cups finely diced onion

2 qt Chicken or Vegetable Broth (pages 15, 18)

Sachet: 1 teaspoon cumin seeds, 1-inch slice of fresh ginger, 1 dry hot chili, and 4 to 5 parsley stems enclosed in a large tea ball or tied in a cheesecloth pouch

Zest and juice of 1 lemon

Salt to taste

Freshly ground black pepper to taste

1 cup sour cream or plain yogurt

½ cup diced fresh tomato

⅓ cup sliced scallion greens

THIS DELICIOUS, HEARTY soup is simple to make, although the soaking and simmering of the beans takes some time. If you're in a hurry, you can substitute 7 cups of drained and rinsed canned black beans. Reduce the simmering time to 30 minutes. The flavor and texture will not be quite the same as if you started from scratch, but you will be sitting down to eat sooner.

MAKES 8 SERVINGS

1. Sort through the beans, discarding any stones or bad beans. Place the beans in a large pot and pour in enough water to cover by at least 3 inches. Bring to a boil, then remove from the heat. Cover and soak for 1 hour. Drain the beans, rinse them in cold water, and set aside.

2. Heat the olive oil in a soup pot over medium heat. Add the garlic, leeks, and onion. Cover the pot and cook, stirring occasionally, until the vegetables are translucent, about 10 minutes.

3. Add the beans, broth, and sachet. Bring to a simmer over medium-low heat and cook, covered, until the beans are tender, 1 to 1½ hours. Stir down to the bottom of the pot from time to time with a wooden spoon to prevent the beans from sticking.

4. Remove and discard the sachet. Purée the soup (page 158) and return it to the soup pot. Bring the soup back to a simmer over medium-low heat. If the soup is too thick, add additional broth and stir well.

5. Just before serving, stir in the lemon juice and grated lemon zest and season the soup to taste with salt and pepper. Serve the soup in heated bowls, garnished with sour cream, tomato, and scallions.

BUTTERNUT AND ACORN SQUASH SOUP

THIS SOUP HAS a rich creamy texture that belies its actual calorie count. Feel free to use only one type of squash or to replace the squash with pumpkin. For a richer soup, whip a little heavy cream to soft peaks, fold in an equal amount of sour cream, and add grated fresh ginger to taste. Place a dollop of this ginger-scented cream on top of each portion.

MAKES 8 SERVINGS

1. Heat the butter in a soup pot over medium heat. Add the onion, carrot, celery, ginger, and garlic. Cook, stirring frequently, until the onion is tender and translucent, 5 to 6 minutes.

2. Add the broth, squashes, and potato. Bring the broth to a simmer over medium-low heat and cook until the squashes are tender enough to mash easily with a fork, about 20 minutes.

3. Purée the soup (page 158) and return it to the soup pot. Return the soup to a simmer over medium-low heat.

4. Season the soup to taste with salt, pepper, and orange zest. Serve the soup in heated bowls.

Peeling Winter Squash

Acorn, pumpkin, butternut, and Hubbard squashes have a hard, thick rind. The rind protects the squash and keeps it from spoiling for long periods, but makes your job a challenge if you want to remove the rind before you cook the squash.

Make an initial cut to create a flat, stable surface that makes it easier and safer to cut up the squash. Cut through a butternut squash at the point where the "neck" meets the rounded "body." Cut through a round squash like acorn squash from stem end to blossom end.

Use a spoon to scoop out the seeds and any filaments in the center of the squash. Then, set your squash, flat side down, on a work surface and use a chef's knife to cut away the skin.

1 tbsp butter

1¼ cups diced onion

⅓ cup diced carrot

½ cup diced celery

1 tbsp minced fresh ginger

1 clove garlic, minced

3 to 4 cups Chicken Broth (page 15)

2 cups cubed butternut squash

1 cup cubed acorn squash

½ cup sliced yellow or white potato (peeled)

¼ tsp salt, or to taste

¼ tsp ground white pepper, or to taste

1 tsp grated orange zest

BLACK BEAN AND
BUTTERNUT SQUASH SOUPS

BUTTERNUT SQUASH SOUP:

½ tbsp butter

¼ cups diced onion

⅓ cup diced carrot

3 cups diced butternut squash

¼ cup honey

¼ tsp ground cinnamon

⅛ tsp ground allspice

Salt to taste

BLACK BEAN SOUP:

1 dried chipotle chile, stemmed

3 cups cooked black beans, drained and rinsed

1 cup water, plus more as needed

¼ tsp dried oregano, preferably Mexican

¼ tsp chopped dried epazote (optional)

¼ tsp ground cumin

Salt to taste

THIS 2-IN-1 SOUP is beautiful to behold and tastes as good as it looks. It's impressive, yet ridiculously easy to prepare. If you'd rather use freshly cooked black beans, start with 1½ cups of dried beans. You can use the bean cooking liquid instead of water to prepare the bean soup.

MAKES 8 SERVINGS

1. Make the butternut squash soup: Melt the butter in a large saucepan over medium-low heat. Add the onion and carrot. Cook until the onion is tender, about 4 to 6 minutes. Add the squash and enough water to cover the vegetables by about 3 inches. Simmer, uncovered, until the squash and carrots are fork-tender, about 30 minutes. Stir in the honey, cinnamon, and allspice and simmer 2 minutes longer. Remove the soup from the heat and let cool for 10 minutes. Purée the soup in a blender until smooth. (Thin the soup with a little water, if necessary.) Pour the soup back into saucepan and bring it to a simmer over medium heat. Season to taste with salt. Reduce the heat to low and keep the soup hot until ready to serve.

2. Make the black bean soup: Grind the chipotle chile into a powder in a spice grinder. Purée the ground chipotle, beans, water, oregano, epazote (if using), and cumin in a blender until smooth. Thin the soup with a little additional water, if necessary. Bring the soup to a simmer in a medium saucepan over medium heat. Season to taste with salt. Reduce the heat to low and keep the soup hot until ready to serve.

3. To serve the soup, simultaneously ladle equal amounts of the soups side by side into heated soup bowls. Swirl the two soups together with a toothpick. Serve immediately.

CALDO VERDE

Portuguese Potato Kale Soup

ALDO VERDE, LITERALLY "green soup" in Portuguese, is a robust and incredibly satisfying concoction of kale, garlic, and smoky meats in a silky puréed potato soup base. Served with a loaf of Portuguese bread, it makes a complete meal. Linguiça is a Portuguese garlic sausage that can be found in many supermarkets and Latin American markets.

MAKES 8 SERVINGS

1. Heat the oil in a soup pot over medium heat. Add the leek, onion, and celery. Cook, stirring occasionally, until the onion is translucent, 4 to 6 minutes.

2. Add the broth, potatoes, and ham hock. Bring to simmer over medium-low heat and cook until all are very tender, about 40 minutes.

3. Meanwhile, bring a large pot of salted water to a rolling boil. Use a paring knife to cut the tough stems away from the kale leaves. Blanch the kale in the boiling water until it wilts, about 3 minutes. Drain the kale, run it under cold water to stop the cooking, and drain again. Slice the kale into thin shreds.

4. Remove the ham hock from the soup base. Purée the soup base and return to a simmer over medium-low heat.

5. When cool enough to handle, remove the meat from the ham hock and dice. Add the ham hock meat, sliced kale, sausage, and bay leaf to the potato purée. Season to taste with salt and pepper and simmer 15 to 20 minutes longer. Serve in heated bowls.

1 tbsp olive oil

¾ cup diced leek (white and light green parts)

¾ cup diced onion

¼ cup diced celery

5 cups Chicken Broth (page 15)

4 russet potatoes, peeled, cut in sixths

1 smoked ham hock

¼ lb fresh kale

2 oz linguiça sausage, diced (about ½ link)

½ bay leaf

Salt to taste

Freshly ground black pepper to taste

PURÉE OF TWO ARTICHOKES

1 large artichoke

2 qt Chicken or Vegetable Broth (pages 15, 18)

½ lb Jerusalem artichokes (about 5 average)

½ lemon

3 tbsp butter

¾ cup diced onion

½ cup diced celery

3 tbsp all-purpose flour

½ cup heavy cream

1 tbsp fresh lemon juice, or as needed

Salt as needed

Freshly ground white pepper as needed

¼ cup thinly sliced chives

2 tbsp thinly sliced scallion greens

Artichoke lovers will adore this soup. It combines the flavors of Jerusalem and regular globe artichokes. Although the Jerusalem artichoke is not truly an artichoke (it's actually the tuber of a type of sunflower), it has a taste and texture not unlike an artichoke heart. It is believed that the name "Jerusalem artichoke" is derived from the Italian word for sunflower: *girasole*. Jerusalem artichokes, also known as *sunchokes*, are usually available from October to March. Choose those that are firm, not soft and wrinkled, and store in a plastic bag in the refrigerator for up to 1 week.

MAKES 8 SERVINGS

1. Cut off all but about two inches of the artichoke stem. Use a paring knife to trim away the tough outer part of the remaining stem. Place the artichoke and broth in a large non-aluminum saucepan and bring to a simmer over medium-low heat. Cover and cook until the outer leaves are tender and pull away easily from the artichoke, about 35 minutes. (If necessary, weight the artichoke down with a small inverted crock or heavy plate to keep it submerged in the broth while simmering.) When tender, remove the artichoke from the broth and set aside to cool. Reserve the broth.

2. Meanwhile, fill a glass or stainless steel bowl with cold water and squeeze the juice from the lemon half into it. Drop the rind into the water as well. Peel the Jerusalem artichokes with a stainless steel paring knife, slicing each one thinly as soon as it is peeled and placing the slices in the lemon water immediately to keep them from turning brown. (You should have about 1 cup.)

3. Melt the butter in a soup pot over medium heat. When the foaming subsides, add the onion and celery and cook, stirring occasionally, until the vegetables are translucent, about 5 minutes. Stir in the flour and continue to cook for another 2 minutes.

4. Whisk in the reserved broth. Drain the Jerusalem artichokes, and add to the broth mixture. Bring to a simmer over medium-low heat and cook, partially covered, for 30 minutes (if the level of liquid drops, add more broth or water to keep it constant).

5. While the soup is simmering, scrape the flesh off the base of each artichoke leaf with the end of a teaspoon and reserve the flesh (the innermost leaves are very thin and will not yield any flesh; discard these). Use the spoon to scoop the hairy choke from the heart and dice the heart. Reserve for the garnish.

6. Add the flesh from the artichoke leaves and the cream to the soup. Purée the soup (page 158). Return the purée to the (cleaned) soup pot and bring it to a simmer over medium-low heat.

7. Season the soup to taste with the lemon juice, salt, and white pepper. Serve the soup in heated bowls, garnished with the reserved diced artichoke heart, chives, and scallions.

ROASTED EGGPLANT AND GARLIC SOUP

Tahini is a paste made from sesame seeds. It can be found in most large supermarkets (often next to the peanut butter), as well as in shops that specialize in Middle Eastern and Asian foods. Roasting the garlic and eggplant in advance adds wonderful flavor and aroma to this hearty soup. Be sure to allow the vegetables enough time to take on a deep rich hue.

To make this a substantial main course soup, add drained, cooked chickpeas, diced roasted peppers, cooked broccoli, and/or cooked cauliflower florets. Serve accompanied with warmed whole wheat pita bread. Garnish the soup with a drizzle of extra-virgin olive oil, chopped fresh parsley, and toasted pine nuts to add a final dash of flavor and texture.

MAKES 8 SERVINGS

4 garlic cloves, unpeeled

2 cups cubed eggplant (peeled)

1¼ cups diced yellow onion

½ cup diced celery

⅓ cup diced carrot

3 tbsp olive oil

1 cup diced yellow or white potato (peeled)

1 qt Chicken Broth (page 15)

1 sprig fresh thyme or ¼ tsp dried leaves

2 tbsp tahini

½ tsp salt, or as needed

¼ tsp fresh ground black pepper, or as needed

Freshly squeezed lemon juice as needed

1. Preheat the oven to 350°F. Wrap the garlic cloves in a square of aluminum foil.

2. Combine the eggplant, onion, celery, and carrot in a baking dish large enough to hold the vegetables in a single layer.

3. Place the garlic directly on the oven rack. Drizzle the olive oil over the vegetables. Cover the pan and roast for 20 minutes. Remove the cover, increase the heat to 400°F, and roast until the eggplant and garlic are very soft, about 15 minutes. When cool enough to handle, squeeze the garlic from its skin.

4. Combine the roasted vegetables with the potato, broth and thyme in a soup pot. Simmer over medium-low heat until the potatoes are tender enough to mash easily, about 25 minutes. Remove and discard the thyme sprig.

5. Add the tahini, salt, pepper, and lemon juice to the soup and whisk to combine the ingredients well. Continue to simmer the soup for another 2 to 3 minutes.

6. Purée the soup (page 158). Return the soup to medium heat and simmer over medium-low heat for 5 minutes, or until reduced to the desired consistency. Check the seasoning and adjust it to taste with additional salt, pepper, or lemon juice. Serve in heated bowls.

POTATO, ESCAROLE, AND COUNTRY HAM SOUP

{PICTURED AT LEFT}

COUNTRY HAMS HAVE an altogether different taste and texture than boiled hams. They have been cured for lengthy periods and have a salty, smoky taste that is unique. Different parts of the country swear by their special curing techniques, as well as the way in which their pigs are fed, as the key to producing the ultimate ham. Ask your deli manager or butcher to help you find country ham or a suitable substitute.

MAKES 8 SERVINGS

1. Heat the butter in a soup pot over low heat. Add the onion, leek, celery, and garlic; stir until they are evenly coated with butter. Cover the pot and cook until the vegetables are tender and translucent, about 6 to 8 minutes.

2. Add the broth, potatoes, and thyme. Simmer over medium-low heat the soup until the potatoes are tender enough to mash easily, about 20 minutes.

3. Remove and discard the thyme sprig. Purée the soup (page 158). Return the soup to the soup pot and bring to a simmer over medium-low heat.

4. Add the escarole and diced ham and simmer the soup until all ingredients are tender, another 12 to 15 minutes.

5. Season to taste with salt and pepper. Serve the soup in heated bowls.

1 tbsp butter

1¼ cups diced onion

1¼ cups minced leek (white and light green parts)

½ cup diced celery

1 garlic clove, minced

1 qt Chicken Broth (page 15)

2 cups diced yellow or white potatoes

1 sprig fresh thyme or ½ teaspoon dried

2 cups chopped escarole

1 cup diced country ham

¼ tsp salt, or as needed

¼ tsp ground black pepper, or as needed

POTATO SOUP

with Mushrooms and Marjoram

2 tbsp olive oil

1 cup diced yellow or white potato

1¼ cups diced onion

3 cups sliced white mushrooms

1¼ cups sliced leek (white part only)

1 tbsp chopped fresh marjoram

1 tbsp chopped fresh chervil (optional)

1 qt Chicken Broth (page 15)

1 cup sour cream

2 tbsp butter

Salt as needed

Freshly ground white pepper to taste

Pinch freshly grated nutmeg or to taste

THIS RECIPE COMES from long-time C.I.A. instructor and Certified Master Chef Fritz Sonnenschmidt. He has been making this soup for nearly 60 years. For him, it recalls fond memories of the master chef to whom he was apprenticed. This recipe was her favorite, and it was a personal honor when she allowed him to cook it for her—despite incurring the jealousy of the other apprentices!

MAKES 6 SERVINGS

1. Heat the olive oil in a soup pot over medium heat. Add the potato and onion and sauté until the onion is golden, 5 to 7 minutes. Add the mushrooms and leek and cook for 2 to 3 more minutes. Add half of the chopped marjoram and chervil (if using).

2. Add the broth and bring to a simmer over medium-low heat. Cook until the potatoes are tender, about 25 minutes.

3. Purée the soup (page 158) and return to the soup pot. Return to a simmer over medium-low heat.

4. Stir in the sour cream and butter. Season to taste with the salt, pepper, and nutmeg. Serve in heated bowls, sprinkled with the remaining marjoram and chervil.

CORN AND SQUASH SOUP

with Roasted Red Pepper Purée

6 cups water

3 fresh basil sprigs

1 garlic head, halved horizontally

2 tbsp butter

1 cup diced onion

2 cups diced yellow squash

3 cups fresh corn kernels

Salt to taste

Freshly ground black pepper to taste

1 recipe Roasted Red Pepper Purée (page 236)

THIS SIMPLE SOUP, based on a freshly made garlic and basil broth, is a wonderful way to take advantage of fresh summer produce. If you crave a taste of summer in the middle of winter, you can also make this soup with frozen corn.

MAKES 4 TO 6 SERVINGS

1. Combine the water, basil, and garlic in a large saucepan. Bring to a simmer over medium-low heat and cook, partially covered for ½ hour, skimming the surface, if necessary. Strain the broth and reserve.

2. Heat the butter in a soup pot over medium heat. Add the onion and cook, stirring frequently, until translucent, about 5 minutes.

3. Add the squash and cook, stirring frequently, for another 5 minutes.

4. Add the corn and reserved broth and bring the soup to a simmer over medium-low heat. Season to taste with the salt and pepper.

5. Purée the soup (page 158), then strain it through a fine sieve back into the soup pot. Return the soup to a simmer over medium-low heat.

6. Adjust the seasoning with more salt or pepper, if necessary. Ladle it into heated soup bowls and swirl some of the red pepper purée through each portion.

PURÉE OF CARROT AND ORANGE

THE AFFINITY of carrots and oranges is highlighted in this fruity soup. The hint of ginger adds an appropriate sparkle. Though this recipe calls for the soup to be served hot, it also makes a delicious cold soup.

MAKES 8 SERVINGS

1. Heat the butter in a soup pot over medium heat. When the foaming subsides, add the leeks and onion. Cover the pot and reduce heat to low. Cook, stirring occasionally, until tender, about 8 to 10 minutes.

2. Add the carrots, broth, juice concentrate, orange zest and juice, and sachet. Bring to a simmer over medium-low heat and cook, stirring occasionally, until the vegetables are very tender, about 30 minutes.

3. Remove and discard the spice sachet. Purée the soup mixture until smooth (page 158). If a slight texture is desired, do not purée completely. Return the soup to the pot, bring to a simmer over medium-low heat, and season to taste with salt and pepper.

4. Serve the soup in heated bowls, garnished with watercress leaves and orange sections (if using).

4 tbsp butter

2½ cups diced leek (white and light green parts)

1¼ cups diced onion

4½ cups diced carrots

1½ qt Chicken or Vegetable Broth (pages 15, 18)

¼ cup orange juice concentrate

Zest and juice of 1 orange

Sachet: 4 to 5 parsley stems and a 1-inch slice of ginger enclosed in a large tea ball or tied in a cheesecloth pouch

Salt as needed

Freshly ground black pepper as needed

¼ cup watercress leaves

8 orange sections (optional)

Make It Different

This soup, like several other recipes in this chapter, can easily be prepared as a cold soup. Cool the puréed soup according to the instructions on page 5, then place the purée in the refrigerator to chill completely prior to serving. Taste the cold soup, adjust the seasonings as necessary, and serve in well chilled bowls. Garnish with a dollop of sour cream, if desired, or the ginger-infused whipped cream used in the Pumpkin Soup with Ginger Cream recipe on page 147.

Bisques & Chowders

CHOWDERS GET THEIR name from the French word *chaudière*, a kettle in which fisherman made their stews. Classically, chowders were made from seafood and included pork, potatoes, and onions, though it is not uncommon for any thick, rich, and chunky soup to be called a chowder. There is also a group of chowders, of which Manhattan is probably most widely known, that are prepared more like a hearty broth. The main flavoring ingredients for chowder are often shellfish, fish, or vegetables, such as corn. Vegetables, whether they are used as main flavoring ingredients or as aromatics, should be well rinsed, then peeled, trimmed, and cut into small and uniform pieces so they cook evenly. (For more information, see pages 6–9, Shopping for Soup Ingredients.)

Bisques are traditionally based on crustaceans, such as shrimp, lobster, or crayfish, and thickened with rice, rice flour, or bread. The crustacean shells are usually pulverized along with the other ingredients before a final straining. The end result is a soup with a consistency like that of a cream soup.

Contemporary bisques may be based on ingredients other than crustaceans and rely on a vegetable purée or roux as the thickener. A vegetable-based bisque is prepared in the same manner as a puréed soup. If the main vegetable does not contain enough starch to act as a thickener, rice, roux, or a starchy vegetable such as potato may be used to provide additional thickness. When the vegetables are tender, the soup is puréed until smooth. Consequently, the distinction between a purée and a bisque is not always clear.

Crustacean meat and shells for bisque should be rinsed well, and then coarsely chopped. Shellfish should be scrubbed clean. Consult specific recipes for guidance. Check the quality of stored fumets, stocks, or broths used to prepare a bisque before use. Bring a small amount to a boil and taste it for any sour or off flavors or odors.

☼ BASIC METHOD FOR BISQUES

A good bisque reflects the flavor of the main ingredient. If you have added cream to round out and mellow the soup, it should not mask the main flavor. All bisques are slightly coarse or grainy, with a consistency similar to heavy cream. A crustacean bisque is pale pink or red in color; a shellfish bisque ivory; and a vegetable bisque a paler shade of the main vegetable.

➡ *PREPARE THE SHELLS:* Rinse the shells well and chop larger shells, such as crab or lobster. Drain and dry them well. Traditional bisques get their color and flavor from shrimp, lobster, crab, or crayfish shells. Use one type of crustacean or a combination. Brown the shells in the cooking fat, stirring frequently, until they turn a bright pink or red and remove them from the pan.

➡ *ADD THE AROMATIC INGREDIENTS:* Add the mirepoix to the pan and cook it over medium heat for 20 to 30 minutes, or until the vegetables are tender and the onions are light brown. Tomato paste is often added at this point and allowed to cook until it has a sweet aroma and a deep rust color. Add spices such as paprika to the shells and other aromatics to cook in the fat.

➡ *THICKEN THE SOUP:* Some bisque recipes indicate the addition of flour to prepare a roux as part of the soup-making process. If necessary, add a bit more oil or butter to the shells, then stir in the flour and cook the result roux, stirring constantly, for 4 to 5 minutes. A good-quality stock or broth is as important to the flavor of a bisque as the shells are. Bring the broth to a simmer while cooking the aromatic vegetables to make cooking more efficient. Also, a more traditional rice-thickener can be used instead of flour that has been cooked into a roux. Once the soup is simmering, add the wine (if called for) and any additional herbs or aromatics, such as a spice sachet or bouquet garni.

➡ *PURÉE THE SOUP:* Taste the soup and make modifications to the seasoning or consistency during cooking. Add more liquid, if necessary, to maintain a good balance between the liquid and solids as the soup cooks. Stir frequently and monitor the heat. A bisque, like any other soup with starchy ingredients, can scorch quickly if left unattended for even a few minutes. A bisque takes about 45 minutes to 1 hour to cook properly. At that point, all ingredients (except, obviously, the shells) should be relatively tender, so they will purée easily. Skim the bisque throughout. Remove and discard the sachet or bouquet garni before puréeing the bisque. Use a blender (immersion or countertop) to purée it to a fairly smooth and even consistency. Pulverizing the shells and puréeing the aromatic vegetables helps to release more flavor into the soup. If time allows, return the puréed bisque to a simmer for several minutes and make any appropriate adjustments to the soup's seasoning or consistency before straining.

➡ *STRAIN THE SOUP:* Use rinsed cheesecloth to strain a shellfish bisque. Cheesecloth removes all traces of the shell and gives the bisque a very fine, delicate texture. This is a two-person task. First, set a sieve or colander in a clean pot. Drape the rinsed cheesecloth in the sieve or colander and pour the bisque through it. Most of the bisque will pass through the cheesecloth. Each person holds two corners of the cheesecloth and lifts the corners up in an alternating sequence (known as the milking method). When only solids remain in the cheesecloth, each person gathers his or her corners together and twists in opposite directions to finish straining the bisque (known as the wringing method). The bisque is ready to finish now, or it may be rapidly cooled and refrigerated for later service.

➡ *FINISH THE SOUP:* Finish the bisque and add any garnish ingredients. Return the bisque to medium heat and bring it to a simmer. Taste the soup and make any seasoning adjustments. Separately, bring the cream to a simmer and add it gradually to the bisque. There should be enough cream to enrich the soup and add a smooth flavor and mouthfeel, but not so much that the cream masks the main ingredient.

SHRIMP BISQUE

¼ cup vegetable oil

¾ to 1 lb shrimp shells

1 tbsp minced shallots

1 cup thinly sliced leek (white part only)

½ cup thinly sliced celery

1¼ cups thinly sliced onion

½ cup tomato purée

1 tbsp sweet paprika

¼ cup brandy

8 cups Fish Broth (page 17)

½ cup white wine

Sachet: 4 to 5 peppercorns, ½ bay leaf, 2 to 3
    parsley stems, 1 sprig fresh thyme or ½ tsp
    dried thyme enclosed in a large tea ball or
    tied up in a cheesecloth pouch

1 cup long-grain white rice

½ cup heavy cream, heated

Salt as needed

Cayenne pepper as needed

1 cup diced cooked shrimp

MUCH OF THE flavor in this soup comes from a somewhat unusual ingredient: shrimp shells. You need ¾ to 1 pound of shrimp shells to make this bisque, and it takes about 4 pounds of shrimp to yield ½ pound of shells. Unless you are really desperate to have this soup, though, don't buy shrimp just to get the shells. Instead, every time you shell shrimp for another use, save the shells in the freezer. When you have accumulated at least ½ pound of shells, then it's time to make bisque.

MAKES 8 SERVINGS

1. Heat the oil in a soup pot over high heat. Add the shrimp shells. Reduce the heat to medium and cook the shells, stirring occasionally, until the shells develop a deep red color, about 10 minutes (see photos below). Add the shallots, leek, celery, and onion. Continue to cook until the vegetables soften, about 4 to 6 minutes.

2. Add the tomato purée and paprika. Cook until the purée darkens, about 3 minutes. Add the brandy and let the liquid boil away until nearly dry. Add the broth, white wine, and sachet. Bring to a simmer and cook for 30 minutes.

3. Add the rice and continue to simmer until the rice is very soft, about 30 minutes more. Remove and discard the sachet. Purée the bisque (including the shells), preferably in a foodmill.

4. Strain the bisque through a fine sieve into a clean soup pot. Return the bisque to a simmer. Remove the bisque from the heat and add the heated cream. Blend well. Adjust the seasoning to taste with the salt and cayenne.

5. Heat the shrimp over low heat in a small amount of bisque. Divide the shrimp evenly between 8 heated bowls. Ladle the bisque over the shrimp and serve.

ROASTED TOMATO BISQUE

ROASTING THE TOMATOES adds an unusual twist to this bisque. If you prefer, you can substitute sun-dried tomatoes (not oil-packed) for the roasted tomatoes.

MAKES 4 TO 6 SERVINGS

1. Heat the oil in a soup pot over medium heat. Add the onion, celery, and leek. Cook, stirring occasionally, until translucent, about 4 to 6 minutes.

2. Add the broth, plum tomatoes, tomato purée, roasted tomatoes, and thyme leaves. Bring to a simmer and cook for 30 minutes.

3. Add the rice and continue to simmer for another 15 minutes. Purée the soup until very smooth (page 158). To give the soup an extremely fine texture, strain it through a fine sieve after puréeing, if you wish.

4. Return the soup to the pot. Stir in the vinegar and smoked tomato. Reheat to just below a simmer. Serve in heated bowls.

Making Roasted and Smoked Tomatoes

To make roasted tomatoes, slice ripe tomatoes about ¼-inch thick, lay them on an oiled baking sheet, and roast in a 400°F oven for about 20 minutes. The tomatoes should deepen in color and lose some moisture. They will keep well in the refrigerator in a covered container for at least 10 days.

The optional smoked tomato garnish for this tomato bisque is quite unusual. Smoked tomatoes add a rich, almost meaty savor to this soup, and can be added to other soups, sauces, and stews. A little goes a long way; too much smokiness in a dish becomes overwhelming. To keep your house from taking on a smoky smell, do this outside on your grill. You can use this technique to smoke mushrooms as well.

Prepare the grill. If using charcoal, stack the coals to one side. Scatter a thin layer of wood chips in the bottom of a disposable aluminum pan (or use aluminum foil to fashion a container for the chips). Cut the tomato in half lengthwise and remove the seeds. Place the pan of chips on the rack above the hottest part of the grill. When the chips begin to smoke, place the tomato halves on the rack over the coolest part of the grill. Close the lid (make sure the air vent is open and positioned above the tomatoes if possible). Smoke for 5 to 7 minutes. Remove the skin and dice the tomato. (Alternatively, if your grill has a built-in smoking compartment, follow the manufacturer's directions for smoking.)

2 tbsp vegetable or olive oil

1¼ cups diced onion

½ cup diced celery

1¼ cups diced leek (white and light green parts)

2 cups Chicken or Vegetable Broth (pages 15, 18)

2 cups chopped plum tomatoes (peeled, seeded, and juices reserved)

1 cup tomato purée

½ cup chopped roasted tomatoes

1 tbsp fresh thyme leaves, chopped

¼ cup long grain white rice

3 tbsp balsamic vinegar, or as needed

1 smoked plum tomato, diced (optional)

{PICTURED AT RIGHT}

1½ qt Fish Broth (page 17)

30 fresh oysters, scrubbed well

1 tbsp butter

¾ cup diced onion

½ cup long-grain white rice

1½ cups heavy cream, heated

¼ tsp salt, or as needed

Tabasco sauce as needed

Worcestershire sauce as needed

1 tbsp chopped parsley

OYSTER BISQUE

T HIS OYSTER BISQUE is quite easy to prepare and makes an elegant starter for a special meal, such as Thanksgiving or Christmas dinner. The bisque has good body and a flavor that is light and oystery, but not overly so.

MAKES 6 TO 8 SERVINGS

1. Bring the broth to a boil in a large pot. Add the oysters, cover, and steam until they open, about 12 minutes. Remove the oysters (discard any that do not open). Strain the broth through a fine sieve, then through a coffee filter. Reserve the broth. Remove the oyster meat from the shells. Chop half the oysters. Set the whole and chopped oysters aside.

2. Heat the butter in a soup pot over medium heat. Add the onion and cook, stirring occasionally, until translucent, 4 to 6 minutes.

3. Add the oyster broth and the rice. Bring to a simmer and cook until the rice is soft, about 20 minutes.

4. Purée the soup (page 158) and place over low heat. Add the chopped oysters and the cream. Heat thoroughly but do not simmer or boil. The oysters' edges should just barely start to curl, as shown in the photo, opposite.

5. Season to taste with the salt, Tabasco, and Worcestershire. Serve in heated bowls, garnished with the whole oysters and chopped parsley.

PUMPKIN BISQUE

2 tbsp butter

2 garlic cloves, chopped

½ cup diced celery

1 cup diced onion

1 cup diced leek (white part only)

3½ cups diced pumpkin (fresh or frozen)

2 qt Chicken Broth (page 15)

2 tbsp white wine

½ tsp grated ginger

Salt as needed

½ tsp ground nutmeg (optional)

B UY A VARIETY of pumpkin meant specifically for eating when you make this bisque. Pumpkins meant for carving are very fibrous and will not make a good soup. For added richness, garnish each portion of the bisque with a dollop of un-sweetened whipped cream. For a playful presentation, serve the bisque in hollowed-out mini pumpkins.

MAKES 6 TO 8 SERVINGS

1. Heat the butter in a soup pot over medium heat. Add the garlic, celery, onion, and leek. Cook, stirring occasionally, until the onion is translucent, about 7 to 10 minutes.

2. Add the pumpkin and broth. Bring to a simmer and cook until all the vegetables are tender, about 30 minutes.

3. Meanwhile, heat the wine in a small saucepan to a simmer. Immediately remove from the heat, add the ginger, and cover. Steep for 10 minutes, then strain the wine and discard the ginger.

4. Strain the solids from the soup, reserving the liquid. Purée the solids and add enough of the liquid to achieve a slightly thick soup consistency.

5. Add the wine to the soup and season to taste with the salt and nutmeg (if using). Serve in heated bowls.

☼ BASIC METHOD FOR CHOWDERS

Good chowders have a rich flavor, balancing the main flavoring ingredient(s) and supporting aromatic and finishing flavors, a velvety texture, and a lightly thickened consistency, similar to heavy cream. If you are making a shellfish-based chowder (clams, mussels, oysters, etc.), before beginning, steam the main ingredient in stock or water until the shellfish open. Strain the broth through a filter or cheesecloth and reserve. Pick the meat, chop, and reserve.

➡ *PREPARE THE ROUX:* Render the salt pork or bacon and add the aromatics. It may be necessary to add additional oil or butter to the rendered fat, depending on how you intend to introduce the roux into the soup. If the roux is to be made as part of the overall process, known as the *singer* method, additional fat is needed.

➡ *ADD THE AROMATIC INGREDIENTS:* White mirepoix is a common aromatic combination for light-colored chowders, though for other chowders a combination of vegetables, such as carrots, onions, celery, leeks, garlic, and peppers, is also used. Cook the aromatics gently in the rendered fat and/or oil over low heat, until the vegetables are tender and translucent and they begin to release their juices.

➡ *THICKEN THE SOUP:* Stir the flour into the fat and cook the roux just long enough for it to take on a pale golden color. Slowly whisk in the reserved broth and/or stock. Bring the soup just up to a simmer, stirring frequently. Check the soup's seasoning and make any necessary adjustments. Certain ingredients are added to the soup at intervals, depending upon how dense they are and the effect extended cooking might have on them. Tender new peas will become gray and pasty if allowed to cook for too long, but potatoes need time to cook. A spice sachet left in the soup too long may lose its fresh flavor. Consult individual recipes for specific instructions on when to add ingredients.

➡ *FINISH THE SOUP:* Simmer until all the ingredients are fully cooked and tender and the soup has good flavor. Stir, skim, and adjust seasoning throughout cooking time. Chowders usually need 1 hour of simmering time to develop flavor and thicken properly. Make any necessary adjustments to the consistency now. The soup is ready to finish now, or it may be rapidly cooled and refrigerated for later service. Return the soup to a simmer over medium heat and add enough hot cream, if using, to enrich the soup, without overwhelming the main ingredient's flavor. Add the garnish or reserved main ingredient back to the chowder. Return the soup to a simmer and adjust seasoning if necessary. Serve at once in heated bowls or cups.

CRAB AND MUSHROOM CHOWDER

5 cups assorted mushrooms (about 1 lb)

¾ cup water

6 tbsp butter

¾ cup diced onion

¼ cup diced celery

½ cup diced leek (white and light green parts)

2 tsp minced garlic

½ cup all-purpose flour

1 qt Chicken Broth (page 15)

2¼ cups diced russet potatoes (peeled)

¾ cup milk

6 tbsp dry sherry

2 tsp heavy cream

1 tsp salt, or as needed

1 tsp freshly ground black pepper, or as needed

10 oz lump backfin crabmeat, picked over for
    shells

M ANY SUPERMARKETS NOW carry a decent selection of "exotic" mushroom varieties, such as shiitake, oyster, and cremini mushrooms. You can make this delicious chowder using a single variety or a combination. Avoid white mushrooms though; they don't have the flavor and texture needed for this hearty soup.

MAKES 8 SERVINGS

1. Cut the stems from the mushrooms and slice the mushroom caps. Set the caps aside. Simmer the stems in the water for 30 minutes to make a mushroom broth. Strain the broth and set aside.

2. Heat 5 tablespoons of the butter in a large soup pot. Add the onion, celery, leek, and garlic. Cook until tender, stirring occasionally, about 4 to 6 minutes.

3. Add the flour and cook, stirring constantly with a wooden spoon, for 3 to 4 minutes. Gradually whisk in the chicken broth and bring to a simmer. Cook for 15 minutes. Strain through a sieve, pressing hard on the solids to recover as much thickened broth as possible. Return the broth to a simmer and discard the solids.

4. Add the potatoes to the broth and simmer until tender, about 15 minutes. Remove the pot from the heat and add the milk, 4 tablespoons sherry, and heavy cream. Season to taste with salt and pepper.

5. Meanwhile, melt the remaining tablespoon of butter in a skillet over medium heat. Add the sliced mushroom caps and sauté until tender, about 7 to 10 minutes. Add the mushroom broth, stirring and scraping the bottom of the pan with a wooden spoon to loosen any particles of mushroom stuck to the pan. Season to taste with salt and pepper.

6. Stir the mushrooms with their liquid and the crabmeat into the chowder. Check the seasoning once more and make any necessary adjustments. Serve in heated bowls, adding the remaining sherry to the individual bowls, if desired.

OPPOSITE, CLOCKWISE FROM UPPER LEFT: *Pick over the crab to remove bits of shell and cartilage before using; trim and discard mushroom stems; press hard on the solids to extract flavor; to finish, either add the sherry to the entire pot or let each diner add it to suit his or her own taste.*

FENNEL AND POTATO CHOWDER

4 tbsp butter

2½ cups diced leeks (white and light green parts)

1¼ cups minced onion

2 tbsp minced shallot

1½ cups diced fennel

6 cups Chicken or Vegetable Broth (pages 15, 18)

4 cups diced yellow or white potatoes (peeled)

1 cup heavy cream or half and half, heated

Salt as needed

Freshly ground white pepper as needed

6 tbsp minced chives or sliced scallions

F ENNEL, WHICH IS sometimes labeled as "anise" in supermarkets, is a vegetable with a broad, bulbous base that can be eaten raw or cooked. It has a delicate and very mild sweet licorice flavor. If you happen to find fennel with the feathery, dill-like tops still attached, chop some to use as a garnish for this chowder.

This is not a thickened chowder, though the cooked potatoes will give it some body. If you prefer a thicker consistency, try puréeing half of the soup and mixing it with the unpuréed half.

MAKES 8 SERVINGS

1. Melt the butter in a soup pot over medium heat. Add the leeks, onion, shallot, and fennel. Stir to coat evenly with butter. Cover the pot and cook until the onion is tender and translucent, about 4 to 5 minutes.

2. Add the broth and potatoes. Bring to a simmer and cook, atirring occasionally, until the potatoes are tender, about 20 to 25 minutes.

3. Skim the surface of the soup as necessary. Add the cream, blend well, and return to a simmer. Adjust the seasoning to taste with salt and white pepper. Serve in heated bowls, garnished with the chives or scallions.

NEW ENGLAND SEAFOOD CHOWDER

THIS THICK, DECADENT-TASTING chowder is packed with fish and shellfish. Round it out with a green salad, some crusty bread, and a bottle of dry white wine for an unforgettable meal.

MAKES 8 SERVINGS

1. Scrub the clams and mussels well in cold water. Place them in a large pot with the 5 cups of water and the peppercorns, thyme stems, parsley stems, and bay leaf. Bring to a simmer, cover, and steam until the shells open, about 7 minutes. Discard any shells that do not open.

2. Remove the clams and mussels and strain the broth through a fine strainer, then through a coffee filter. Set the broth aside. Remove the clams and mussels from their shells and dice the meat. Set aside.

3. Heat a soup pot over medium heat and add the salt pork or bacon. Cook, stirring frequently, until the fat melts and the bits of meat become crisp, about 6 to 8 minutes.

4. Add the onion and celery. Cook until tender, stirring occasionally, about 5 minutes. Reduce the heat to low, add the flour, and cook for 3 to 4 minutes, stirring constantly with a wooden spoon. Stir in the thyme, then add the reserved broth gradually, using a whisk to work out any lumps between each addition. Simmer for 30 minutes. Add the potatoes and simmer until tender, about 20 minutes.

5. Add the cod fillet and simmer until cooked through, about 4 to 6 minutes. Remove the cod, flake it apart, and return to the chowder.

6. Add the clams, mussels, scallops, milk, and cream. Heat gently, but do not simmer, until the scallops are cooked, about 3 minutes.

7. Season to taste with the salt and pepper. Serve in heated bowls.

8 chowder clams

1¼ lb mussels, debearded (see page 47)

5 cups water

5 black peppercorns, crushed

2 fresh thyme stems

2 parsley stems

½ bay leaf

2 tbsp ground salt pork or 3 strips bacon, minced

2 cups diced onion

1 cup diced celery

½ cup all-purpose flour

1 tbsp fresh thyme leaves

2 large yellow or white potatoes, peeled and diced

4 oz cod fillet (about 1 small fillet)

4 oz sea scallops, diced

1 cup milk

1 cup heavy cream

Salt as needed

Freshly ground black pepper as needed

NEW ENGLAND CLAM CHOWDER

{PICTURED AT LEFT}

THE CULINARY INSTITUTE of America's version of the American classic—a silky, rich chowder based upon simple, wholesome ingredients.

MAKES 8 SERVINGS

1. Scrub the clams well under running water. Shuck the clams, reserving the juices. Cut the larger clams in half. Mix the reserved juices with enough bottled clam juice to equal 3 cups.

2. Cook the bacon slowly in a soup pot over medium heat until lightly crisp, about 7 minutes. Add the onion and cook, stirring occasionally, until the onion is translucent, about 4 to 6 minutes. Add the flour and cook over low heat, stirring with a wooden spoon, for 2 to 3 minutes.

3. Whisk in the clam juice, bring to a simmer, and cook for 5 minutes, stirring occasionally. The liquid should be the consistency of heavy cream. If it is too thick, add more clam juice to adjust the consistency. Add the potatoes and simmer until tender, about 20 minutes.

4. Meanwhile, place the clams and cream or half and half in a saucepan and simmer together until the clams are cooked, 5 to 8 minutes.

5. When the potatoes are tender, add the clams and cream to the soup base. Simmer for 5 minutes. Stir in the sherry. Season to taste with salt, pepper, Tabasco and Worcestershire sauce. Serve in heated bowls with crackers on the side.

---

3 dozen chowder clams

2½ cups bottled clam juice, or as needed

2 slices bacon, minced

1¼ cups diced onion

2 tbsp all-purpose flour

4 cups diced yellow or white potatoes (peeled)

3 cups heavy cream or half and half

6 tbsp dry sherry, or as needed

Salt as needed

Freshly ground black pepper as needed

Tabasco sauce as needed

Worcestershire sauce as needed

Oyster or saltine crackers as needed

{PICTURED AT RIGHT}

2 slices bacon, minced

2½ cups diced leeks (white and light green
    parts)

1¼ cups diced onion

⅓ cup diced carrot

⅓ cup diced celery

1 cup diced red bell pepper (seeds and ribs
    removed)

1 tsp minced garlic

2 canned plum tomatoes, seeded and coarsely
    chopped

2 cups diced yellow or white potatoes (peeled)

3 cups bottled clam juice

1 cup tomato juice

1 bay leaf

Pinch dried thyme

3 dozen chowder clams, shucked, juices reserved

Salt as needed

Freshly ground black pepper as needed

Tabasco sauce as needed

MANHATTAN CLAM CHOWDER

THIS IS THE classic mid-Atlantic clam chowder, not to be confused with New England's version. So controversial was the inclusion of tomatoes to New Englanders that a piece of legislation attempting to ban tomatoes from any true chowder was once introduced in Maine. Fresh clams will, of course, make the best chowder, but if you wish, you can substitute ¾ cup canned clam meat and ¾ cup bottled clam juice for the fresh clams and juices.

MAKES 8 SERVINGS

1. Cook the bacon in a soup pot over medium heat until crisp and browned, about 10 minutes.

2. Add the leeks, onion, carrot, celery, pepper, and garlic. Cover the pot and cook over medium-low heat, stirring occasionally, until the vegetables are soft and translucent, about 10 minutes.

3. Add the tomatoes, potatoes, clam juice, tomato juice, bay leaf, and thyme. Bring to a simmer and cook until the potatoes are tender, about 15 to 20 minutes. Add the clams with their juices and simmer until the clams are cooked, about 5 to 10 minutes more.

4. Using a shallow, flat spoon, remove any fat from the surface of the chowder and discard. Remove the bay leaf and season to taste with salt, pepper, and Tabasco. Serve in heated bowls.

FRESH CORN CHOWDER

with Chiles and Monterey Jack

I F FRESH CORN is out of season and you are desperate for corn chowder, you may substitute 3 cups of frozen corn kernels which have been thawed. To avoid this situation altogether, though, make an extra batch or two at the height of corn season and freeze to enjoy later in the dead of winter when fresh corn is but a distant memory.

MAKES 8 SERVINGS

1. Cut the corn kernels from the cobs with a sharp knife, capturing as much of the juice as possible. Reserve ¾ cup of the corn kernels and purée the rest with the heavy cream in a food processor or blender. Set aside.

2. Cook the bacon in a soup pot over medium heat until crisp, about 8 minutes. Add the onion, pepper, celery, and garlic. Cover and reduce the heat to low. Cook, stirring occasionally, until the vegetables are tender, about 10 to 12 minutes.

3. Add the broth, potatoes, and tomatoes, including their juices. Bring to a simmer and cook, covered, until the potatoes are tender, about 20 minutes. Skim any fat from the surface of the soup and discard.

4. Add the puréed corn and cream, the reserved corn kernels, chiles, and cheese. Warm the soup. Season to taste with salt, pepper, and Tabasco. Serve in heated bowls, garnished with tortilla strips (if using).

{PICTURED AT LEFT}

6 ears of corn, shucked

1 cup heavy cream

2 slices bacon, minced

1¼ cups minced onion

1 cup minced red bell pepper

½ cup minced celery

1 garlic clove, minced

1½ qt Chicken Broth (page 15)

3 cups diced yellow or white potatoes (peeled)

3 cups chopped tomatoes (peeled, seeded, and juices reserved)

One 4-oz can green chiles, drained and chopped

1 cup grated Monterey Jack cheese

Salt as needed

Freshly ground black pepper as needed

Tabasco sauce as needed

1 cup corn tortilla strips, toasted (optional)

Cold Soups

JUST AS A steaming hot bowl of soup can warm you to the core on a freezing winter's day, so a cold soup holds the power to cool you on a blazing hot summer's day. Cold soups are served as appetizers, palate cleansers in a multicourse meal, as a drink, or a dessert.

Many of the soups found in the previous chapters, especially the cream soups, adapt very well to being served cold. Cold soups can be rich, as in the case of the Vichyssoise (page 208), or bold and robust, like our Cold Carrot Bisque (page 207).

Whenever you intend to serve any food chilled, be sure to taste it carefully when it is at the correct temperature for serving it—that is after it is completely chilled, not just cooled down to room temperature. Cold foods almost always require a heavy hand when you are seasoning them or they can seem bland.

The caveat about allowing some soups enough resting time for their flavors to develop applies to cold soups as well as hot soups. Some soups are at their best and ready to serve as soon as they are prepared—Chilled Cream of Avocado Soup (page 205) or Cold Cantaloupe Soup (page 216), for example—while others are best after they mellow, like Chilled Potato Soup with Tomato and Basil (page 208).

Cold Vegetable and Fruit Soups

Cold vegetable and fruit soups are often popular hot-weather offerings. You'll find them throughout various cuisines, ranging from Lebanese Kh'yaaf b'Lubban (Chilled Cucumber and Yogurt Soup, page 210) to an Indian-inspired Fresh Spring Pea Purée with Mint (page 201).

Vegetable or fruit soups are usually made by puréeing or chopping vegetables and/or fruits fine enough that they reach a soup-like consistency. Gazpacho (page 202) is the perfect example. These soups range in texture from pleasantly coarse and chunky to the velvety smoothness of a chilled melon soup. Broth or juice is often added to the vegetables or fruits to loosen the purée enough to create a good consistency. Other ingredients, such as cream, milk, buttermilk, garnishes, or granités can be added to the soup for extra flavor, color, or texture.

Cold Cream Soups

Vichyssoise (page 208) is a classic example of a cold creamed soup. It is made by preparing a chilled purée of potato and leek that is enriched with cream. After chilling, they are typically finished by adding chilled cream, yogurt, buttermilk, or crème fraîche.

When you taste and evaluate your cold cream soup, pay attention to the texture and consistency, too. Cold cream soups should have the same velvety smooth texture as hot cream soups. Cold soups may thicken as they cool, so be certain that you adjust the consistency to make a soup that is creamy but not stiff. Good cold creamed soups should not leave your mouth feeling coated with fat, so keep the amount of cream in proportion to the other ingredients.

Cold Clear Soups

Cold clear soups, like the Chilled Infusion of Fresh Vegetables on page 213, require a rich, full-bodied, clarified broth. Infusions, essences, or well-strained purées are often used to create the special character of these soups. Some clear soups are thickened with a little gelatin. Jellied clear soups should barely hold their shape and should melt in your mouth instantly.

FRESH SPRING PEA PURÉE WITH MINT

THIS DELICATE SOUP captures the essence of fresh peas. It's a great recipe to try if you find a bumper crop of peas—either in your own garden or at your local farm stand—or if you're looking for an unusual soup to serve as the first course for a special spring meal. Technically, you could make this soup with frozen peas, but it's not recommended; the flavor just won't be the same.

MAKES 8 SERVINGS

1. Heat the olive oil in a soup pot over medium heat. Add the leeks and onions. Cover and cook, stirring occasionally, until the onions are soft and translucent, about 4 to 6 minutes. Add the peas, cover, and cook for 2 minutes.

2. Add the vegetable broth and sachet. Bring to a simmer, cover, and cook until all the ingredients are very tender, about 45 minutes.

3. Add the lettuce and simmer until wilted, about 5 minutes.

4. Remove and discard the sachet. Purée the soup in a food processor or blender until smooth. Cover and chill thoroughly.

5. Just before serving, add the chilled cream or half and half to the soup. Season to taste with salt and pepper. Stir in the mint and serve in chilled bowls.

2 tbsp olive oil

1¼ cups minced leeks (white and light green parts)

1¼ cups minced onions

6 cups fresh peas

5 cups Vegetable Broth (page 18)

Sachet: 6 parsley stems and 3 white peppercorns enclosed in a large tea ball or tied in a cheesecloth pouch

4 cups shredded green leaf lettuce

¾ cup heavy cream or half and half, cold

½ tsp salt, or to taste

½ tsp freshly ground white pepper, or to taste

2 tbsp finely shredded mint chervil

{PICTURED AT RIGHT}

3 cups diced tomato (peeled, seeded, and juices reserved)

2 cups diced cucumber (peeled and seeded)

1¼ cups minced onion

1 cup minced red bell pepper

2 garlic cloves, minced

2 tbsp tomato paste

2 tbsp extra-virgin olive oil

2 tbsp minced fresh herbs such as tarragon, thyme, or parsley

3 cups canned tomato juice

¼ cup red wine vinegar, or to taste

Juice of ½ lemon, or to taste

¼ tsp salt, or to taste

¼ tsp cayenne pepper, or to taste

1 cup Croutons (page 222)

½ cup thinly sliced chives or scallion greens

GAZPACHO

THIS TANGY MARRIAGE of fresh tomato, cucumber, pepper, and onion is a summer favorite. The flavor of gazpacho improves if allowed to chill overnight, but thereafter this soup has a short shelf life because the tomatoes sour very quickly. It is best prepared no more than a day or two before it will be eaten.

MAKES 8 SERVINGS

1. Reserve 2 tablespoons each of the tomato, cucumber, onion, and pepper for the garnish.

2. Purée the remaining tomato, cucumber, onion, and pepper in a food processor or blender along with the garlic, tomato paste, olive oil, and herbs until fairly smooth but with some texture remaining.

3. Transfer to a mixing bowl and stir in the tomato juice along with the red wine vinegar, lemon juice, salt, and cayenne to taste. Cover and chill thoroughly, at least 3 hours but preferably overnight.

4. After chilling, recheck the seasoning and adjust as needed. Serve in chilled bowls garnished with the reserved vegetables, croutons, and chives.

If the soup is too thin for your taste, add about 1 cup of freshly made white bread crumbs before chilling. If it's too thick, the consistency can be thinned by adding more tomato juice or water. Part of the tomato juice can be replaced with fish broth or clam juice, an apt substitution if the soup will be served before a seafood main course.

CHILLED CREAM OF AVOCADO SOUP

{PICTURED AT LEFT}

THIS SOUP, ONE of the easiest in this book, manages to preserve the elusive flavor of the avocado. Use only very ripe avocados for this soup. If you buy avocados that aren't ripe yet, you can speed the ripening process by placing them in a paper bag with an apple and folding the top of the bag closed. The apple will give off ethylene gas, which accelerates ripening.

MAKES 4 TO 6 SERVINGS

1. Cut each avocado in half from top to bottom, following the contour of the pit in the center. Remove the pit and scoop out the avocado flesh.

2. Purée the flesh in a food processor or blender with 4 cups of the broth, the chili powder, coriander, and lime juice until very smooth. If the soup is too thick, add more broth to correct the consistency. Transfer to a bowl, cover, and chill thoroughly.

3. Just before serving, blend in the yogurt. Adjust the seasoning to taste with salt and white pepper. Serve in chilled bowls, garnished with the tomato and tortilla strips (if using).

Make It Different

You can garnish this soup with the tomato and tortilla strips called for in the recipe, or for a more elegant (albeit expensive) touch, try the crabmeat, corn, and pepper garnish pictured at left. You will need about 4 oz picked over crabmeat, ½ cup cooked corn kernels, ⅓ cup finely diced red pepper, 2 tsp fresh lime juice, and salt and pepper as needed. Combine the ingredients and toss to coat evenly with the lime juice. Add about 2 tbsp of the garnish to each serving.

2 large ripe avocados

4 to 5 cups Vegetable Broth (page 18) or water

½ tsp chili powder

¼ tsp ground coriander

Juice of 1 lime

1 cup plain yogurt or heavy cream

Salt to taste

Freshly ground white pepper to taste

2 ripe plum tomatoes, peeled, seeded, and diced (optional)

2 corn tortillas, cut into strips and fried (optional)

COLD CARROT BISQUE

{PICTURED AT LEFT}

I F YOU DON'T own a juicer, look for fresh carrot juice at your local natural foods store. Garnish with a dollop of whipped cream and a sprinkling of sliced chives, or for a touch of sweetness, homemade Candied Orange Zest (page 220).

MAKES 8 SERVINGS

1. Melt the butter in a soup pot. Add the onion, shallots, ginger, and garlic and sauté until the onion is translucent, about 4 to 6 minutes.

2. Add the carrots, broth, wine, cardamom, and orange juice. Bring to a simmer and cook until the carrots are tender, about 30 minutes.

3. Purée the soup in a food processor or blender until smooth. Cover and chill thoroughly.

4. Just before serving, stir in the light cream. Thin the soup with carrot juice to a barely thick consistency. Adjust the seasoning to taste with salt and serve in chilled bowls.

2 tsp butter

⅓ cup minced onion

3 tbsp minced shallots

2 tsp minced fresh ginger, or to taste

1 garlic clove, minced

5½ cups thinly sliced carrots

5 cups Vegetable Broth (page 18)

2 tbsp white wine

½ tsp ground cardamom

2 cups orange juice

½ cup light cream, cold

1½ to 2 cups fresh carrot juice

2 tsp salt, or to taste

CHILLED CARAWAY SQUASH BISQUE

A ROMATIC CARAWAY SEEDS complement the subtle flavor of yellow squash in this delicate and unusual soup. Small squash are the best choice for this soup because they have small seeds. If you can only find large squash, remove any large seeds. Select squash that are firm, bright, and free of spots or blemishes.

MAKES 8 SERVINGS

1. Melt the butter in a soup pot over medium heat. Add the onion, celery, carrot, and leek. Stir to coat evenly with the butter. Cover the pot and cook until the onion is tender and translucent, about 6 to 8 minutes.

2. Add the broth, squash, potato, and sachet. Bring to a simmer and cook, stirring occasionally, until the potato is tender, about 25 minutes.

3. Remove and discard the sachet. Strain the soup through a sieve, reserving the liquid. Purée the solids and return to the soup pot. Add enough of the reserved liquid to achieve a soup consistency. Blend well and return to a simmer for 2 minutes. Transfer to a bowl and chill thoroughly.

4. Add the heavy cream and blend well. Season to taste with the salt and white pepper. Serve in chilled bowls, garnished with toasted caraway seeds.

4 tbsp unsalted butter

1¼ cups minced onion

½ cup minced celery

⅓ cup minced carrot

1 cup minced leek, (white part only)

6 cups Vegetable Broth (page 18) or water

4 cups diced yellow squash

1 cup diced yellow or white potato (peeled)

Sachet: 1 tsp caraway seeds, 1 garlic clove, 1 sprig fresh thyme or ½ tsp dried thyme enclosed in a large tea ball or tied up in a cheesecloth pouch

¾ cup heavy cream. chilled

Salt to taste

Freshly ground white pepper to taste

1 tsp lightly toasted caraway seeds

{PICTURED AT RIGHT}

2 tbsp vegetable oil

3 cups finely chopped leeks (white parts only)

¾ cup minced onion

5 cups Chicken or Vegetable Broth (pages 15, 18)

3 cups diced russet potatoes (peeled)

*Sachet: 2 whole cloves, 2 parsley stems, 2 black
    peppercorns, ½ bay leaf enclosed in a large
    tea ball or tied up in a cheesecloth pouch*

1½ cups heavy cream, chilled

1 tsp salt, or as needed

White pepper, as needed

¼ cup thinly sliced chives

VICHYSSOISE

THIS IS THE Culinary Institute of America's rendition of the traditional classic that was first prepared by French chef Louis Diat at New York City's Ritz Carlton Hotel in 1917. Diat's chilled potato and leek soup sprinkled with chives was inspired by a favorite hot soup made by his mother in France.

MAKES 8 SERVINGS

1. Heat the oil in a soup pot over medium heat. Add the leeks and onion and cook until tender and translucent, about 4 to 5 minutes. Add the broth, potatoes, and sachet. Bring to a simmer and cook until the potatoes are starting to fall apart, about 25 minutes. Remove and discard the sachet.

2. Purée the soup (page 158). Chill thoroughly in the refrigerator for at least 2 and up to 24 hours before adding the cream and serving the soup.

3. Just before serving, add the chilled cream to the soup and season to taste with the salt and white pepper. Serve and garnish with the chives.

1 bacon slice, chopped

1¼ cups chopped onion

2½ cups sliced russet potatoes (peeled)

1 qt Chicken or Vegetable Broth (pages 15, 18)

1 bay leaf

½ cup half and half, chilled (optional)

½ tsp salt, or to taste

¼ tsp freshly ground black pepper, or to taste

Tabasco sauce to taste

1 plum tomato, finely diced

2 tbsp shredded fresh basil

CHILLED POTATO SOUP

with Tomato and Basil

INSPIRED BY VICHYSSOISE, the classic cold leek and potato soup, this soup is updated with a topping of fresh tomatoes and basil, a favorite flavor pairing. When fresh tomatoes are out of season, substitute sautéed or deep-fried leeks or onions.

MAKES 4 TO 6 SERVINGS

1. Cook the bacon in a soup pot over medium heat until the fat is rendered and the bacon bits are crisp, about 6 to 8 minutes. Add the onion and cook, stirring frequently, until the onion is tender and translucent, 3 to 4 minutes.

2. Add the potatoes, broth, and bay leaf and simmer until the potatoes are tender enough to mash, about 20 minutes. Remove and discard the bay leaf.

3. Let the soup cool slightly and then purée it. Transfer the soup to a bowl, cool to room temperature, and refrigerate overnight. If necessary, the consistency of the soup may be adjusted by adding additional broth. Add the half and half (if using) to the chilled soup and blend well. Season to taste with the salt, pepper, and Tabasco.

4. Serve in chilled bowls, garnished with the chopped tomato and basil.

CHILLED INFUSION OF FRESH VEGETABLES WITH FAVA BEANS

{PICTURED AT LEFT}

Y OU CAN ADJUST the suggested vegetable garnish in this soup to suit your taste, using more or less of any particular vegetable. Or, you can use different vegetables entirely. It's up to you. Fava beans, also known as broad beans, resemble large lima beans. Some supermarkets carry frozen fava beans. In the spring you may be fortunate enough to find fresh favas. Fava beans have a tough outer skin that must be removed before cooking: Blanch the beans for about 30 seconds in boiling water, then cool slightly and slip the beans from the skins. If the skins do not come off easily, blanch the beans again for another 30 seconds. If you cannot find fava beans, simply substitute fresh or frozen lima beans.

MAKES 8 SERVINGS

1. Make the vegetable infusion: Combine the leeks, celeriac, shallots, parsley, chives, garlic, thyme, bay leaf, salt and pepper with 1½ quarts of the water in a soup pot. Cover and simmer gently for one hour. Add a little water to bring it back to its original level, and return briefly to a boil. Remove from the heat and allow to cool. Strain through a fine-mesh sieve or cheesecloth. Cover and chill thoroughly.

2. Meanwhile, make a tomato broth: Combine the tomatoes with 1½ cups of the remaining water. Simmer gently for 30 minutes, and then strain through a fine sieve or cheesecloth. Cover and chill thoroughly.

3. Bring about 1 inch of water to a boil in a saucepan. Add the carrots, cover, and pan-steam until tender. Using a slotted spoon, transfer the carrots to a colander and rinse under cold water to stop the cooking. Drain well and transfer to a bowl. Repeat this process with the peas, fava or lima beans, and asparagus tips, cooking each vegetable separately until tender. Add the tomatoes to the cooked vegetables and toss to combine. Cover and chill thoroughly.

4. Mix the tomato broth and the vegetable infusion. Taste and adjust the seasoning as needed. Serve in chilled bowls, garnished with the diced tomato and parsley leaves (if using).

3½ cups sliced leeks (white and light green parts)

1 cup sliced celeriac

½ cup minced shallots

1¼ cups minced parsley

2 tbsp sliced chives

1 tsp minced garlic

1 thyme sprig

½ bay leaf

1 tbsp salt, plus more to taste

¾ tsp freshly ground black pepper, plus more to taste

2 qt water, or as needed

3 cups quartered ripe tomatoes

¼ cup sliced baby carrots

¼ cup small green peas (fresh or frozen)

¼ cup fava or lima beans (fresh or frozen)

¼ cup asparagus tips

¼ cup diced tomato (peeled and seeded)

8 fresh flat-leaf parsley leaves (optional)

COLD TOMATO AND ZUCCHINI SOUP

4 cups chopped plum tomatoes (peeled and
    seeded)

2 cups tomato juice

1 cup chopped onion

1 cup chopped red pepper (seeded and ribs re-
    moved)

¾ cup chopped cucumber (peeled and seeded)

1½ cups chopped zucchini

¼ cup chopped fresh cilantro

¼ cup chopped fresh basil

¼ cup chopped fresh parsley

5 tsp prepared horseradish (drained)

1 tbsp red wine vinegar

3 garlic cloves, chopped

Vegetable Broth (page 18) or water, as needed

Tabasco sauce to taste

Salt to taste

Freshly ground black pepper to taste

½ cup Croutons (page 222)

THIS FRESH-TASTING SOUP is a great way to make use of a summer bounty of fresh vegetables and herbs. If time permits, make it a day ahead of serving to let the flavors blend. Don't store it more than 2 to 3 days, though—tomatoes can sour quickly.

MAKES 8 SERVINGS

1. Combine all the ingredients *except* the broth, Tabasco, salt, pepper, and croutons in a blender or food processor, in batches if necessary. Process the soup in short pulses to a coarse purée.

2. Pour the soup into a bowl. If it is too thick, thin it slightly with broth or water. Season to taste with the Tabasco, salt, and pepper. Refrigerate for at least 30 minutes before serving.

3. Serve in chilled bowls, garnished with croutons.

Handling Zucchini

Tender, tiny zucchini need no special treatment beyond a thorough rinse and trimming the ends away, but larger specimens do. To remove any bitterness from the seeds, cut the zucchini in half lengthwise and scoop out the seeds. You can leave the skin on as long as it is not too thick or tough.

COLD STRAWBERRY SOUP

1 qt strawberries, hulled and quartered

⅓ cup sugar

¼ cup Grand Marnier or strawberry liqueur

3 cups heavy cream, cold

3 cups apple juice, cold

½ cup honey

1 tsp lemon juice

Strawberry slices for garnish

CHOOSE THE REDDEST, most fragrant strawberries you can find for this cold soup. You could substitute other cordials or liqueurs for the Grand Marnier, like Chambord, a raspberry-flavored liqueur, or Amaretto, an almond-flavored liqueur.

MAKES 8 SERVINGS

1. In a large non-reactive bowl, combine the quartered strawberries, sugar, and liquor and refrigerate for at least 2 and up to 24 hours.

2. Purée the berries with their juices until smooth (page 158). Add the heavy cream, apple juice, honey, and lemon juice to the purée. Chill the soup at least 4 and up to 24 hours.

3. Serve the soup in chilled cups garnished with a slice of strawberry.

CHILLED RED PLUM SOUP

THIS SWEET AND spicy soup is a beautiful purple color that hints at the fullness of the fruit flavor it contains. It makes the perfect beginning or end to a summer luncheon or outdoor dinner. Choose plums that are ripe, but not extremely soft. If red plums are unavailable, black plums will do well in this soup also.

MAKES 8 SERVINGS

1. Combine the plums, apple juice, sachet, and honey in a soup pot. Bring to a simmer and cook until the plums are tender, about 20 minutes. Remove and discard the sachet.

2. Purée the soup until it is very smooth. Season to taste with the lemon juice. Chill the soup thoroughly for at least 4 and up to 24 hours.

3. Serve in chilled bowls, garnished with a dollop of the sour cream and a scattering of toasted, slivered almonds.

When plums are in season, you'll find a rainbow of colors—light red, yellow streaked with red, crimson, deep purple, and green. Try whichever variety is juiciest.

6 cups chopped red plums (pitted)

3 cups unsweetened apple juice

Sachet: 3 to 4 black peppercorns, 1 large slice fresh ginger, 1 whole allspice berry, and ½ cinnamon stick enclosed in a large tea ball or tied in a cheesecloth pouch

¼ cup honey

Fresh lemon juice to taste

6 tbsp sour cream

2 tbsp slivered almonds, toasted

WHITE GRAPE GAZPACHO

with Toasted Almonds and Dill

WHITE GRAPES ARE a surprising ingredient in this refreshing soup. Cream cheese, an unusual soup ingredient, gives the soup body. English cucumbers, otherwise known as hothouse or seedless cucumbers, are less bitter than regular cucumbers and have very few seeds. Because they are not coated with food-grade wax like most regular cucumbers found in supermarkets, they can be used peel and all.

MAKES 10 TO 12 SERVINGS

1. Peel and halve 18 of the grapes. Reserve for a garnish.

2. Purée the remaining grapes with the cucumber, scallions, half and half, yogurt, cream cheese, vinegar, olive oil, and ½ cup of the dill.

3. Season to taste with the salt and white pepper. Chill thoroughly.

4. Serve the soup in chilled bowls, garnished with the remaining chopped dill, the grape halves, and the almonds.

6 cups seedless white grapes, rinsed well

3 cups diced English cucumber (do not peel)

⅓ cup thinly sliced scallions (green parts only)

1½ cups heavy cream, chilled

1¼ cups plain yogurt, chilled

¼ cup cream cheese (about 2 oz)

2 tbsp white wine vinegar

2 tbsp extra-virgin olive oil

½ cup plus 2 tbsp chopped fresh dill

Salt to taste

Freshly ground white pepper to taste

¼ cup sliced almonds, toasted

{PICTURED AT RIGHT}

4½ cups cubed cantaloupe (peeled and seeded)

Juice of 2 oranges

¼ cup cornstarch

Juice of 1½ lemons

3 cups sparkling water or seltzer water

2¼ tsp orange zest

2¼ tsp lemon zest

½ cup sugar, or to taste

1 cup diced strawberries (hulled)

You could also serve this soup garnished with Lime Granité (page 220) in place of the strawberry garnish.

4½ cups cubed cantaloupe (peeled and seeded)

2 cups apricot nectar

Juice of ½ lemon

2 tbsp honey, or to taste

Sachet: ½ tsp ground ginger, 3 whole allspice berries, 1 whole clove, and one 2-inch cinnamon stick tied up in a cheesecloth pouch

1 cup plain yogurt, chilled

8 mint leaves

CANTALOUPE SOUP

THIS CHILLED MELON soup is perfect to serve at an elegant brunch. Choose a cantaloupe that is fragrant and feels heavy for its size. The netting on the cantaloupe should be well raised and the blossom end should yield slightly to gentle pressure.

MAKES 8 SERVINGS

1. Purée the melon and orange juice in a blender.
2. Dissolve the cornstarch in the lemon juice. Bring the water, orange zest, and lemon zest to a boil in a large saucepan. While stirring, add the cornstarch solution and continue to stir until the liquid returns to a simmer and thickens. Remove from the heat.
3. Add the melon purée and sweeten to taste with sugar.
4. Serve in chilled bowls, garnished with diced strawberries.

COLD CANTALOUPE CREAM SOUP

THIS IS A surprisingly delicate and pleasant starter to any meal served on a hot summer day. Sparkling wine or seltzer may be added to the soup just before serving. For an unusual presentation, serve the soup in wine glasses. Dip the rims of the glasses into lightly whipped egg whites, then into granulated sugar, and chill.

MAKES 8 SERVINGS

1. Place the melon, apricot nectar, lemon juice, honey, and sachet in a soup pot. Bring to a simmer over low heat and cook, stirring frequently, until the melon is tender, about 10 to 15 minutes.
2. Remove and discard the sachet. Purée the soup in batches in a food processor or blender. Transfer to a bowl or storage container, cover and refrigerate until thoroughly chilled.
3. Whisk half of the yogurt into the soup. Serve in chilled wine glasses or bowls, garnished with a dollop of the remaining yogurt and a mint leaf.

Accompaniments

LIME GRANITÉ

2 cup water

1 cup sugar

¼ cup fresh lime juice (from about 2 limes)

Zest of 2 limes, minced

G ranité is the French word for what is known in English as an *ice* and in Italian as a *granita*. Not only does this easy-to-make lime granité complement the Cantaloupe Soup on page 216 beautifully, but it also makes a refreshing summertime treat all by itself. Granités are stirred frequently during freezing to give them a granular texture and keep them from freezing solid. Don't forget to remove the zest from the limes before juicing them.

MAKES ABOUT 2 CUPS

1. Combine all ingredients in a shallow pan. Stir well to combine.

2. Place the pan in the freezer and stir every 25 minutes for 3 hours. Freeze the granité until firm.

CANDIED ORANGE ZEST

1 orange

½ cup water

½ cup sugar

The reserved syrup has several different applications: use it to poach other fruits, especially plums and apricots, to sweeten cold drinks like iced tea, or to brush on cakes for added moisture and flavor.

C andied orange zest makes an interesting garnish for the Cold Carrot Bisque on page 207. Candy the zest a day ahead of when you want to use it so it has time to dry and crystallize. Try to remove as little of the bitter white pith as possible when zesting the orange. Any leftover syrup can be saved for other uses (see note).

MAKES ABOUT ¼ CUP FOR 10 GARNISH SERVINGS

1. Use a zesting tool to cut the zest from the orange in thin shreds, or use a vegetable peeler to peel off strips, and then slice the strips into shreds.

2. Boil the water and sugar in a small saucepan until the sugar dissolves. Add the zest and simmer for 20 minutes. Using a fork, lift the zest from the sugar syrup, drain briefly, then transfer to wax paper and spread in a single layer. Allow the zest to dry completely before storing in an airtight container.

CHEDDAR RUSKS

Rusks are slices of bread that have been toasted until they are crisp and golden brown. In France, rusks are called *biscotte* and in Germany they are known as *zwieback*. Try experimenting with other cheeses as well.

MAKES 8 RUSKS

1. Toast the bread until golden brown on both sides.
2. Preheat the broiler. Scatter the cheese evenly over the toasted bread and broil just until the cheese bubbles and begins to brown.

8 slices French or Italian bread (½ inch thick)
1 cup grated cheddar cheese

GOAT CHEESE RUSKS Top each slice of toasted bread with a ¼-inch-thick slice of goat cheese. Sprinkle with chopped fresh herbs (rosemary, basil, thyme, etc.) or freshly ground black pepper. Heat in a 325°F oven to soften the cheese. Do not brown.

RYE RUSKS

MAKES 8 RUSKS

1. Cut the crusts off the bread and square off the corners to make rectangles out of the bread. Toast the bread until lightly browned.
2. Preheat the broiler. Mix the cheeses, butter, mustard, and cayenne pepper together. Spread the cheese mixture on the bread. Cut each slice on the diagonal to make 2 triangles. Place the rusks under the broiler until the cheese browns.

4 slices rye bread
½ cup grated sharp cheddar cheese
¼ cup grated Parmesan cheese
1 tbsp butter, softened
1½ tsp Dijon mustard
Pinch cayenne

BEAN AND CHEESE RUSKS

If you cannot find a serrano chile, substitute about 1 teaspoon minced jalapeño. Try serving these rusks with the Chicken Vegetable Soup Azteca (page 23) or any other Southwestern- or Mexican-style soups.

MAKES 8 RUSKS

1. Toast the bread until golden brown on both sides.
2. Mince the garlic clove. Sprinkle with the salt and mash to a paste using the side of a large knife.
3. Combine the garlic with the beans, onion, bacon, chile, and pepper. Mix well.
4. Preheat the broiler. Spread the bean mixture on the toast and top with the cheese. Broil until the cheese is melted and lightly browned.

8 slices French bread (½ inch thick)
1 garlic clove
¼ tsp kosher salt
⅔ cup cooked pinto beans, mashed
¼ cup minced onion
2 slices raw bacon, chopped
½ serrano chile, minced
¼ tsp freshly ground black pepper
1 cup grated Monterey jack cheese

3 slices white bread

4 tbsp melted butter or olive oil

¼ tsp salt, or to taste

You can cut these basic croutons to any size you desire. As you increase or decrease the size of the croutons, remember that you'll need to adjust the baking time accordingly.

CROUTONS

THIS RECIPE MAKES enough croutons to generously garnish about 8 servings of soup. Croutons keep well for several days in an airtight container, so the recipe can easily be multiplied. Cut the croutons into any size you desire, from tiny cubes for garnishing soups in cups to large cubes for garnishing soups served in soup plates or salads. Just don't make them any bigger than a soup spoon (so they fit in the mouth) and remember to adjust the baking time appropriately.

MAKES ABOUT 2 CUPS OF ½-INCH CROUTONS

1. Remove the crust from the bread, if desired. Cut the bread into cubes. (If the bread is very fresh, let the bread cubes dry out in a 200°F oven for 5 minutes.)

2. Preheat the oven to 350°F. Toss the bread cubes, butter or oil, and salt together in a large bowl.

3. Spread the bread cubes in a single layer on a baking sheet and bake until golden, about 8 to 10 minutes. Stir the croutons once or twice during baking so they brown evenly.

Make It Different

Add one of these flavorings to the basic plain crouton recipe, or experiment with different flavor combinations of your own:

GARLIC-FLAVORED CROUTONS Mince 1 clove of garlic. Sprinkle with ¼ tsp of kosher salt and mash to a paste with the side of a large knife. Add the garlic paste to the butter or oil before tossing with the bread cubes. Bake as directed.

CHEESE CROUTONS After the bread cubes have been tossed with the butter, toss with ½ cup very finely grated Parmesan, Romano, or other hard grating cheese (a rotary cheese grater or a microplane grater will give you the finest texture and help the cheese adhere to the bread). Bake as directed.

HERB-FLAVORED CROUTONS Add 3 tablespoons chopped fresh or dried herbs (such as oregano or rosemary) to the butter or oil. Toss with the bread cubes and bake as directed.

FOCACCIA

1 cup milk

1 tsp sugar

1 envelope active dry yeast

3½ cups all-purpose flour, plus as needed for
dusting dough and work surface

¾ cup water, about 70° F, plus 1 tbsp for topping

½ cup olive oil

3 tsp kosher salt

You can replace up to half of the all-purpose
flour called for here with whole-wheat flour
for a more wholesome version.

Focaccia is enjoyed in parts of Italy as a snack or quick meal accompanied with a fresh salad, or split and stuffed with fresh salami and cheeses to make flavorful sandwiches, perfect to pair with a soup for a satisfying meal. You can also choose to dress up focaccia with a number of toppings as it bakes: olives, goat cheese, feta cheese, pine nuts, caramelized onions, sun-dried tomatoes, grilled vegetables, and chopped herbs are just a few suggestions. Pick a combination of flavors that complement the soup you are serving.

MAKES 8 SERVINGS

1. Warm the milk to around 100°F over very low heat (this happens quickly; it shouldn't boil). Remove it from the heat, let it cool slightly, and then add the sugar and yeast. Stir until dissolved. Let the mixture rest 15 minutes; you will see a thick foam on the surface.

2. Combine the flour, yeast mixture, water, 2 tablespoons olive oil, and 2 teaspoons salt in a large bowl. Mix by hand or with a dough hook until a smooth, elastic dough is formed, about 10 to 15 minutes.

3. Dust the surface of the dough with a sprinkling of flour, and cover the bowl tightly with plastic. Leave the dough to rise at room temperature until it doubles in bulk, about 1 hour.

4. Transfer the dough to a floured work surface. Press the dough out into a rough square, and then pull the four corners in toward the center. Turn it over so the upper surface is smooth. Drape the ball of dough with the plastic you used during the first rise and let it rest until it has relaxed, about 30 minutes.

5. Brush a baking sheet (with sides) or a jelly roll pan liberally with about 2 tablespoons of olive oil. Uncover the dough and spread and pull it into a rectangle about the same dimensions as your pan. Lift the dough into the pan and brush the surface with 2 tablespoons of olive oil. Drape the plastic wrap over the surface and let the dough rise until it has nearly doubled in volume, about 30 minutes.

6. Preheat the oven to 475°F. Position a rack in the bottom third of the oven.

7. Before the focaccia goes into the oven, whisk together the remaining 2 tablespoons olive oil, 1 tablespoon water, and 1 teaspoon salt; it should thicken. Remove the plastic wrap, and, using your fingertips, poke dimples into the dough in a random pattern. Pour the oil mixture over the dough.

8. Bake the focaccia until the edges are slightly golden in color, about 10 to 12 minutes. Remove from the oven and a cool on a rack for about 10 minutes. The focaccia is ready to cut into squares and serve.

BREAD STICKS

1. Combine the water and yeast in the bowl of an electric mixer or a large mixing bowl if working by hand. Stir until the yeast is dissolved. Add the flour, 4 teaspoons of oil, and the salt. Mix and knead the dough with a dough hook or by hand until smooth and elastic, about 10 minutes.

2. If using an electric mixer, transfer the dough to a large mixing bowl. Cover the bowl and allow the dough to rise in a warm place for 40 minutes.

3. Preheat the oven to 425°F. Line 2 baking sheets with parchment paper. Sprinkle with the cornmeal.

4. Transfer the dough to a floured work surface. Press the dough out into a rough square, then pull the four corners in toward the center. Turn it over so the upper surface is smooth. Drape the ball of dough with the plastic you used during the first rise and let it rest on the work surface, loosely covered, until it has relaxed, 30 minutes.

5. Cut the dough into 10 even pieces (about 1½ ounces each). Roll each piece into a long, thin stick and place on the prepared baking sheets. Brush with olive oil and scatter the salt or seeds (if using) over the breadsticks. Cover loosely with a cloth or plastic wrap and let rise until nearly doubled in volume, about 15 minutes. Bake in a preheated 425°F oven until golden, about 10 to 12 minutes. Cool on wire racks.

¾ cup tepid water (95 to 100°F)

1 tsp active dry yeast

1⅔ cup bread flour

4 tsp extra virgin olive oil, plus more as needed

1 tsp salt

Cornmeal for dusting

Toppings: Coarse salt, poppy seeds, or sesame seeds

OLIVE BREAD

THIS BREAD IS best eaten the day it is made. Dry-cured (as opposed to brine-cured) olives, identifiable by their slightly wrinkled skin, are ideal to use in this bread.

MAKES ONE 1-POUND LOAF

1. Mix the yeast and the sugar with 3 tablespoons of water. Let the yeast develop for 15 minutes in a warm (not hot) place.

2. Combine the flour and salt in bowl of an electric mixer or a large mixing bowl if working by hand. Add the remaining ¼ cup of water, the yeast mixture, and 1½ tablespoons of the olive oil. Mix and knead the dough with a dough hook or by hand until elastic, 8 to 10 minutes. Add the olives and mix well.

3. If using an electric mixer, transfer the dough to a large mixing bowl. Rub the remaining ½ tablespoon of oil on the dough to prevent a skin from forming. Cover and let rise in a warm place for 30 minutes. *(recipe continues)*

1½ tsp active dry yeast

½ tsp sugar

3 tbsp plus ¼ cup tepid water (95 to 100°F)

1⅔ cups bread flour

¼ tsp salt

2 tbsp virgin olive oil

½ cup pitted dry-cured olives, chopped

If you are making olive bread on a very hot day, use cool water (60 to 70°F) or the dough may rise too quickly.

4. Punch down the dough, cover, and let rise until the dough has doubled in volume, about 30 minutes more.

5. Punch down and shape the dough into a loaf. Place on a parchment paper-lined baking sheet. Cover and let rise until doubled, about an hour. Meanwhile, preheat the oven to 475°F.

6. Bake until the loaf sounds hollow when tapped on the bottom, about 30 minutes. (If the loaf gets too dark on the bottom during baking but does not yet sound hollow, lower the oven temperature to 400°F and continue to bake.) Cool on a wire rack.

BUTTERMILK BISCUITS

1½ cups buttermilk

1 egg

3 cups all-purpose flour

2 tbsp sugar

1½ tsp baking powder

½ tsp baking soda

1½ tsp salt

½ cup cubed butter, cold

Egg wash of 1 egg yolk whisked with
2 tablespoons milk

Mix the ingredients until they just come together to form what is known as a *shaggy mass.* Don't overmix the dough, and these biscuits will turn out light and fluffy. This recipe doubles easily, and you can freeze any unbaked biscuits to bake another time. Prepare and cut out the biscuits as described below, then freeze them on a lined baking sheet (do not apply eggwash to the biscuits you plan to freeze). Once they are solid, transfer them to freezer bags or containers. You can bake them directly from the freezer, without thawing, increasing the baking time by about 5 minutes.

MAKES 12 BISCUITS

1. Preheat the oven to 425°F. Prepare a baking sheet by spraying it lightly with cooking spray or lining with parchment paper.

2. Combine the buttermilk and egg in a small bowl and blend until evenly mixed. Set aside.

3. Sift the flour, sugar, baking powder, baking soda, and salt into a large bowl. Add the butter and cut it into the dough until it looks like a coarse meal. You should still be able to see small pieces of butter.

4. Add the buttermilk mixture to the flour mixture, stirring until barely combined. The dough will look coarse and shaggy at this point.

5. Transfer the dough to a lightly floured work surface and press into a ball and knead once or twice. Press or roll out to a thickness of ½ inch. Cut out the biscuits using a 2½-inch cutter. Gather scraps together, re-roll, and cut additional biscuits. Place the biscuits on the prepared pan about 1 inch apart and lightly brush the tops with egg wash.

6. Bake the biscuits until they have risen and the tops are golden brown, about 18 to 20 minutes. Serve very hot, directly from the oven.

CHEDDAR CHEESE AND WALNUT ICEBOX CRACKERS

THIS SAVORY VERSION of an icebox (refrigerator) cookie is simple to make and goes well with many of the soups in this book.

MAKES ABOUT 2 DOZEN CRACKERS

1. Cream butter with an electric mixer until fluffy. Add the cheese and mix well.
2. Add flour and salt. Mix well. Blend in the nuts.
3. Roll out into a log about 1½ inches in diameter. Wrap well and chill for at least one hour or overnight.
4. Preheat the oven to 350°F. Line 2 baking sheets with parchment paper. Cut the dough into ¼-inch-thick slices and place on the baking sheets. Bake until crisp and golden, about 15 minutes. Cool on wire racks and store in an airtight container for up to 3 days.

2 tbsp butter, softened

1 cup grated aged cheddar cheese

⅓ cup all-purpose flour

¼ tbsp salt

2 tbsp finely chopped walnuts

BLUE CHEESE AND PECAN ICEBOX CRACKERS
Substitute an equal amount of blue cheese for the cheddar and pecans for the walnuts.

PEPPER JACK AND OREGANO CRACKERS

TO KEEP THE crackers from browning too quickly during baking, use an insulated baking sheet. If you don't have an insulated baking sheet, double two regular baking sheets, or place an empty sheet on an oven rack below the rack you bake the crackers on to deflect heat.

MAKES ABOUT 2 DOZEN CRACKERS (2 INCHES IN DIAMETER)

1. Combine the cheese, flour, oregano, salt and pepper in a food processor or by hand. Add the oil and pulse or mix by hand just until a coarse meal consistency is achieved. Add the water gradually until the dough forms a cohesive ball that pulls away from the sides of the bowl. Wrap the dough and refrigerate for at least ½ hour.
2. Preheat the oven to 325°F. Roll the dough by hand or through a pasta machine to a ⅛-inch thickness.
3. Cut the dough into desired shapes using a knife, pizza cutter, or shaped cutters. Place on an insulated or double-layered baking sheet. Combine the sugar, salt, and cayenne. Sprinkle the crackers with the mixture.
5. Bake until lightly golden, about 5 to 10 minutes. Turn and bake until medium golden brown, another 5 to 10 minutes. Cool on wire racks and store in an airtight container for up to 3 days.

1 cup grated pepper Jack cheese

¼ cup all-purpose flour

½ tsp dried oregano or ¾ tsp chopped fresh oregano

Pinch salt

Pinch ground black pepper

2 tbsp vegetable oil

2 to 3 tbsp water

1 tsp sugar

1 tsp kosher salt

¼ tsp cayenne pepper

If the dough becomes soft during rolling or cutting, chill it.

{PICTURED AT RIGHT}

1 cup sifted all-purpose flour

½ tsp salt

2 large eggs

1 cup milk

Melted butter or oil, as needed

POPOVERS

To GET THE full dramatic effect of popovers, serve them as soon as you take them from the oven. The big "puffs" will start to deflate almost immediately.

MAKES 6 LARGE POPOVERS

1. Preheat the oven to 450°F. Position a rack in the lower third of the oven. Preheat a popover pan or custard cups on a baking sheet while the oven preheats.

2. Mix together the flour and salt in a bowl. Whisk together the eggs and milk separately. Stir the milk mixture into the dry ingredients, stirring until just mixed and smooth, but do not beat the batter.

3. Take the popover pan or cups out of the oven (still on the baking sheet) and brush them with butter or oil. Immediately pour or ladle the batter into the cups, filling them about half full. Bake for 20 minutes, and then turn the heat down to 375°F. Bake until the popovers are a deep golden brown on the top and sides, an additional 20 minutes.

4. Shut off the oven; leave the popovers in the oven until the sides are firm and crusty, about 10 minutes. If they are taken out of the oven too soon, the popovers collapse and lose their magnificent puffs. Serve immediately.

Make It Easier

You can prepare the popover batter (step 2) up to 24 hours before baking them. Store the batter in a covered container in the refrigerator. If you use the batter directly from the refrigerator, the baking time may be increased by 2 or 3 minutes.

GOUGÈRES

Gruyère Cheese Puffs

1 cup water

½ cup butter

½ tsp salt

1 cup all-purpose flour, sifted

4 eggs

¾ cup grated Gruyère cheese

I N ADDITION TO being a great snack item, these puffs lend texture to cream or purée soups. Try them with the Purée of Cauliflower (page 171) or the Cheddar Cheese Soup (page 140). They are best when served warm from the oven, but they can be cooled, held in airtight containers, and served at room temperature, if necessary. This recipe makes a large amount because it is difficult to make a lesser quantity of dough, but you can freeze any that you won't eat within a few days. To reheat, defrost at room temperature for 10 minutes, then crisp in a 350°F oven for 5 to 10 minutes.

MAKES ABOUT 50 PIECES

1. Preheat the oven to 400°F. Line 2 baking sheets with parchment paper. Combine the water, butter, and salt in a saucepan and bring to a boil.

2. Add the sifted flour all at once and stir in well. Cook, stirring constantly, until the dough begins to come away from the sides of the pot.

3. Immediately transfer the dough to a mixer and beat on medium speed for about 1 minute. Add the eggs one at a time, mixing well after each addition to achieve a stiff but pliable texture.

4. Add the grated cheese and continue mixing for 1 minute.

5. Transfer the dough to a pastry bag with a plain tip, pipe out in 1-inch diameter balls (or other shapes as desired) onto the baking sheets.

6. Bake in the oven until golden brown and puffed, about 5 minutes, and then reduce the oven temperature to 325°F and continue to bake until cooked through, about 20 minutes more.

PAILLETTES

Cheese Sticks

CHEESE STICKS ARE a quick and simple way to add a signature look to your table. The sticks may be twisted, curled, or shaped as desired before baking. The fanciful shapes reaching from tall glasses or jars serve as eye-catching edible decorations. Look for puff pastry in the frozen foods section of your supermarket, and follow package directions for handling and storage.

MAKES 35 TO 40 PIECES

1. Preheat the oven to 400°F. Beat the egg yolk with the milk.
2. Brush one side of the puff pastry sheet with the egg mixture.
3. Sprinkle the cheese and paprika evenly over the puff pastry.
4. Cut the pastry lengthwise into ¼-inch strips.
5. Line several baking sheets with parchment paper and transfer the pastry strips to the baking sheets, leaving an inch of space between each strip to allow for expansion. Bake until golden brown, about 10 minutes.

1 egg yolk

1 tbsp milk

8 oz puff pastry (one 10- by 10-inch sheet)

½ cup grated parmesan cheese

Sweet paprika to taste

Cajun spice blend, cayenne, poppy seeds, and sesame seeds may also be used to flavor the sticks.

PALMIERS WITH PROSCIUTTO

THIS IS A savory variation of a classic French pastry, the *palmier,* which is made of puff pastry sprinkled with granulated sugar. The name reflects the palm-leaf shape of the pastry. These "palm leaves" are lined with prosciutto and a dusting of Parmesan cheese replaces the sugar. Look for puff pastry in the frozen foods section of your supermarket, and follow package directions for handling and storage. The palmiers can be made up in batches and frozen. They can then be baked from the frozen state as needed and served warm.

MAKES 35 TO 40 PIECES

1. Preheat the oven to 400°F. Brush one side of the pastry with the tomato paste.
2. Lay the prosciutto over the tomato paste, then dust with the cheese.
3. Simultaneously roll both long sides in toward the center until they meet to create the palmier shape. Slice ¼-inch thick and bake on parchment-lined baking sheets until golden brown, about 10 minutes. (A sheet of parchment paper on top will help the palmiers to stay flat. The paper can be removed for the last few minutes of baking to allow for browning.)

8 oz puff pastry (one 10- by 10-inch sheet)

6 tbsp tomato paste

12 thin slices prosciutto

¼ cup finely grated Parmesan cheese

FRESH PASTA

Egg Noodle Dough

USE THIS BASIC dough to make egg noodles, flat pastas like linguini or tagliatelli, or filled pastas including ravioli and tortellini.

MAKES ABOUT 1 POUND

3⅔ cups all-purpose flour

4 large eggs

Water, as needed

1. Put the flour into a bowl and make a well in the center. Add the eggs in the center of the well.

2. Using a fork and working as rapidly as possible, incorporate the flour into the eggs little by little working from the outside toward the center, until a shaggy mass forms. As the dough is mixed, adjust the consistency with additional flour or a few drops of water to compensate for the natural variations in ingredients, humidity, and temperature.

3. Once the dough is mixed, turn it out onto a floured surface and knead until its texture becomes smooth and elastic. Use the heels of your hands to push the dough away from you, and then reverse the motion, folding the dough over on itself toward you. Give the dough a quarter turn periodically so that it is evenly kneaded (about 10 to 12 minutes).

4. Divide the dough into balls about the size of an orange, place in a bowl, and cover loosely with a cotton towel. Allow the dough to rest at room temperature for at least 30 minutes. This will relax the dough and make it easier to roll out.

5. Working with one ball of dough at a time, flatten the ball into a rectangle about ½ inch thick. Set the rollers of your pasta machine to the widest opening, guide the flattened dough through the machine as you turn the handle. Roll the dough to form a long, wide strip. Pass the dough through the widest setting 2 or 3 times, folding the dough in thirds each time. Narrow the opening by adjusting the setting, lightly dusting the dough with flour before rolling it in the machine. Continue, narrowing the opening after each pass through the machine without folding the dough, until it reaches the desired thinness. Cut and shape the pasta as needed.

OPPOSITE: *Using fresh pasta dough to form tortellini for the Tortellini in Brodo, page 28. If you don't have a pasta machine, you can roll the dough out by hand, on a lightly floured surface with a rolling pin. Turn the pasta dough often as you roll it, until you get the dough to the desired thickness.*

1¼ lb yellow potatoes (about 4)

¾ cup all-purpose flour

1 egg

1 tbsp extra virgin olive oil, plus more as needed

1 tbsp salt

½ cup grated dry jack or Parmesan cheese

2 tbsp chopped fresh sage

OPPOSITE: *Roll each dumpling over the tines of a fork to shape, just as you would an Italian gnocchi. These dumplings are a component of the Roast Turkey Broth recipe on page 24.*

SAGE DUMPLINGS

THESE DUMPLINGS ARE an herbed version of Italian *gnocchi* (potato dumplings). You can substitute any other fresh herb for the sage, if you like. There are two keys to getting them light and fluffy. First, mix the dough until the ingredients just come together. Overmixing will develop the gluten in the flour and cause the dumplings to become tough. Second, don't let the water simmer too hard while you cook the dumplings. Vigorous simmering will rough up the dumplings and misshape them. If you plan on storing the cooked dumplings rather than adding them directly to soup, rinse them under cold water, drain, and lightly toss them in olive oil to keep them from sticking together.

MAKES ABOUT 60 PIECES

1. Peel the potatoes and cut into sixths. Place the potatoes in a pot of cold, salted water. Bring to a simmer over medium heat and cook gently until just tender, about 20 minutes. Drain and return the potatoes to the pot. Place over medium heat again for a few minutes to drive off excess moisture. Shake the pot frequently until steam no longer rises from the potatoes.

2. Pass the potatoes through a medium-holed food mill or potato ricer. Spread the potatoes in a thin layer on a baking sheet and refrigerate or set aside until cool.

3. Place the potatoes in a large bowl and add the flour. Chop the flour into the potatoes with a rubber spatula until a grainy texture has formed.

4. Mix the egg, oil, and salt together. Add to the potato mixture along with the cheese and sage. Mix gently by hand until just incorporated.

5. Place the dumpling dough in a pastry bag without a tip and pipe the dough into 6-inch logs onto a floured cutting board. Gently roll the dough by hand into smooth logs approximately the diameter of a dime.

6. Cut the logs into ½-inch lengths and roll onto a fork to imprint with ridges. Store the dumplings in a single layer on a floured jellyroll pan until ready to cook.

7. Cook the dumplings in heavily salted, gently simmering water until just firm, about 1½ minutes. Lift the dumplings out of the water with a slotted spoon and add directly to soup.

ROASTED RED PEPPER PURÉE

1 red bell pepper

3 tsp olive oil

½ tsp balsamic vinegar

Salt to taste

Cayenne pepper to taste

THIS COLORFUL ACCOMPANIMENT is quick and easy to make. You can substitute ½ cup bottled red peppers, but omit the oil in the recipe if your bottled peppers are oil-packed. Store the purée tightly covered in the refrigerator for up to 5 days.

MAKES ½ CUP

1. Preheat the broiler.
2. Brush the pepper with 1 teaspoon of the oil. Place the pepper under the broiler and turn as it roasts so that it blackens evenly on all sides.
3. Put the pepper in a small bowl and cover the bowl. Let the pepper steam for 10 minutes, then remove it from the bowl and pull off the skin. Use the back of a knife to scrape away any bits that don't come away easily. Remove the seeds, ribs, and stem from the pepper. Chop the flesh coarsely.
4. Purée the pepper with the remaining oil and the vinegar. Season to taste with the salt and cayenne.

HARISSA

9 dried New Mexico or other large hot red chiles

1 garlic clove, peeled

¼ tsp salt

¾ tsp ground caraway

¼ tsp ground coriander

¼ tsp ground cumin

1 tbsp extra virgin olive oil

HARISSA IS A spicy-hot Tunisian condiment that traditionally accompanies couscous. It is also frequently used to flavor soups and stews. For the best flavor, grind caraway, coriander, and cumin seeds yourself just before making the harissa (a spice/coffee grinder will give you the finest grind). Covered tightly, harissa will keep in the refrigerator for months.

MAKES ABOUT ⅔ CUP

1. Stem, seed, and break up the chiles. Soak in cold water for 15 minutes. Drain well, wrap in cheesecloth or place in a strainer and press out any excess moisture.
2. Chop the garlic, sprinkle with the salt, and mash to a paste using the side of a knife.
3. Grind the chiles, garlic, caraway, coriander, and cumin in a mortar and pestle. (A spice grinder may also be used, but it may smell like harissa forever after.)
4. Place in a small jar or other suitable container and drizzle the oil over the harissa to make a thin layer.
5. Cover tightly and store in the refrigerator.

BASIL OIL

(Basic Fresh Herb Oil)

YOU CAN USE this technique to make any herb-flavored oil you like: chives, tarragon, oregano, or chervil, for instance. With the exception of basil and parsley, it is not necessary to blanch the herb leaves first. To use this flavored oil, pour a few drops on top of each bowl of soup. The heat will release the aroma and flavor of the herbs.

MAKES 1 CUP

1 cup packed basil leaves

¼ cup packed flat-leaf parsley leaves

1 cup extra-virgin olive oil

1. Blanch the basil and parsley leaves in salted water for 20 seconds. Shock in cold water and drain on paper towels.

2. Combine the blanched herbs with half the oil in a blender and purée very fine. Add this purée to the remaining oil. Let the oil rest for at least 12 hours. Strain the oil through a coffee filter or cheesecloth into a clean storage container or squirt bottle. Keep chilled. Use within 3 to 4 days.

RED PEPPER OIL

TRY THIS WITH yellow or green peppers. For a spicy variation, use chiles and omit the mustard.

MAKES 1 CUP

4 red peppers

2 tbsp prepared mustard (Dijon-style)

1 cup extra-virgin olive oil

Salt as needed

1. Wash the peppers, remove the stems and seeds, and rough cut into small dice.

2. Purée the peppers very fine in a blender. Place this purée juice in a sauce pan and reduce over medium heat to one-fourth its original volume. Strain through a fine-mesh sieve into a bowl and cool.

3. When the pepper purée is cool, stir in the mustard, and then add the olive oil. Season with salt.

4. Transfer to a storage container or squirt bottle. Keep chilled. Use within 2 to 3 days.

FRIED SHALLOTS

2 shallots

½ cup all-purpose flour

Salt to taste

Cayenne to taste (optional)

½ cup milk

2 cups vegetable oil or as needed for frying

THESE CRISPY SHALLOTS are the finishing touch for several soups in this book, and are an great-looking and flavorful garnish. If you don't have a thermometer, you can test the temperature of the oil by adding 1 shallot ring. If the oil is hot enough, it will immediately bubble around the shallot.

MAKES 8 GARNISH SERVINGS

1. Peel and slice the shallots into ⅛-inch-thick rings. Separate the rings.
2. Season the flour with salt and cayenne (if using).
3. Dip the shallots in the milk. Strain or use a slotted spoon to remove. Dredge the shallots in the flour.
4. Fry in 325°F oil until golden, about 5 minutes. Drain on paper towels. Season to taste with salt.

Fried Shallots are the perfect finishing touch for soups like Soto Ayam (page 41), shown here, or Potage Solferino (page 170). Be sure to keep an eye on the shallots as they cook in the oil—they can burn easily.

VEGETABLE CHIPS

A BASKET OF THESE chips makes a great snack as well as an accompaniment to many of the soups in this book. Follow the main recipe, or choose your own assortment (see note below). The best way to get thin slices of these vegetables is to use a *mandoline*, which is a hand-operated slicing tool. Professional stainless steel versions of this tool are fairly expensive ($150 to $200), but many stores carry plastic versions that retail for $20 to $50 and generally produce excellent results.

MAKES ABOUT 15 SERVINGS

½ taro root

½ russet potato

½ sweet potato

1 parsnip

1 carrot

1 small beet

½ plantain

Vegetable oil for frying as needed

Salt as needed

1. Peel all the vegetables. Slice all very thin (¹⁄₁₆ inch). Keep the taro and potato slices separately in cold water; all other vegetables may be held dry. Keep them separate because they may all require different cooking times.

2. Heat the oil in a deep fryer or kettle to 325°F. Pat the taro and potato slices dry before frying. Fry each vegetable separately until crisp, about 3 to 5 minutes, depending up the thickness of the slice and the type of vegetable, drain on paper towels, and season with salt.

3. Serve immediately or cool and store in an airtight container. Serve within 24 hours for the best quality.

Make It Different

Aside from the assortment of vegetables called for in the main recipe, there are a number of items that would be great substitutions. Here are a few ideas:

ARTICHOKE CHIPS Remove the choke and some of the stem. Slice trimmed artichokes very thin and fry in 350°F vegetable oil until crisp. (If not frying right away, keep sliced artichokes in a bowl of water with a lemon squeezed into it. Pat dry before frying.) Drain and salt to taste.

FENNEL CHIPS Remove stem ends from fennel, trim root end, and halve or quarter (depending on the size of the fennel bulb). Slice very thin. Fry in 350°F vegetable oil until crisp. Drain and salt to taste.

GARLIC CHIPS Use large garlic (elephant garlic) and slice peeled cloves very thin using a knife or a garlic slicer. Fry in 350°F olive oil until lightly browned. Reserve the flavored oil for another use, if desired.

APPLE OR PEAR CHIPS Remove the core from rinsed apples or pears, slice thin, and bake on a silicone baking mat or a lightly oiled baking sheet in a 375°F oven until crisp, 20 to 30 minutes.

PISTOU

{PICTURED AT LEFT}

PESTO IS ONE of Italy's most popular culinary exports; *pistou* is the subtly different French version of this fragrant herb paste. While pesto typically includes
nuts, pistou may or may not. The key ingredients for both are basil, olive oil, garlic,
and cheese. In fact, the first version of pistou was essentially a cheese paste—basil
may have been a later addition.

MAKES ABOUT ¾ CUP

1. Purée the basil, Parmigiano, and garlic to a fine paste in a food processor or
blender.

2. With the machine running, add ⅓ cup of the olive oil in a thin stream. Scrape
the sides of the bowl or blender jar as necessary. Purée until the oil is completely incorporated.

3. The pistou is ready to use now. To hold for later use, pour a thick layer of olive
oil over the surface and store it in a covered container in the refrigerator for up to 2
weeks, or in the freezer for up to 2 months.

Pesto

FOLLOW THE RECIPE above, adding 2 tbsp toasted pine nuts (see note at right about
pan-roasting nuts) to the food processor or blender when puréeing the other ingredients. Proceed with the recipe as directed.

Make It Easier

If you have an herb garden that produces large amounts of basil (or find it in abundance at your
local farm stand), make big batches of pistou or pesto at the end of the season and freeze it in
ice cube trays. Once the cubes are frozen solid, you can transfer them to freezer bags for use in
even the darkest days of winter, thereby avoiding the premium prices for out-of-season fresh
basil or commercially prepared pesto.

1 cup chopped fresh basil leaves

½ cup grated Parmigiano-Reggiano

2 garlic cloves, chopped

⅓ cup olive oil, plus as needed

Pan-Roasting Nuts

Let a heavy-bottomed skillet or sauté pan get
very hot over high heat. Add the nuts to the
pan in an even layer. Swirl the pan gently to
keep the ingredients in motion constantly. The
aromas will open up and deepen dramatically.
Once the nuts begin to give off a noticeable
aroma, keep a close eye on them. They can go
from perfect to overdone in a few seconds.
Pour them out of the pan into a bowl just before they are the shade of brown you want.

INDEX

A Note on the Type

This book was set in the OpenType version of Monotype Bell.
In 1931, the Monotype Design Studio released a revival of this typeface by the
eighteenth-century English type cutter, Richard Austin. Austin created his type in 1788, while
working for John Bell's British Type Foundry, where it was used in the production of Bell's newspaper,
The Oracle. The face was Austin's effort to create an English version of the contemporary typefaces being
cut in France by Firmin Didot. Considered to be the first English Modern typeface, Bell displays the
extreme modulation of stroke and highly decorative forms that were characteristic of the faces of Didot and
his Italian contemporary, Giambattista Bodoni. Austin's typeface (like many typefaces of the period, Bell
was named for the man who commissioned its creation, rather than the actual designer) is unique in that
it was designed with uniform, three-quarter height numerals, versus the more traditional "text
figure" numerals that accompanied most typefaces of the period. The digital revival of the
Monotype version was created under the supervision of Robin Nicholas, based on the
original Monotype models by Stephenson Blake, and includes the decorative
uppercase swash variants that were part of Austin's original design.

Art direction, design, and composition by Kevin Hanek

Printed in Singapore by Imago Worldwide Printing